RN

WITHDRAWN

Western Europe and Germany

German Historical Perspectives Series
General Editors: Gerhard A. Ritter and Anthony J. Nicholls

ISSN: 0953–363X

German Historical Perspectives/IX

Western Europe and Germany

The Beginnings of European Integration 1945–1960

Edited by
CLEMENS WURM

BERG PUBLISHERS
Oxford/Washington, USA

English edition.
First published in 1995 by
Berg Publishers Ltd
Editorial offices:
150 Cowley Road, Oxford, OX4 1JJ, UK
13590 Park Center Road, Herndon, VA 22071, USA

© Clemens Wurm

Library of Congress Cataloging-in-Publication Data

A catalogue record for this book is available from the Library of Congress.

British Library Cataloguing in Publication Data

A catalogue record for this book is available from the British Library.

ISBN 1 85973 052 3

Printed and bound in Great Britain by WBC, Bridgend, Mid Glam.

Contents

Editorial Preface

The purpose of this series of books is to present the results of research by German historians and social scientists to readers in English-speaking countries. Each of the volumes has a particular theme which will be handled from different points of view by specialists. The series is not limited to the problems of Germany but will also involve publications dealing with the history of other countries, with the general problems of political, economic, social and intellectual history as well as international relations and studies in comparative history.

We hope the series will help to overcome the language barrier which experience has shown obstructs the rapid appreciation of German research in English-speaking countries.

The publication of the series is closely associated with the German Visiting Fellowship at St Antony's College, Oxford, which has existed since 1965, having been originally funded by the Volkswagen Stiftung, later by the British Leverhulme Trust, by the Ministry of Education and Science in the Federal Republic of Germany, and, starting in 1990, by the Stifterverband für die Deutsche Wissenschaft with special funding from C. & A. Brenninkmeyer Deutschland. Each volume is based on a series of seminars held in Oxford, which has been conceived and directed by the Visiting Fellow and organised in collaboration with St Antony's College.

The editors wish to thank the Stifterverband für die Deutsche Wissenschaft for meeting the expenses of the original lecture series and for generous assistance with the publication. They hope that this enterprise will help to overcome national introspection and to further international academic discourse and co-operation.

Gerhard A. Ritter   Anthony J. Nicholls

Notes on Contributors

Werner Abelshauser is presently holding the Chair of Economic and Social History at the University of Bielefeld, Germany. He has been Professor of European History at the European University Institute, Florence (1989–91). Among his main publications are *Umweltgeschichte* (Göttingen, 1994); *Wirtschaftsgeschichte der Bundesrepublik Deutschland* 7th edition (1993); 'American Aid and West German Economic Recovery: A Macroeconomic Perspective', in C.S. Maier and G. Bischof (eds), *The Marshall Plan and Germany* (1991); 'The First Post-Liberal Nation: Stages in the Development of Modern Corporatism in Germany', *European History Quarterly* 14; 'West German Economic Recovery 1945–51: A Reassessment', *The Three Banks Review* 135; *Konflikt und Kooperation. Strategien europäischer Gewerkschaften im 20. Jahrhundert* (1988); *Die Weimarer Republik als Wohlfahrtsstaat* (1987).

Werner Bührer was formerly Research Fellow at the Institut für Zeitgeschichte, Munich, and now teaches contemporary history at the Technical University of Munich. He has published *Ruhrstahl und Europa* (1986), *Vom Marshallplan zur EWG* (co-editor, 1990), a documentation on the Adenauer era (1993) and several articles on European integration, Franco–German relations since 1945, the West German steel industry and economic associations in the Federal Republic. He has just finished a study on Germany and the OEEC.

Hartmut Kaelble is Professor for Social History at the Humboldt University, Berlin. His main field of research is comparative social history of Europe during the nineteenth and twentieth centuries, especially the history of social mobility, social inequalitiy, business elites, strikes, the active population and the welfare state. Recent books include *Social Mobility in the 19th and 20th Centuries* (1985); *Industrialisation and Social Inequality in the 19th Century Europe* (1986); *A Social History of Western Europe 1880–1980* (1990); with Y.S. Brenner and M. Thomas (eds), *Income Distribution in Historical Perspective* (1991); *Nachbarn am Rhein* (1991) (Divergences and Convergences between French and German Society since 1880).

Hanns Jürgen Küsters, at Bonn University, Faculty of Political Science since 1987, and chief of the editorial staff of the *Dokumente zur Deutschlandpolitik* of the Ministry of Home Affairs since 1992, conducting contemporary history research and providing several contributions on the developments of the European Communities and Western European questions in the 1950s, on the international aspects of the Germany policy after the Second World War and on Konrad Adenauer. He is preparing a study on 'The Four-Power Conferences on Germany 1945–1955'. Principal publications include *Die Gründung der Europäischen Wirtschaftsgemeinschaft* (1982) (French version, *Fondements de la Communauté Économique Européenne* (1990); Adenauer, *Teegespräche 1950–1961*, series *Adenauer Rhöndorfer Ausgabe*, 3 vols (1984–1988).

Wilfried Loth is Professor of Modern and Contemporary History at the University of Essen. He has published widely, in particular on the history of the German Kaiserreich, political Catholicism, French contemporary history, and international relations after the Second World War. Among his publications are *The Division of the World 1941–1955* (1988); *Documents on the History of European Integration 1945–1950* (with Walter Lipgens, 2 vols, 1988–1991); and *Der Weg nach Europa. Geschichte der Europäischen Integration 1939–1957* (1990, 2nd edn 1991).

Gustav Schmidt has been Full Professor of International Politics, Faculty of Social Sciences, Ruhr-University Bochum since 1976. Visiting Professorships include St. Antony's College, Oxford (1979–80), Emory University, Atlanta (1984), University of Toronto (1985–86), and Cornell University (1990–91). Publications include *Deutscher Historismus und Parlamentarische Demokratie. Untersuchungen zu den politischen Gedanken von Meinecke-Troeltsch-Max Weber* (1964); *England in der Krise. Grundlagen und Grundzüge der britischen Appeasement-Politik 1930–1937* (1981), (*The Politics and Economics of British Appeasement*, 1985) and *Der europäische Imperialismus 1890–1914* (1985). He has edited *Konstellationen internationaler Politik. Politische und wirtschaftliche Faktoren in den Beziehungen zwischen Westeuropa und den Vereinigten Staaten 1924–1932* (1983); *Großbritannien und Europa – Großbritannien in Europa* (1989); with Karl Rohe und Hartmut Pogge von Strandmann, *Deutschland, Großbritannien, Europa* (1991); and *Ost-West-Beziehungen: Konfrontation und Détente 1945–1989*, 2 vols

(1993). Articles on Germany and Britain before World War I include 'War Aims, Peacemaking, and the demise of the "Versailles System", 1917–21'; 'International Politics in the World Depression 1930–32'; 'The North Atlantic Triangle: U.S. – Canada – Britain'; 'The Role of Germany in Anglo-American Relations 1955–1967'; 'Nuclear Diplomacy and East-West Relations, 1950–1961'; and 'Divided Germany – Divided Europe, 1950–1961'.

Klaus Schwabe is Professor of Contemporary History at the University of Technology at Aachen. Has held guest professorships at Ohio State University, Columbus, Ohio (1984), Sorbonne, Paris IV (1985), Georgetown University 1990–91), and since 1992 is holder of a Monnet Professorship of the European Communities. Publications include *Wissenschaft und Kriegsmoral. Die deutschen Hochschullehrer und die politischen Grundfragen des Ersten Weltkrieges* (1969); *Woodrow Wilson* (1971); *Gerhard Ritter. Ein politischer Historiker in seinen Briefen* (1984); *Woodrow Wilson, Revolutionary Germany, and Peacemaking 1918–19* (1985). He edited *The Beginnings of the Schuman Plan 1950–51* (1988), and, with Martin Broszat, *Die deutschen Eliten und der Weg in den Zweiten Weltkrieg* (1989). A monograph dealing with American policies with regard to the integration of Europe, 1947–1955 is in preparation.

Clemens Wurm is Professor of West European History at the Humboldt University of Berlin. He has published on the history of France and Britain, on the history of international relations in the twentieth century and on European integration. His main publications include: *Die französische Sicherheitspolitik in der Phase der Umorientierung 1924–1926* (1979); *Industrielle Interessenpolitik und Staat. Internationale Kartelle in der britischen Außen- und Wirtschaftspolitik während der Zwischenkriegszeit* (1988); *Business, Politics and International Relations: Steel, Cotton and International Cartels in British Politics 1924–1939* (1993). He edited *Internationale Kartelle und Außenpolitik. Beiträge zur Zwischenkriegszeit/International Cartels and Foreign Policy: Contributions on the Interwar Period* (1989), *Wege nach Europa. Wirtschaft und Außenpolitik Großbritanniens im 20. Jahrhundert 1992*, and, with Harm G. Schröter, *Politik, Wirtschaft und internationale Beziehungen. Studien zu ihrem Verhältnis in der Zeit zwischen den Weltkriegen* (1991).

List of Tables

CLEMENS WURM

Introduction

The momentous events of 1989–90 have radically changed the political map of Europe. The Soviet Union has disintegrated, and with it the systems of alliance and integration in Eastern Europe over which it presided. The Warsaw Pact and the Council for Mutual Economic Assistance (COMECON) have broken up. The division of Europe into two hostile blocs has ended. Germany is reunited.

The current situation is, however, contradictory and paradoxical. The developments hold new possibilities but are full of uncertainties and risks; the euphoria of 1990 has faded. The Central and Eastern European countries are embarked upon a difficult and highly uncertain process of transition from centrally directed economies under single-party rule to democratic and liberal-capitalist systems. The division of Europe continues in economic and social respects. We are experiencing a revival of nationalism and the flaring up of bloody conflicts. Old problems of boundaries and nationalities have been revived. The danger of a new fragmentation of the European continent is great.

Disintegration in Eastern Europe has been accompanied by ambitious steps towards integration in Western Europe. The European Community – officially the European Union since the ratification of the Treaty of Maastricht – continues to be seen as an anchor of stability, as both a centre of gravity and an agent of change in Europe. Despite internal conflicts over security, immigration and responses to the economic crisis, the EC is holding to its ambitious aims of political and monetary union. Its attractiveness seems unbroken, despite some disillusionment and disappointments over its failure in the crisis in ex-Yugoslavia. Along with

1

NATO, the EC is the organisation whose membership is most striven for by the reforming countries of Central and Eastern Europe. The question is being asked, as much in Western as in Eastern Europe, whether and to what extent institutions like the EC can help to safeguard democracy, settle conflicts peacefully, and promote growth and stability in Middle and Eastern Europe.

The basic structure of today's European institutions was established in the second half of the 1940s and in the 1950s. The 'Quinze Décisives', as the years 1945–1960 have accurately been called in an allusion to the title of a well-known book by Jean Fourastié[1], were the years of European reconstruction. After the austerity of the early post-war years they were a period of increasing prosperity and strong economic growth that continued until the beginning of the 1970s. The long boom was a basic requirement for the stabilisation of Western European societies and democracies. The two decades after the war were crucial for European integration, and they have been for some time an object of intense historical research. In these years a network of organisations with different objectives, areas of competence and memberships was established, which has shaped the structure of Europe up to the present day. Of these institutions, the EC has shown itself to be the most stable and the most significant.

The division of Germany, and the division of Europe into two hostile blocs and the creation of two different systems of integration organised around the ECSC, the EEC and NATO in the West, and COMECON and the Warsaw Pact in the East, also occurred in the 1940s and 1950s. Integration had quite different meanings in East and West Europe after 1945. In the East it was founded on compulsion, not on free choice and popular consent as in the West, and it never got beyond the first stages. The system of bilateral treaties in the East was more important than forms of integration. The leading power of the Eastern bloc, the Soviet Union, was a member of both COMECON and the Warsaw Pact, which were conceived as instruments of Soviet power politics. The USA supported Western European integration from the beginnings until the end of the 1950s, after which its attitude became more ambivalent. Its direct participation in European integration, however, was never up for discussion. Its aim was to make Western Europe stronger and more self-supporting. The USA long hoped to be able to reduce its direct political and military engagement in Europe through the process of European integration, and to be able to reduce the number of its troops or even to withdraw them completely.

With the onset of the Cold War in 1947–8, integration became an important object of the practical politics of Western European governments. Stalin had largely established the boundaries of his empire in Eastern Europe and pushed the Soviet area of influence forward to the Elbe. With the Marshall Plan, Western Europe constituted itself as a 'new unit'[2] that organised itself first economically and then politically and militarily within the larger framework of 'the West'. By the start of the Korean War at the latest, West European integration had become an element in the clash of opposing systems and an important function of the cold war. The restriction of the integration process to Western Europe was artificial and a product of the power-political and ideological circumstances of the time. It was a consequence rather than a cause of the division of Europe, even if it stabilised and entrenched this division. The origins of the European idea and of the European unity movement lie further back, as can be seen from the Briand plan, and earlier plans for some form of political, economic or cultural European unity were of course directed towards the whole of Europe – irrespective of the fact that in the past there has always been disagreement how Europe should be defined in the geographical, political or cultural sense.

Since the historic events of 1989–90 and the end of the cold war in Europe, we are in a way experiencing a return to earlier historical periods. The ideological and systemic obstacles to European-wide structures and solutions have fallen away. The question of European identity presents itself in a new form. Europe is no longer, as it was from the Second World War onwards, dominated by the politics of the Super-Powers. The years from 1945 to 1989 seem now to have marked a comparatively distinct period in the history of Europe, and the year 1989 appears as a caesura, a decisive break with far-reaching consequences both for the future and even for the analysis of developments and policies since 1945. The upheaval and the events in the East of Europe affect Germany the most, and Germany was their main beneficiary. Yet they will have enormous repercussions on Western Europe and on the future shaping of the European continent as a whole. With the end of the East-West conflict, the end of the division of Europe, and the end of the division of Germany, many commentators consider that the prerequisites and conditions that aided, made possible or motivat-

ed cooperation and integration in Western Europe have vanished.
Some therefore even assume – a view that I do not share – that
even the EC itself will prove to have been merely a product of the
Cold War and an ephemeral phenomenon.[3]

Against this background, the question of the origins and driving
forces of integration in Western Europe gains new significance.
Was post-war European integration the product of external factors
and a response to the changed geopolitical and ideological position in Europe after the Second World War, or did it result from
the internal domestic motivations of Western European countries?
Was it a result of the forces of the Cold War, pressure from the
USA or the desire to restrain and integrate Germany? Or did its
origins lie in historical experiences, in a changed European political consciousness and in the imperatives of the search for growth
and prosperity? What relative importance did the different factors
have in the overall picture of a complex development? These questions are not merely of academic interest: they are crucial for an
understanding of the current situation in Europe. A reply to them
would shed light on the conditions likely to lead to integration or
disintegration in Europe. The question of the longer-term historical causes or preconditions for integration and cooperation in
Europe also gains in importance when seen from this angle.

The considerations set out above were the background and the
reason for using my stay at St Antony's College, Oxford, in the
summer term of 1993 to hold a seminar on Western Europe and
the beginnings of European integration, and to invite visiting
German speakers to present the results of their research for discussion. This volume brings together the lectures held under these
auspices. The subjects dealt with reflect the conception of the seminar, the directions of current German research into these subjects
and the availability of contributors. Painful gaps could not be
avoided. It was not intended to try to present a neat and consistent
explanation, but to look at the complex process of European integration from various angles. In this respect the contributions
reflect the general state of research into European integration,
where widely differing approaches prevail. The central focus of the
book is on the years from 1945 to around 1960, but it is not limited
to them. Several chapters go beyond these years and consider the
whole period from the Second World War to the present.

In the opening chapter Clemens Wurm deals with the different
perspectives on early Western European integration and the dif-

ferent approaches to the topic. In an overview of the state of research he distinguishes between three views on early European integration. Debates centre principally around the significance of internal or external factors in the process of integration and the relationship between the nation-state and supranationality. As well as showing the clash of different historiographical approaches, he indicates two areas – the 'German problem' and the role of France – where there is a large measure of agreement among the scholars.

The 'German problem' was a crucial motive for Western European integration. Werner Abelshauser discusses the stages of the re-integration of West Germany into the world economy and its rise to become the dominant economy in Europe. This re-integration took place in close connection with the reconstruction of Western Europe. West Germany was faced from the beginning with a conflict between integration of trade on the one hand, and political integration on the other. Germany's joining of the EEC represented a political calculation and less a consideration of economic interests. Abelshauser is sceptical about how far membership of the EC gave new momentum to West Germany's economic development.

The primacy of political objectives is also emphasised by Hanns Jürgen Küsters in his overview of West Germany's integration policy. Despite the importance that was accorded in Bonn to European integration as a political aim, there were considerable differences as to the form and method of integration. Even Konrad Adenauer was not committed to one particular approach. Integration was for Germany a means of freeing itself from external controls, of re-gaining sovereignty and international recognition. Germany was in this respect in quite a different situation to, for example, France. West Germany was meant to become a West-oriented, calculable and reliable power, with its security guaranteed by the Western powers.

The role of industrial and economic interest groups in European integration has up to now been little researched. The predominant academic view is that the attitude of Western European industry was in general one of scepticism or outright rejection. Werner Bührer shows that this was different in the case of Germany: West German industry supported European integration and the building of new institutions. As with the German government, it was concerned primarily (but not solely) with the regaining of sovereignty and the removal of Allied controls. Its attitude changed from almost full support at the beginning through

cautious reluctance to 'pragmatic participation' by 1960. The conclusion of the chapter, that German industrialists are 'pragmatic
Europeans', should be of particular interest today, after the establishment of German unification, since the real commitment of the
Federal Republic to European integration is questioned by many
outside Germany.

The role of external factors in European integration is presented by scholars from different points of view. Klaus Schwabe discusses the stance of the USA. Successive American governments
supported European integration almost from its beginnings up to
the Treaties of Rome. They found themselves confronted early on
with the conflict between 'widening' and 'deepening' which has
accompanied European integration to this day: a tighter structure
would make the accession of new members difficult, while an
expansion of membership would endanger the cohesiveness and
effectiveness of European institutions. The USA was in favour of
the supranational approach but stuck to its line that European
integration must be devised by the Europeans themselves and not
by Washington. Schwabe credits the USA with considerable consistency in its conception of the future political structure of a
European union.

The firm anchoring of West Germany in the West was a common aim of Western governments, but, as Gustav Schmidt shows,
how Germany should best be accommodated in the Western
framework and into which system it should be integrated
remained subjects of dispute. While in forms of economic integration the principle of equal treatment ruled (and was followed in
the ECSC and the EEC), it was withheld from West Germany in the
area of defence and security policy. Here the differences between
Great Britain, France and Germany were to remain. The tensions
between defence, equality and the anchoring of Germany in the
West were not successfully resolved in a comprehensive system of
integration. American policies had unintended consequences for
European integration. As Schmidt shows, the nuclear issue proved
particularly divisive. Great Britain insisted – in this as in other matters – on its special status; France strove towards its own nuclear
weapons and caused the failure of the EDC partly for this reason.

Great Britain and France had much in common and were confronted after the war with similar challenges. Yet both countries
adapted to the post-war world in quite different ways. Clemens
Wurm examines from a comparative perspective the fundamental

principles, the underlying continuities and the driving forces of both countries' European and integration policy since the Second World War. In order to protect growth, rank and influence, Britain leaned on the Commonwealth and the USA, whereas France turned to an increasing extent to Western European integration. Britain and France pursued conflicting policies on integration; they were the advocates of different forms of integration and had different views on the construction of European institutions and the role of Europe in the world. The basic attitude of both countries to integration has remained remarkably stable since around 1950.

Very different motivations and driving forces have been cited by scholars as lying behind European integration. In his account of the integration process, Wilfried Loth emphasises political objectives and the role of political movements, pressure groups and individuals. Since the First World War, European integration has been striven for, with varying intensity, as an alternative to the nation-state system. Such plans, Loth argues, aimed at the creation of supranational structures since the nation-state was no longer considered an adequate or appropriate framework for providing peace, security and welfare. The most ambitious plans have not been realised; the actual outcome was the result of a combination of the endeavours of the European movement and divergent national interests. There has been progress towards economic integration, while resistance to a politically united Europe has up to now remained strong.

Integration is a multi-dimensional concept. It does not extend merely to the building of political communities. Hartmut Kaelble argues in his contribution for a broader and more comprehensive approach to the historical analysis of European integration. Are we on the way towards a European society? According to Kaelble, the societies of West European countries have become more similar since the war. European social similarities and European social peculiarities, however, do not imply anything similar to a national society. Social developments will not lead automatically to peace and political integration; these remain matters for political decisions.

The contributions to the book show clearly the central role of Germany and the German problem in the early stages of integration. West European integration resulted neither purely from internal, nor purely from external factors. It was a complex, historically novel process. Monocausal explanations cannot do justice to the complexity of the subject matter. The Western European states were fortunate insofar as integration was made easier by the coincidence of exceptionally favourable factors such as high economic growth from the early 1950s and the support of the USA. National strength and prosperity came to be regarded as a function of political and economic interdependence and integration. Political motives dominated, and this applies especially to West Germany. Although the formation of political communities was in the foreground, integration also took place with varying intensity and at varying speeds on other levels. It remains a task for historical research to establish the relationship between political, economic and social integration and the factors and circumstances which were decisive in Europe. In this way too, well-supported statements of a more general kind about processes of regional integration or disintegration may be arrived at that go beyond the specific Western European case.

I would like to thank the authors for their cooperation. Many thanks are due to the Stifterverband für die Deutsche Wissenschaft for its financial support, which made possible the holding of the seminar and provided funds for the travel and accommodation of the German guest speakers. I would also like to thank St Antony's College for its generous hospitality and the participants of the seminar for the lively discussions. Finally, special thanks are due to Tony Nicholls for his assistance in holding the seminar and for his rendering of the contributions into a comprehensible and readable English.

Notes

1   René Girault, Preface to Gérard Bossuat, *La France, l'aide américaine et la construction européenne 1944–1954*, Paris, 1992, pp. XV–XVI; Jean Fourastié, *Les Trente Glorieuses ou la Révolution invisible de 1946 à 1975*, Paris, 1979

2   Charles S. Maier, 'Die konzeptuellen Grundlagen des Marshall-Plans', in Othmar Nikola Haberl and Lutz Niethammer (eds), *Der Marshall-Plan und die europäische Linke*, Frankfurt am Main, 1986, p. 53

3. See for example Hans Arnold, *Europa am Ende? Die Auflösung von EG und NATO*, München, 1993

CLEMENS WURM

Early European Integration as a Research Field: Perspectives, Debates, Problems

Research by historians on early European integration is more intense than ever. A strong boost was given to historical research by the release of new archives and the availability of unpublished public sources from around the end of the 1970s onwards, and historians from several countries and from different historical disciplines have taken up the subject. Scholars with a special interest in long-term trends and developments are exploring the historical roots of European integration. Others are concentrating on more specific issues like the building of European institutions. Centres of research such as the European University Institute at Florence are examining the topic as also are research groups and the European Community Liaison Committee of Historians. The European University Institute's research project on 'Challenge and response in Western Europe' is investigating the history of European integration in its widest sense.[1] The research projects launched on the initiative of René Girault in Paris consider 'Perceptions of power in Western Europe' and the 'Emergence and development of a European conscience in the 20th century'.[2] The Liaison Committee, a group of historians from Western European countries connected with the European Community, seeks to contribute to our knowledge on European integration by organising conferences, advancing cooperation between scholars and encouraging new research.[3] At the beginning of the 1980s Hans-Peter Schwarz, a German political scientist

9

and a leading member of the Liaison Committee, blamed historians for not really being interested in European integration.[4] Since then, however, the situation has completely changed.

European integration is not being analysed by a single historical discipline. In accordance with integration as a multidimensional concept, historians from different specialisms are exploring the subject. The initial focus soon after the war was provided by the historians of political ideas.[5] They investigated the history of the idea of European unity, an idea stretching back into the Middle Ages, and attempted to determine the common cultural features of Europe, the roots, the essence and the limits of a distinctly European culture. Their topic was, in the words of Theodor Schieder, 'cultural Europe'.[6] The next focus was by economic historians. They dealt with the emergence, the decline and the rebirth (after 1945 in a divided Europe) of a European market since the nineteenth century. They investigated the internationalisation of economic activities in Europe, concentrating on the free movement of capital, goods and labour. They looked at movements or antecedents that built up the tradition in which the Common Market was possible. Today they are also analysing the interrelationship of economic and political factors and the creation of common institutions.[7]

More recent is the concern of social historians for European integration. Hartmut Kaelble has devoted his attention to the comparative investigation of European societies since the end of the nineteenth century, to social integration and to the emergence of a distinctly European society. Other social historians are examining the history of social classes or social strata in Europe.[8] Finally, the political and diplomatic historians have proved the by far most productive group of all. Their main interest is directed towards the political and economic history of early European integration, comprising roughly the period from the Second World War until around 1960. It is with research on this period that this paper deals.

What are the main themes of their studies? Their works explore the sources and the evolution of the political and economic reconstruction of Western Europe. They examine the origins, the building and the nature of European institutions, the sources of European integration and the role of the various forces involved in this process including governments, civil servants, the 'founding fathers' of Europe, European pressure groups and the European

Movement, the extra-European powers, in particular the United States and the Soviet Union, and the impact of the Cold War.

Historical research on early European integration has led to important new results. Earlier views have been questioned, modified or even revised. A whole range of new facts, considerations and analyses has been brought forward. The integration process is now being seen in a completely different light from that which prevailed twenty or even ten years ago. Yet, there is no agreed or common view on early European integration; on the contrary, conflicting and opposing views are being put forward. It is the different perspectives, views and approaches to the topic which form the subject of this paper.

Two preliminary remarks are necessary. First, Western European integration took place against the background of important developments in Europe and the wider world: the cold war, the division of Germany and Europe and the formation of political, military and economic blocs in Eastern and Western Europe. After the upheaval of the war and the austerity of the early post-war years, the Western European economies entered a period of sustained economic growth at the end of the 1940s. The economic boom of the 1950s and 1960s combined with dramatic improvements in average incomes, standards of living and the possession of consumer goods. The structure and attitude of European society changed profoundly. 'Paralleling the unprecedented levels of growth was an equally impressive extension of government welfare provision.'[9] There was virtually no unemployment. Another important factor was decolonisation and the disintegration of the European Empires; by 1965 nearly all the former colonies had become independent. Early European integration has to be explored against this wider background. It was itself an integral part of these complex and interacting developments, and must, in fact, be analysed as such.

The second preliminary remark concerns the term *integration*. There is no agreed definition of integration. The term is employed in very different ways by the various categories of historians mentioned earlier. Very generally speaking, we can take integration to mean the amalgamation of or the formation and maintenance of close patterns of interaction between previously autonomous units. These patterns can be of a political, social or economic nature. For most of the studies under discussion here, integration means the process for the creation of political communities. Integration is a dynamic concept, which changed in nature after the war. The term became popular at the end of the 1940s when it began to replace the term federation, and even began to imply the political and institutional meanings contained in the latter.[10]

Basically, the debates on European integration centre on two closely connected sets of questions. First, what were the driving forces behind European integration? Who inspired the movement? What was the motor? Was European integration the product of internal or external forces? Did it grow out of European impulses, out of the European idea, European personalities, the European Movement and the long-term trends of the European economies and societies? Or was it the product of external constraints such as the Cold War and the pressure of extra-European powers, particularly the United States and the Soviet Union? 'How much of this integration grew out of the peculiar conditions of the Cold War, and how much of it would have happened if the struggle had never occurred?' The question is a crucial one now,[11] for institutions, practices and values rooted in the Cold War may well prove ephemeral and disappear with the end of the East-West conflict.[12] Disintegration and fragmentation characterise the situation in large parts of Eastern Europe, and disintegrative tendencies have begun to arise even in Western Europe.

Second, what is the relationship between European integration and the nation-state? Was European integration an attempt to overcome or to supersede the European nation-state by creating supranational institutions, or even a federal state, or was it on the contrary an attempt to strengthen the European nation-state? The answers given to these questions can best be illuminated by an overview of research into European integration. Three different views can be distinguished.

The first view may be called the extra-European, cold war or US-centred perspective on European integration. In a number of studies on the early post-war period, Western European integration appears as merely the product of the Cold War and the antagonism between the superpowers, the United States and the Soviet Union. These studies date from the 1950s and the 1960s and were mostly written by American scholars, either by American historians and political scientists or by those who had been active in government in these years. These works were studies not of European integration but of American foreign policy and the origins, sources and the evolution of the Cold War.[13] For 'traditionalists' like Herbert Feis, William McNeill or Norman Graebner – the traditionalist view blames the USSR for the Cold War – the USA was not only the external federator of Europe but 'the primary catalyst of both the ideas and even institutions' of the European unity movement.[14] The USA was portrayed as the 'positive' external federator, whereas the Soviet Union and communism appeared as a sort of 'negative' external federator. Even in the studies of the 'revisionists' – for the revisionist school the USA was responsible for the conflict – the possibilities and limits of European integration were circumscribed by the global superstructure of the Cold War.

Even in the recent works of American scholars – particularly those of Charles S. Maier or Michael J. Hogan – the crucial role of the USA in European integration and the reconstruction of Western Europe is being elaborated.[15] In contrast to earlier works, these authors are less interested in the Cold War. They are interested in the sources of Western European reconstruction and the contribution American concepts, American ideas and American experiences such as the New Deal made to the rebuilding of Europe after World War II. Limited government intervention, trade liberalisation and cooperation between government, trade unions and business, between capital and labour instead of class conflict, helped to engineer economic growth, productivity, welfare and high consumption for all. 'Be like us' was the American message after the war. The American model, the American way of life and the American way of doing things guided the reconstruction of Western Europe. That applied also to the institutions and the forms of European unity. In order to overcome the old conflicts and rivalries between the European states, the ideal was to create a 'United States of Europe' – on the model of the United States of America. The Marshall Plan and the European Recovery Program were, besides the dependence of the Europeans on the US for their political and military security, the most important channels for the American vision. Marshall Plan aid and the impulses that grew out of it helped create the broad framework for interdependence, within which European integration could take place. In view of their superior economic and military strength, and in view of the weakness of the Europeans, and their need for aid and their hunger for dollars, the USA, according to these studies, was largely successful in achieving its aims – at least in the long run.[16]

American scholars once again have long had a strong influence on even the theoretical study of European integration. 'In fact, the major contributions to a better understanding and conceptualisation to the process of European integration', said a German social scientist in 1965, 'have come from across the Atlantic.'[17] In particular the most influential theory of integration, the concept of neo-functionalism, was developed by a small circle of American scholars including Ernst B. Haas, Philippe Schmitter, Leon Lindberg, Stuart Scheingold or Joseph S. Nye. Theories of integration exercised a great fascination in the 1950s and 1960s, but, in view of their inadequacies and their limited predictive value, they were abandoned in the middle of the 1970s. Neo-functionalism, however, with the Single European Act und the Single Market, has experienced a revival at the end of the 1980s.[18]

Like neo-functionalism, the federal view of European integration, the second perspective discussed here, presumed that the nation-state would wither away. The leading protagonist of the federal view on European integration was Walter Lipgens, who must be regarded as the Nestor of historical research on integration. He pioneered the archive-based study of the origins of European integration, concentrating on the European ideal among resistance groups and the European Movement.

The federal view starts from three interrelated positions: first, from the political and economic decline of Europe since the First World War and the gradual rise of the USA and the USSR as the new world powers; second, from the devastating effects of nationalism, fascism and national socialism; and third, from the perceived anachronism of the nation-state. The European-nation state, according to this view, was no longer capable of fulfilling its traditional functions, namely to provide security to its citizens and to enhance material welfare. The high levels of unemployment, the great depression and the beggar-my-neighbour policies of the 1930s had revealed its failure in the economic and social field. The two world wars had demonstrated that the traditional states system was a source of international rivalry, inter-state conflict and war.

According to Lipgens these experiences – the two world wars, the great depression, the decline of the European powers, resistance to national socialism and to German occupation – effected a profound change in the political consciousness of leading people in the politics and societies of Europe. The solution to Europe's problems lay in European union, in the creation of a European federation or in supranational political structures, structures that were to limit national sovereignty and to supersede the nation-state. The powerlessness and the ultimate failure of the League of Nations which had not affected the sovereignty of its members was adduced as additional proof that supranational solutions were required in order to provide peace and security. Only a federal Europe would be able to secure democracy and welfare. Only a united Europe was strong enough to stand up to the new superpowers and play an independent role in world politics.

What are, according to this view, the driving forces behind European unification? The main actors are, first of all, the European Movement and European pressure groups. Building on the informal groups in exile, these groups were formed during and shortly after the Second World War in all European countries. Second, there are the leading personalities, visionaries, and great Europeans, the 'founding fathers' – politicians like Paul-Henri Spaak, Robert Schuman, Alcide de Gasperi, Konrad Adenauer or Jean Monnet. A high degree of idealism, insight and political will motivated these people. 'Political will', the wish to create new European structures, to overcome the shortcomings of the old European order and the inherent dangers of the sovereign nation-state, played a crucial role in European integration.

How is a united Europe to be created? The best way, according to the Federalist view, is the constitutional method: a European assembly works out a European constitution leading to a European federal state, democratically controlled by a directly elected European Parliament. It is important to stress that, on the European continent, federalism does not mean a centralized European superstate.

Walter Lipgens taught modern history at Saarbrücken University, Germany, before he was appointed Professor at the European University Institute, Florence; he was, from 1976–79, the first person to hold the chair of contemporary history there. Lipgens had already written on the Briand plan of 1929–30, and in a number of studies he collected documentary evidence of plans and concepts for European union. He devoted particular attention to the plans worked out during the Second World War and in the early post-war period, developed in exile by the resistance movements and by the European Movement, by leading personalities and by national political parties and pressure groups, as well as by transnational European parties and pressure groups. His extensive study on the beginnings of European integration remained uncompleted because of his sudden death.[19]

A remarkable degree of inner consistency characterises the federal perspective. It is, to a large extent, a normative approach and a powerful political model. However, the federal view faces considerable difficulties when it tries to demonstrate the extent and importance of federalism in the practical politics of the period under discussion. Numerous questions then arise, such as, how important was the European Movement? How strong was the influence of its leading representatives on the practical politics of the countries concerned? With reference to Britain – admittedly in many respects not a typical example – Donald Watt has called them 'outsiders, distinguished outsiders and distinguished nobodies'.[20] Moreover, the European Movement was extremely heterogeneous, a point seriously underestimated by Lipgens but stressed by Wilfried Loth, one of Lipgens' former students.[21] It was divided into 'federalists', the advocates of a federation (Bundesstaat), on the one hand and 'unionists', the advocates of a confederation (Staatenbund), on the other. There were also advocates of a 'United Socialist States of Europe' and those who, on the contrary, wanted a liberal, capitalist Europe. A third dividing line was between the protagonists of a European Third Force, especially in France, and those like Winston Churchill – he played (with Duncan Sandys) a leading role in the European Movement – who on the contrary wanted to integrate Western Europe firmly into the Atlantic World. And what about the idealism of the 'founding fathers', Schuman, Monnet and Adenauer; were they idealists and 'Europeans', or politicians who thought in terms of power and the interests of their own country? Did the politicians, the governments and the civil servants of the time really aim at weakening or superseding the nation-state? Were federalism, idealism and a change in popular political consciousness really the motor of European integration?

Questions like these were the starting point for a third perspective on early European integration, which may be termed the national interest or European nation-state view. The leading representative of this view is Alan S. Milward.[22] Central assumptions of his approach are shared by scholars such as Frances M. B. Lynch or Ruggero Ranieri and also, with reservations, by Richard T. Griffiths.[23] Most of them were formerly or are still attached to the European University Institute in Florence. Milward taught there in the 1980s, and when in 1987 he moved to the London School of Economics and Political Science, he was succeeded by Griffiths from the Free University, Amsterdam.

Both Milward and Griffiths are economic and social historians. Both combine political and economic analysis. Both can be termed historical political economists, unlike Lipgens who basically was a historian of political ideas. Their studies are based, like those of Lipgens, on a wide range of archives and unpublished sources. Yet, whereas Lipgens' works were based on the archives of European pressure groups, political parties or leading members of the European Movement, the main sources for Milward and Griffiths are government or public archives: a crucial difference. Lipgens mainly dealt in his studies with concepts and plans for European union. Milward, Griffiths and others like them explore the actions and decisions of political systems and governments in their widest sense.

Milward, always revisionist and provocative, rejects, first, the external, US-centred view of European integration. Interestingly enough, on this point his view largely corresponds to the federalist perspective – though for quite different reasons and motives. However, and second, in complete opposition to the federalist view, he stresses the crucial importance of national interests and of the nation-state for European integration. According to Milward, the weakness and the powerlessness of Europe after the war have been greatly exaggerated in the literature – as has the importance of Marshall Aid for the reconstruction and integration of Europe. Contrary to the predominant view, the Marshall Plan was not necessary for postwar European reconstruction.[24] The European states pursued their own strategies and were strong enough even in 1947 to reject American plans. Western European integration was basically a European matter undertaken by Europeans for the solution of European problems. The Organisation for European Economic Cooperation (OEEC) remained a strictly intergovernmental body. It had little in common with the aims the Americans had hoped to achieve: 'The terms on which European reconstruction was finally settled were more European than American.' The Europeans created their own institutionalised framework for interdependence and reconstruction. Its pillars were the Schuman Plan and the European Payments Union: 'In the EPU it was the strength of Britain's position which had to be acknowledged, in the Schuman Plan that of France.'[25] The European Coal and Steel

Community and the European Economic Community were not
the product of American ideas or American concepts, but grew out
of internal European forces, needs and pressures.

This view thus stresses the strength and the self-confidence of
Western Europe even after the War. There is a parallel here to
Cold War historiography, where in the 1970s and 1980s a new
approach emerged which began to 'depolarize' the Cold War
years.[26] This school of thought sought to challenge the until then
dominant view of the Cold War which had regarded the US and
the USSR as virtually the only actors in the global contest and had
painted Western Europe as the 'passive victim of superpower politics'.[27] Instead, it stressed the role of Europe, in particular that of
Britain, in the early Cold War period.[28] Both views – the 'depolar-
ized' perspective on the Cold War and the national interest view of
early European integration – were connected with international
developments of the 1970s and 1980s. They reflected in a way the
gradual decline of the superpowers and the growing confidence
and independence of Europe.

Milward and others, second, reject the federal perspective,
according to which the politicians of the time did not pursue a
national policy, wilfully renounced national sovereignty and aimed
at a federal Europe and the withering away of the nation-state. The
reverse, according to their view, was true: the European governments aimed at the solution of national problems and the national
interest was predominant. It means not the 'objective' national
interest but the 'perceived' national interest, the product of the
search for an internal balance of forces within government structures and the political system.[29] The new European institutions
were the result of efforts to solve national problems on a European
level and in an international context. Supranationality was not a
priori the goal of European politics. The form was of secondary
importance: it might be national, sectoral or supranational.
Europe's politicians were thus much more pragmatic or empirical
than the federal perspective seems to suggest.

The European nation-state was not weakened, but was instead
'rescued' by European integration. Keynesianism, the incorporation of labour into the machinery of policy formulation, state support for incomes in the agricultural sector, the national welfare
regimes, strategic industrial intervention, the requirements of
defence and rearmament all led to a vast growth in the expenditure and the power of the postwar nation-state. There is no

antithesis between European integration and the nation-state; on the contrary, the building of institutions and the Europeanisation of national policies were an integral part of its reassertion. Without integration the European nation-state might well not have regained the allegiance and support of its citizens in the way it did. The 'fathers' of early European integration, statesmen like Spaak, Schuman, Adenauer, de Gasperi or Monnet, regarded the nation-state and integration not as separate and opposed, but as mutually reinforcing entities. Monnet was the architect of French modernisation as well as the author of the Schuman Plan.[30]

Integration was not an inevitable or pre-determined process. It was not the result of long-term trends nor of changes in popular political consciousness. It was the result of a complex bargaining process between the nation-states involved. Parts of national sovereignty were only abandoned if such a policy corresponded to the national interests of the countries concerned; only if those national interests could mutually be satisfied and if this mutual satisfaction of interests represented the best solution was integration in a limited form accepted as a necessary aspect of European post-war politics. Among the various motives for European integration, the federal approach (Lipgens) regarded the political motives as predominant: these included peace, security, democracy and Europe's role in the world. The third – national interest or nation-state – view stresses on the contrary the importance of economic and social motivations such as welfare, expansion and economic growth.

Domestic, not foreign, policy considerations were decisive for European integration. Over the past few years several historians – among them members of the European Community Liaison Committee[31] – have elaborated the importance of national diplomacy for European integration. The impact of military and political security considerations has been stressed by works on military integration, the Brussels Pact, the European Defence Community, NATO and the Western European Union.[32] According to this view France in particular, through European integration, sought to tie Germany firmly to the West and to prevent a new 'Rapallo'. For Adenauer, reconciliation with France was the first priority, which he wished to achieve by forging binding ties between the two countries. European integration was the stepping-stone to regaining sovereignty and to returning to world politics.[33] Integration and common institutions were meant to serve as further guarantees of peace in Western Europe.

Alan Milward accepts these motivations, yet he does not regard them as crucial. The difference between his views and those outlined above may be illustrated by one example, the French government's acceptance of the Rome Treaties. According to Pierre Guillen, the Suez fiasco was the major catalyst for the French decision to abandon objections to the common market treaty. European integration came to be seen as a means to free the French from excessive dependence on the United States and to reassert Europe's voice in the world.[34] According to Alan Milward und Frances Lynch, however, the economic foundation of the treaties was more fundamental. Domestic economic and social choice pushed France down the path of integration. In any case, political motives were not separable from the economic ones. Moreover, the government in Paris had made up its mind before the international events of October–November 1956 took place.[35]

'Changes in the economy, society and political organizations which are closely linked in the post-war state have been the motivation for the choice of integration'.[36] By combining political and economic analysis, the third view considerably widens the perspective. It puts European integration in the wider context of European reconstruction, the welfare state and the imperatives of expansion and growth. It marks an important step in research on integration and offers even a new theory of European integration. However, it is far from clear that the right balance between all the factors involved in European integration has been found. Milward underestimates the role of the Marshall Plan and of the USA for early European integration.[37] He admits the importance of foreign policy considerations and the impact of the international environment for European integration, but these are not integrated into his analytical or theoretical framework.

To conclude, after listing so many points of disagreement or clashes between historiographical approaches, two areas will be mentioned where there is a large measure of agreement among the scholars. The first concerns the role of Germany and the 'German problem' for Western Europe and European integration. Most historians support the view that the control of Germany's resources within and by European institutions was a crucial motive for Western European integration. After two world wars a constructive answer had to be found to the question of what to do with Germany ('que faire de l'Allemagne?'); a Germany moreover, whose resources were deemed crucial for European reconstruction, the containment of the Soviet Union and the security of the Western powers. Was European integration launched in order to cope with the Germans and keep them under control? Integration helped reconcile Germany's recovery with Western European (particularly French) economic and political security needs. In the 1950s West Germany became the economic powerhouse and the centre for Western Europe's foreign trade network, replacing the USA as the most important market and supplier of capital goods.[38]

The second area of agreement concerns the role of France. There is a wide measure of agreement among scholars that the initiatives by Robert Schuman and Jean Monnet in 1950, leading to the European Coal and Steel Community, were among the most important decisions for European integration. France became prepared to accommodate Germany and to move without Britain.[39] For Alan Bullock, Monnet's idea was 'as bold and imaginative as any in European history'.[40] John Gillingham regards the Schuman Plan as a 'substitute peace treaty'.[41] Milward praises the plan as 'the central tie in western European reconstruction which was so conspicuously missing in the 1920s'.[42] Even if, as recent literature suggests, the ECSC and the functioning of the High Authority had little in common with Monnet's original ideas, most scholars are ready to admit that Schuman and Monnet deserve praise for their courage. The Paris-Bonn axis became the foundation for European integration. The integration process advanced the 'West-Integration' of Germany sought by Adenauer and became the framework for Franco-German rapprochement. Many scholars assume that it is precisely in this field that the most important achievements of West European integration can be seen.

Notes

1. On the aims, the current research projects and the state of the project see EUI Research Project Report No 4, *Challenge and Response in Western Europe: The History of European Integration*, by Richard T. Griffiths, EUI, Florence, January 1992.
2. Josef Becker and Franz Knipping (eds), *Power in Europe?*, vol I, *Great Britain, France, Italy and Germany in a Postwar World, 1945–1950*, Berlin, 1986; Ennio di Nolfo (ed.), *Power in Europe?*, vol. II, *Great Britain, France, Germany and Italy and the Origins of the EEC, 1952–1957*, Berlin, 1992. René Girault (ed.), *Les Europe des Européens*, Paris, 1993; Girault (ed.), *Identité et Conscience Européennes au XXe Siècle*, Paris, 1994.

3. So far four volumes based on conferences have been published: Raymond Poidevin (ed.), *Histoire des Débuts de la Construction Européenne (Mars 1948–Mai 1950)*, Bruxelles, 1986; Klaus Schwabe (ed.), *Die Anfänge des Schuman-Plans 1950/51*, Baden-Baden, 1988; Enrico Serra (ed.), *Il Rilancio dell'Europa e i Trattati di Roma*, Milano, 1989; Gilbert Trausch (ed.), *Die europäische Integration vom Schuman-Plan bis zu den Verträgen von Rom. Pläne und Initiativen, Enttäuschungen und Mißerfolge*, Baden-Baden, 1993.

4. Hans-Peter Schwarz, 'Die Europäische Integration als Aufgabe der Zeitgeschichtsforschung. Forschungsstand und Perspektiven', *Vierteljahrshefte für Zeitgeschichte*, vol. 31, no. 4, 1983, pp. 555–72.

5. As examples may be cited Geoffrey Barraclough, *European Unity in Thought and Action*, Oxford, 1963; Heinz Gollwitzer, *Europabild und Europagedanke. Beiträge zur deutschen Geistesgeschichte des 18. und 19. Jahrhunderts*, 2nd edn, München, 1964 (1st edn, 1951); Martin Göhring (ed.), *Europa – Erbe und Aufgabe. Internationaler Gelehrtenkongress Mainz 1955*, Wiesbaden, 1956 (a volume highly instructive of the ideas, thoughts and endeavours of the mid-1950s); Pierre Renouvin, *L'Idée de Fédération Européenne au XIXe Siècle*, Oxford, 1949; Jean-Baptiste Duroselle, *L'Idée d'Europe dans l'Histoire*, Paris, 1965; Rolf H. Foerster, *Europa. Geschichte einer politischen Idee*, München, 1967; Derek Heater, *The Idea of European Unity*, Leicester, 1992.

6. Theodor Schieder, 'Vorwort zum Gesamtwerk. Begriff und Probleme einer europäischen Geschichte', in Theodor Schieder (ed.), *Handbuch der europäischen Geschichte*, vol. 1, *Europa im Wandel von der Antike zum Mittelalter*, Stuttgart, 1976, pp. 1–21; Schieder, 'Nationalbewußtsein und europäische Einigung', in Otto Dann and Hans-Ulrich Wehler (eds), *Theodor Schieder. Nationalismus und Nationalstaat. Studien zum nationalen Problem im modernen Europa*, Göttingen, 1991, pp. 360–76.

7. Again a few works only can be cited: Sidney Pollard, *European Economic Integration 1815–1970*, London, 1974; Pollard, *The Integration of the European Economy since 1815*, London, 1981; William O. Henderson, *The Genesis of the Common Market*, London, 1962; Henderson, 'The German Zollverein and the European Economic Community', *Zeitschrift für die gesamte Staatswissenschaft*, vol. 137, no. 3, 1981, pp. 491–507; Helmut Berding (ed.), *Wirtschaftliche und politische Integration in Europa im 19. und 20. Jahrhundert*, Göttingen, 1984; Alan S. Milward, *The Reconstruction of Western Europe 1945–51*, London, 1984; Carl Strikwerda, 'The Troubled Origins of European Economic Integration: International Iron and Steel and Labor Migration in the Era of World War I', *The American Historical Review*, vol. 98, no. 4, 1993, pp. 1106–29.

8. Hartmut Kaelble, *Auf dem Weg zu einer europäischen Gesellschaft. Eine*

Sozialgeschichte Westeuropas 1880–1980, München, 1987. (Translation: *A Social History of Western Europe, 1880–1980*, Dublin, 1990); Hartmut Kaelble (ed.), *The European Way. Essays on Social Peculiarities of Europe During the 19th and 20th Centuries* (in preparation with Berghahn Publishers); 'Europäische Identität und gesellschaftliche Besonderheiten Europas im 20. Jahrhundert', in *Bericht über die 38. Versammlung deutscher Historiker in Bochum, 26 bis 29. September 1990*, Stuttgart, 1991, pp. 210–20 (in particular the contributions by Hartmut Kaelble, René Girault and Michael Mitterauer); Jonathan Morris, 'Towards a European History of the *Petite Bourgeoisie*', in Mary Fulbroock (ed.), *National Histories and European History*, London, 1993, pp. 183–203; Dick Geary, 'Working-Class Identities in Europe', 1850–1914, in ibid, pp. 204–15.

9. Derek Urwin, *Western Europe since 1945. A Political History*, 4th edn, London, 1992, p.162; on the economic and social developments of Europe since 1945 see Frank B. Tipton and Robert Aldrich, *An Economic and Social History of Europe from 1939 to the Present*, Basingstoke, 1987; Derek H. Aldcroft, *The European Economy, 1914–1980*, London, 1980; Andrea Boltho (ed.), *The European Economy: Growth and Crisis*, Oxford, 1982; Hermann Kellenbenz (ed.), *Handbuch der europäischen Wirtschafts- und Sozialgeschichte*, Vol. 6, Wolfram Fischer (ed.), *Europäische Wirtschafts- und Sozialgeschichte vom Ersten Weltkrieg bis zur Gegenwart*, Stuttgart, 1987; Peter Flora (ed.), *Growth to Limits: The Western European Welfare States since World War II* (planned 5 vols.; so far published vols. 1, 2 and 4), Berlin, 1986–87.

10. Ludolf Herbst, 'Die zeitgenössische Integrationstheorie und die Anfänge der europäischen Einigung 1947–1950', *Vierteljahrshefte für Zeitgeschichte*, vol. 34, no. 2, 1986, pp. 161–203; Heinrich Schneider, *Leitbilder der Europapolitik*, vol. 1, *Der Weg zur Integration*, Bonn, 1977, ch. VII.

11. John Lewis Gaddis, 'The Cold War, the Long Peace, and the Future', in Michael J. Hogan (ed.), *The End of the Cold War: Its Meaning and Implications*, Cambridge, 1992, p. 35.

12. However, even if it could be shown (which is highly unlikely) that European integration was the mere product of the Cold War, this would not necessarily mean that the European Community would disappear after the end of the Cold War. Institutions and practices that have been formed in the Cold War era may have become so deeply rooted that they survive even the end of the East-West conflict with its disciplinary and integrative function.

13. There are numerous surveys of the Cold War. On its history, nature and historiography, see John Lewis Gaddis, *The Long Peace: Enquiries into the History of the Cold War*, Oxford, 1987; Michael Dockrill, *The Cold War 1945–1963*, Basingstoke, 1988; Hogan (ed.), *The End of the*

Cold War (with a helpful bibliographical essay); Gustav Schmidt (ed.), *Ost-West Beziehungen: Konfrontation und Détente 1945–1989*, 2 vols., Bochum, 1993 (especially vol. 1, parts I and IV).

14. Pierre-Henri Laurent, 'Historical Perspectives on Early European Integration', *Revue d'Intégration Européenne*, vol. 12, nos. 2–3, 1989, p. 91.

15. Charles S. Maier, 'The Two Postwar Eras and the Conditions for Stability in Twentieth Century Western Europe', in Maier (ed.), *In Search of Stability: Explorations in Historical Political Economy*, Cambridge, 1987, pp. 153–83; Michael J. Hogan, *The Marshall Plan: America, Britain, and the Reconstruction of Western Europe, 1947–1952*, Cambridge, 1987.

16. The distinction between the long-term and the short-term is also stressed by David W. Ellwood, *Rebuilding Europe: Western Europe, America and Postwar Reconstruction*, London, 1992.

17. Karl Kaiser, '*L'Europe des Savants*: European Integration and the Social Sciences', *Journal of Common Market Studies*, vol. 4, no. 1, 1965, p. 37.

18. A useful collection of theoretical texts from the 1950s and 1960s is Michael Hodges (ed.), *European Integration: Selected Readings*, Harmondsworth, 1972. For a critical overview of the theories of integration see Jürgen Bellers and Erwin Häckel, 'Theorien internationaler Integration und internationaler Organisationen', in Volker Rittberger (ed.), *Theorien der internationalen Beziehungen. Bestandsaufnahme und Forschungsperspektiven*, Opladen, 1990, pp. 286–310; James E. Dougherty and Robert L. Pfaltzgraff, *Contending Theories of International Relations*, 3rd edn, New York, 1990, ch. 10; Ruth Zimmerling, *Externe Einflüsse auf die Integration von Staaten. Zur politikwissenschaftlichen Theorie regionaler Zusammenschlüsse*, Freiburg, 1991, chs 2–3.

19. Walter Lipgens (ed.), *Europa-Föderationspläne der Widerstandsbewegungen 1940–1945. Eine Dokumentation*, München, 1968; *Die Anfänge der europäischen Einigungspolitik 1945–1950, Erster Teil: 1945–1947*, Stuttgart, 1977 (enlarged English edition *A History of European Integration, vol. 1: 1945–47*, Oxford, 1982); *Sources for the History of European Integration (1945–1955): A Guide to Archives in the Countries of the Community*, Leyden 1980; (ed.), *Documents on the History of European Integration*, vol. 1, *Continental Plans for European Union 1939–1945*; vol. 2, *Plans for European Union in Great Britain and in Exile, 1939–1945*, New York-Berlin 1985–6. Volumes 3 and 4 in this series were edited by Wilfried Loth. Vol. 3, *The Struggle for European Union by Political Parties and Pressure Groups in Western European Countries 1945–1950*; vol. 4, *Transnational Organizations of Political Parties and Pressure Groups in the Struggle for European Union 1945–1950*, Berlin-New York, 1988–90. Major articles include 'Europäische Einigungsidee 1923–1930 und Briands Europaplan im Urteil der deutschen Akten', *Historische Zeitschrift*, vol. 203, 1966, pp. 46–89 and 316–63; 'Die

Bedeutung des EVG-Projekts für die politische europäische Einigungsbewegung', in Hans-Erich Volkmann and Walter Schwengler (eds), *Die Europäische Verteidigungsgemeinschaft. Stand und Probleme der Forschung*, Boppard am Rhein, 1985, pp. 9–30.

20. Cited by Hans-Peter Schwarz, 'Die Strassburger Anfänge multinationaler Integrations-Historiographie', in Poidevin (ed.), *Histoire des Débuts*, p. 453.

21. Wilfried Loth has published extensively on early European integration. His major publications include *Der Weg nach Europa. Geschichte der europäischen Integration 1939–1957*, Göttingen, 1990. For his views see ch. 8 of this volume.

22. Milward has published on a wide range of subjects. His main writings on the issues under discussion here include *The Reconstruction of Western Europe 1945–51*, London, 1984; (with the assistance of George Brennan and Federico Romero), *The European Rescue of the Nation-State, London 1992*; with Frances M. B. Lynch, Ruggero Ranieri, Federico Romero and Vibeke Sørensen, *The Frontier of National Sovereignty: History and Theory 1945–1992*, London, 1993.

23. Griffiths currently directs the EUI Research Project on 'Challenge and Response in Western Europe: The History of European Integration'. Griffiths has published on Dutch economic and political history in the 19th and 20th centuries and on early European integration; e.g. Richard T. Griffiths (ed.), *The Netherlands and the Integration of Europe*, Amsterdam, 1990.

24. Alan S. Milward, 'Was the Marshall Plan Necessary?', *Diplomatic History*, vol. 13, no. 2, 1989, pp. 231–53.

25. Milward, *Reconstruction*, passim (quotations pp. 333–4).

26. Robert M. Hathaway, *Ambiguous Partnership: Britain and America, 1944–1947*, New York, 1981, p. 2.

27. David Reynolds, 'The Origins of the Cold War: The European Dimension, 1944–1951', *The Historical Journal*, vol. 28. no. 2, 1985, p. 499.

28. For historiographical overviews see Reynolds, 'Origins', pp. 497–515; Lawrence S. Kaplan, 'The Cold War and European Revisionism', *Diplomatic History*, vol. 11, no. 2, 1987, pp. 143–56; Donald C. Watt, 'Britain and the Historiography of the Yalta Conference and the Cold War', *Diplomatic History*, vol. 13, no. 1, 1989, pp. 67–89. For monographs see Anne Deighton, *The Impossible Peace: Britain, the Division of Germany, and the Origins of the Cold War*, Oxford, 1990; Deighton (ed.), *Britain and the First Cold War*, Basingstoke, 1990; on France, see John W. Young, *France, the Cold War and the Western Alliance, 1944–49: French Foreign Policy and Post-War Europe*, Leicester, 1990.

29. Richard T. Griffiths, 'A la Recherche des Débuts de L'Intégration Européenne', *Revue de Synthèse*, vol. 11, no. 3, 1990, p. 251 (a useful article that surveys historical research on early European integration, attacks mono-causal explanations and sets out a framework for analysis.

Parts of the article are reproduced in EUI Research Project Report No. 4, *Challenge and Response*).

30. Alan S. Milward, 'États-Nations et Communauté: Le Paradoxe de L'Europe?', *Revue de Synthèse*, vol. 111, no. 3, 1990, pp. 253–70; Milward, *European Rescue*, passim. Milward shares the view of Charles Maier (see note 15) that by incorporating the unions and other producer groups into the political system there was a shift of political power and in the political machinery. For both Milward and Maier the new political consensus and the pressure that grew out of it partly explain the high levels of postwar economic growth.

31. See the works mentioned in note 3.

32. For the literature on military integration see the titles cited in the select bibliography at the end of the book.

33. Hans-Peter Schwarz, *Adenauer*, 2 vols. (vol. 1, *Der Aufstieg: 1876–1952*; vol. 2, *Der Staatsmann: 1952–1967*), Stuttgart, 1986–1991; Ludolf Herbst, *Option für den Westen. Vom Marshallplan bis zum deutsch-französischen Vertrag*, München, 1989.

34. Pierre Guillen, 'L'Europe Remède à l'Impuissance Française? Le Gouvernement Guy Mollet et la Négociation des Traités de Rome (1955–1957)', *Revue d'Histoire Diplomatique*, vol. 102, 1988, pp. 319–35; Guillen, 'La France et la Négociation des Traités de Rome: L'Euratom', in Enrico Serra (ed.), *Il Rilancio dell'Europa e i Trattati di Roma*, Milano, 1989, pp. 513–24.

35. Milward, *European Rescue*, pp. 208, 214f.; Frances M.B. Lynch, 'Restoring France: the Road to Integration', in Milward et al., *The Frontier*, pp. 59–87, 208–10.

36. Milward et al., *The Frontier*, p. xi.

37. For recent assessments of the impact of the Marshall Plan on European integration and on European reconstruction see Gérard Bossuat, *L'Europe Occidentale à l'Heure Américaine. Le Plan Marshall et l'Unité Européenne (1945–1952)*, Bruxelles, 1992; Bossuat, *La France, l'Aide Américaine et la Construction Européenne 1944–1954*, 2 vols., Paris, 1992. Unfortunately Bossuat fails to address Milward's findings and the conclusions of foreign-language (above all English-language) research.

38. Milward, *European Rescue*, ch. 4.

39. Raymond Poidevin, *Robert Schuman. Homme d'État 1886–1963*, Paris, 1986, chs xiii–xiv; Schwabe (ed.), *Die Anfänge des Schuman-Plans*; Douglas Brinkley and Clifford Hackett (eds), *Jean Monnet: The Path to European Unity*, London, 1991; Loth, *Weg nach Europa*, ch. 4.

40. Alan Bullock, *Ernest Bevin: Foreign Secretary 1945–1951*, Oxford, 1985, p. 769.

41. John Gillingham, *Coal, Steel, and the Rebirth of Europe, 1945–1955: The Germans and French from Ruhr Conflict to Economic Community*, Cambridge, p. xii.

42. Milward, *Reconstruction*, p. 418.

WERNER ABELSHAUSER

The Re-Entry of West Germany into the International Economy and Early European Integration

The term 'integration' has many different meanings. Economic and political integration should be seen as a process of intra-regional economic development, which for analytical reasons can be divided into three basic steps:[1]

1 — Integration of trade, i.e. free movement of goods and services across borders.
2 — Integration of factors, i.e. free movement of capital, labour and other factors of production across borders.
3 — Integration of policy, i.e. a process of political cooperation leading to supra-national institutions and sovereignty.

According to these definitions, integration of trade is clearly fundamental to the early process of European integration. It was necessary in the first instance to reverse a process of disintegration that culminated in the Great Depression of the early 1930s, the ramifications of which still determined the structure of trade within Europe after 1945. The manner of West Germany's re-entry into the international economy was of crucial importance, not least because of its sheer economic weight.

For West Germany, there was not the slightest possibility of a reorientation on the lines of the practices of the pre-war period. Even the slightest thought of autarky was hopeless, given the shrinking of Germany's economic space and the consequent dislocation of the country's economic structure. The East German areas which had generated large agrarian surpluses were no longer available to supply West Germany. While the Third Reich had been obliged to import some 20 per cent of its food requirements, the Federal Republic now had to meet one-half of its requirements through imports. The effects of the partition of Germany created similar problems for its industrial structure.

The overall trade policy framework had also changed. The once preferred hinterland for bilateral trade relations in Eastern and Southeastern Europe now lay behind the Iron Curtain. From the perspective of 1947, West Germany, in relation to the world economy, had become a 'larger Belgium', as the then economics minister of the State of Hamburg and later economics minister of the Federal Republic, Karl Schiller, put it. Nor was the Federal Republic of Germany in a position to determine its foreign economic strategy on its own; it had to adopt the role which had been laid down for it by the occupying powers in the context of the reorganisation of the world economy after the Second World War. The USA had in effect assumed responsibility for West German economic policy in December 1947, and West Germany had to accommodate itself into the US conception of a liberalised, multilateral and open system of world trade.

One of the main goals of the European Recovery Programme (ERP) launched by US Secretary of State George C. Marshall in June of 1947 was to safeguard this vision of a new order of world economy which should emerge from the British-American Agreement of Bretton Woods. This master plan of re-organising the world economy was, however, threatened by an acute crisis of Western European balance of payments caused by the chronic dollar gap and culminating in the failure of the British attempt to make the pound sterling freely convertible in July 1947. Marshall Aid was then seen as a means to fuel the new machinery of the world economy and Germany was to play a crucial part in this strategy. The perspective of 'European Integration' was part of this concept of the ERP – even if, in the long run, a European trade block could develop into a threat to the original vision of a multilateral and anti-protectionist world trade system.

Against this background, Germany's foreign economic policy had to cope with a dilemma from the very beginning. Economic interests represented by the economics ministry and a majority of export industries opted for the world market as their system of reference. 'European integration' did not stand in the way of this strategy as long as it was restricted to integration of trade and production factors. For the mainstream of German foreign policy, represented by the Foreign Office and the Federal Chancellor, 'European integration' was more than just an economic area favourable to economic growth; priority was given to political stability. At the beginning of Germany's re-entry into the international economy both strategies could easily be combined, but there was a built-in conflict right from the beginning.

The most concrete way to throw light on the process of West Germany's re-entry into inter-European trade, and therefore on the first stage of European economic integration, is to look at Germany's role in the Marshall Plan. Alongside material Marshall Aid, which was designed to balance the trade deficit of the recipient country with the dollar area and to promote the recovery of Western Europe, the Marshall Plan also developed techniques which were to further the goal of European economic integration.

The foreign aid packages adopted by the US Congress in the spring of 1948, entitled the Economic Cooperation Act (ECA), contained the legal basis for the ERP. One of Congress's primary goals was stated to be the promotion of economic cooperation among the European countries.[2] The mechanics of the Marshall Plan itself, however, initially took little account of this. The reconstruction of Western Europe under the auspices of the Marshall Plan was foreseen according to the so-called Long Term Plan, which was expected to develop out of the coordination of the individual plans of the participating countries; but this scenario soon proved entirely unrealistic.[3] The linking of US economic aid to the financing of the European dollar deficit, and accordingly to the bilateral relations of individual European participants with the USA, even gave rise to the fear that 'the Marshall Plan will not only fail to prevent the Balkanisation of the Western European economic area, it will in part even promote it'.[4] Measured against this opening position, the so-called 'Intra-European' or (in contrast to the 'Large') 'Little' Marshall Plan assumes a pioneering role in the reassumption of multilateral trade relations in Europe. Under its auspices a network of intra-European economic aid developed, which – although unintentionally and inadequately – meant that the ERP became at least partially a device for self-aid.

Even though intra-European economic aid in the framework of the Little Marshall Plan was implemented mainly through the leverage of American dollar aid, there were also European elements in its development. Germany's readiness to proceed towards the integration of Western European trade did not merely reflect an absence of alternatives or of room to manoeuvre. It was also based on the national and trade policy myth of the German *Zollverein*. As its role model it took the 'magnificent growth that the German economy achieved after the removal of barriers between states in the last century'.[5] For generations this effect had been presented as the driving force behind the industrialisation of Germany and its national integration;[6] it was now believed capable of making an even stronger contribution to the regeneration of the European economy and its integration, since 'the possibilities for complementary development among the European participants [in the Marshall Plan] are obviously much greater than those within Germany's borders in the last century'.[7]

The American recovery programme also owed something to this model, in which the establishment of a 'large internal market' assumed attributed central importance as a catalyst of economic and political integration accordingly. One of the programme's main aims was to break down the system of bilateralism in world trade relations and to re-establish the open and multilaterally-organised world economy that typified European capitalism in its 'golden age' before the First World War. Post-war Europe was still far from that goal. The weaker among Europe's trading nations were not the only ones to take recourse to protectionism even after the end of the Second World War; large countries also continued with trade policies that had become unavoidable under the pressure of the Great Depression of the early 1930s. At this point, when the world trade system had not yet overcome its chronic weakness, this policy permitted a volume of foreign trade that would not have been maintained under the full application of the Most Favoured Nation (MFN) principle to all trading partners.

By 1947 over 200 bilateral treaties had been concluded, extended or renewed in Europe. Even Switzerland conducted three-quarters of its foreign trade on a bilateral basis. With the exception of Belgium and Switzerland, all the European countries had a quota system which they could use to regulate imports completely. In August 1947, Great Britain had to abandon the attempt it had made, under American prompting, to make sterling convertible and to dismantle preferences for the sterling block countries. The British example shows that dollar aid alone could not restore multilaterality in European trade. The Convention for European

Economic Co-operation (OEEC) of 16 April 1948 underlined this wish: Article Four imposed on participating states the duty to 'continue the efforts already initiated to achieve as soon as possible a multilateral system of payments among themselves, and will cooperate in relaxing restrictions on trade and payments between one another, with the object of abolishing as soon as possible those restrictions which at present hamper such trade and payments.'[8]

The previous attempt to set up a European 'Clearing Union', even before the implementation of the ERP, had failed miserably.[9] On 18 November 1947, Belgium, Luxembourg, the Netherlands, France and Italy had agreed to this union in Paris. The 'non-permanent' members of the Union, Great Britain, Denmark, Sweden, Norway, Greece and Switzerland, refused to agree to the transfer of balances in their respective currencies without prior approval. Great Britain in particular, still reeling from the preceding sterling crisis, wanted to ensure that no sterling assets could be converted into gold or dollars. This possibility would arise should sterling assets be transferred for example to Belgium, which was entitled to demand the conversion of surplus sterling.

The United States attempted to overcome bilateralism in Western Europe through the workings of the Marshall Plan. The Agreement for Intra-European Payments and Compensations, which was signed on 16 October 1948, was modest in its aspirations. Whereas the treaty on the 'Clearing Union' of the previous year had been entitled the 'First Agreement on Multilateral Monetary Compensation', the new arrangement envisaged only a plan for 'limited balance'. It was to last 'until it is possible to undertake further steps towards the creation of a fully multilateral payments system'.[10] It was nevertheless a first step towards setting Western Europe on the road to economic integration, even if the European countries followed the United States along this path only after considerable economic pressure. The ERP (the 'Large' Marshall Plan) aimed at establishing equilibrium in the deficit of the participating countries with the dollar area, and therefore in the first instance with the United States itself. The 'Little' Marshall Plan aimed at bringing equilibrium to the balance of payments situation between the European participants. The ERP assumed a new dimension in that potential surplus countries like Great Britain, Belgium/Luxembourg, Italy and West Germany were forced to give economic assistance to potential deficit countries.

The 'Large' Marshall Plan continued in the first instance the wartime systems of Lend-Lease and emergency supplies (GAR-IOA), which the United States had provided for many European countries after the end of the war. The continuation of aid was necessary for two reasons. Most countries were still not in a position to cover their import surplus from the dollar area, which was regarded as essential to recovery. Secondly, the exceptional condition of postwar Europe meant it was impossible to conduct commercial transactions on credit. The gaps in European trade balances were closed through the supply of goods to the amount of the estimated deficit arising. ERP participants were not allocated 'free' dollars to cover their import requirements, but instead received allotments in the form of goods consignments of a specified volume and type. These in turn were set in bilateral import plans and were subject to a complicated authorisation procedure in which the interests of both sides were considered. The wishes of the recipient were to be balanced against the domestic economic preferences of the donor country.

This mechanism of the ERP made only a limited contribution to inter-European trade links. Where the goods involved were foodstuffs, raw materials and manufactured products of American provenance, there was no such effect. 'Offshore purchases', where the United States bought goods in a European country and forwarded them to the recipient countries, were another matter, but this was done only to a very limited extent. Transactions under the ERP were generally conducted strictly on the basis of bilateral agreements between the US and the respective European participating country. The OEEC, set up as the European coordination agency for the Marshall Plan, functioned solely as a control and intermediary agency.

The 'Little' or 'European' Marshall Plan which arose out of the Intra-European Payments and Compensations Agreement of 16 October 1948 was based on the same principle, in that the equilibrium of balances of payments between surplus and deficit countries was foremost. The group of net creditors (Great Britain, Belgium/Luxembourg, Italy, Sweden, Turkey and Bizonia) were in the same position vis-à-vis the other European participants, the net debtors, as the United States was with respect to Europe as a whole. Up to the implementation of the 'Little' Marshall Plan, the net debtors had to cover their balances with the creditor group with gold or foreign exchange, of which they had very little. As a consequence, inter-European trade – just like trade with the Dollar Area – was faced with a further decline due to import limitation.

In order to prevent and then reverse this tendency towards disintegration, the 'Intra-European Payments Plan' envisaged drawing rights. Each participant was to provide a non-refundable drawing right in its own currency to each country with which it had a payments surplus which could not be balanced through other means, to the amount of the positive balance involved. In other words, each presented its trading partner with the means needed to balance the payments deficit.[11] Alongside the supplies provided through the 'Large' Marshall Plan, debtor countries received additional resources in the form of drawing rights which allowed them to finance increased imports from other participating countries. Countries which were obliged to issue such drawing rights on account of surplus balances estimated in advance only received allotments under the Marshall Plan on fulfilment of this obligation. US aid for European creditor countries to the amount of the drawing rights thus became 'Conditional Aid'. The overall amount of aid supplied (conditional and unconditional aid added together) was unchanged, but the net effect of foreign aid for creditor countries was reduced, to the extent that they now had to allow debtor countries unreciprocated access to their own resources through the framework of the drawing rights. The net amount of foreign aid for debtor countries rose correspondingly, since the extent of aid under the ERP remained unchanged.

The results of this policy were evident in Year One of the ERP, in the form of considerable shifts in the distribution or net foreign aid among the participating countries (see Table 1). As long as the creditor countries had hoped to convert their surpluses in inter-European trade either entirely or in part into dollars (on the lines of the 'offshore purchases') and to supplement their ERP allotments, they set very high estimations for their surplus balances. In the early stages of the Paris talks, Great Britain and the sterling block reported a surplus of $600 million, and Belgium a surplus of $400 million. Italy promised the delivery of fruit and vegetables, Greece and Turkey offered dried fruits and tobacco, Belgium offered steel and Sweden promised iron ore.[12]

As it became clear during the negotiations that the drawing rights would have to be deducted from the actual foreign aid, if not indeed the dollar aid, of each country, the participants

Table 1 **Economic Aid within the framework of the ERP (1948–49 $millions)**

	ERP (1 + 2) (1)	incl.: conditional aid = drawing rights to give 'European' (2)	drawing rights to take *Marshall Plan* (3)	total foreign aid (1./.2) + 3 = (4)
Belgium/Luxembourg		219	11	40
Denmark	248	5	12	116
Western Germany				
Bi-zone	109	109	99	401
French-zone		15	16	100
France		10	333	1304
Greece	411	–	67	212
Great Britain	99	320	30	949
Ireland	–	–	–	78
Iceland	981	–	–	5
Italy		47	27	535
Netherlands	145	11	82	541
Norway	123	16	48	115
Austria	9	3	67	279
Portugal	78	–	–	–
Sweden	5	35	10	22
Switzerland	–	–	–	–
Triest	555	–	–	18
Turkey		29	17	28
Reserve	470	–	–	13
	83			
	215			
	–			
	47			
	–			
	18			
	40			
	13			
Total	4756	818	818	4756

Source: Der Länderrat des VWG, Hauptref. für ERP-Angelegenheiten,
　　　Die Grundlinien des gesamten Marshallplan-Systems, Anlage I,
　　　(3.9.1949) BA, Z14/41.

became eager to keep their planned exports to other countries as low as possible and to register large import needs at the same time. In each case the calculation had to be preceded by some estimate of the trade between each pair of ERP countries, for only after those calculations had shown the extent to which Europe's needs could be satisfied out of Europe's resources could any reasonable estimate be made of the gap that would remain to be filled by the United States. Circumstances dictated that the estimation of supplementary needs and the corresponding export surpluses was a political exercise, and was not possible by means of purely economic calculations. As a result, the surpluses offered at the beginning of the Paris talks disappeared as if by magic. Every country naturally tried to keep its exports to other European countries to a minimum and to inflate its imports from European countries as far as decency would allow. With great effort, and with the application of dollar aid, deliberations stretching over months arrived at a minimum programme, and this in itself represented a clear improvement of the status quo.

The largest supplementary requirement under the new scheme was that of $323 million allocated to France, although contemporary observers were aware that France's difficulties 'are due to mismanagement rather than to misfortune'.[13] The further allocations of drawing rights were $71 million to the Netherlands, $67 million to Greece, $64 million to Austria, $32 million to Norway, and $7 million to Denmark.[14] Great Britain had to bear the lion's share ($290 million) of inter-European economic aid in the first year of the ERP. Belgium ($208 million), Sweden ($25 million), Italy ($20 million), Turkey ($12 million) and West Germany ($9 million)[15] were also constrained to pass on a part of their dollar aid in their own currency to other European participants in the Marshall Plan (see Table 1).

In the first year of the ERP, drawing rights had an exclusively bilateral character. They could only be used by each country to balance payments with one other participating country. They thus allowed a greater degree of inter-European economic integration than would otherwise have been possible and promoted the export trade of the creditor countries, but they did not contribute to the re-establishment of genuine competitive conditions for international trade. On the contrary, the system presupposed a high degree of bureaucratic guidance. Within the OEEC, around 110 different balances of payments had to be predetermined before the level of drawing rights could be fixed.[16] This process had considerable political implications, and to some contemporaries the organisation seemed 'to be burdened with the legacy of political resentments and national efforts at autarky more strongly than is tolerable for the task at hand'.[17]

The implementation of another goal of the October 1948 Agreement also proved difficult. It envisaged the possibility of clearing such balances as arose out of existing bilateral payments agreements 'provided that this is in accordance with the transfer policy of the individual countries and with the conditions of the payment agreements they have concluded'.[18] The Basel-based Bank for International Settlements (BIS) acted as agent for the European central banks in inter-European payments and compensation agreements; but the terms under which it was allowed to clear balances without the prior agreement of the countries concerned were extremely narrow. The primacy of bilateral arrangements is unmistakeable.[19]

The renewal of the Intra-European Payments and Compensations Agreement took place in Paris in July 1949. The talks addressed a US-sponsored proposal to make all drawing rights transferable and therefore usable on a multilateral basis. This would mean that buyers in the receiving countries could seek out the markets in which they could buy at the cheapest and most favourable terms. The USA thus wanted not only full competitiveness in international trade within Europe, but also between Europe and North America. Conditional aid, hitherto distributed in each case to the full extent, would in future be provided only to the extent that drawing rights were actually exercised in respect of the issuing country. Britain in particular sought to block this proposal; after its dollar exports fell sharply in the spring of 1949 it was more dependent on its reserves of gold and currency. The proposal would mean less dollar aid for surplus countries in general and for relatively uncompetitive ones such as Britain in particular. This was not the least of the reasons behind the dropping of the demand for the convertability of the drawing rights into dollars. The second Paris Payments and Compensations Agreement of 7 September 1949 elaborated a compromise: the transferable proportion of the drawing rights, and therefore the extent of the multilateralisation of the system, was limited to 25 per cent.[20]

At the same time the 'Little' Marshall Plan assumed greater

importance in terms of overall foreign aid. The drawing rights amounted to about one-sixth of total aid in the first year, but this share rose to almost one-quarter in the second year, principally because of the reduction of 20 per cent in the large Marshall Plan (see Table 2). The distribution of inter-European economic aid also shifted considerably. England (together with the sterling block countries) was the most affected; aid transfers fell from $290 million to $60 million. It had become evident in the previous year that a large portion of the drawing rights issued by Great Britain could not be used because of the high level of sterling export prices.

Britain was thus succeeded as the most important surplus country by Belgium, followed at some distance by West Germany. Belgium's position in respect of the Little Marshall Plan was somewhat exceptional. The European creditor countries as a rule had deficits with the USA which well exceeded their net surplus towards the participating European countries. But Belgium had a trade surplus of around $400 million in Europe, compared with a deficit of just $200 million with the USA. Accordingly only half of the Belgian surplus was eligible for financing through Marshall Plan consignments. In order to secure the full involvement of Belgium in the Little Marshall Plan, the country received additional transfers under the Marshall Plan above and beyond the covering of its dollar deficit: $50 million in the form of goods consignments of specified type and volume, according to the usual ECA procedure, and a further $62.5 million in 'free' dollars. This was a way of compensating Belgium for being, uniquely among the European participants, a net donor rather than a net recipient of foreign aid.[21]

These special conditions did not apply to West Germany. A serious row about the level of German participation in the 'Little' Marshall Plan broke out in the first year of the Marshall Plan; the conflict between the USA, representing German interests, and the potential recipients of German credits assumed ugly dimensions.[22] The prospective balance of trade between West Germany and the rest of Europe symbolised all the political issues that revolved round the future of the Ruhr. Calculations on this question were bound to crystallise all the differences over the future location of industry in Western Europe and the priority to be given to the industrial reconstruction of the Ruhr. Though the Western

European countries demanded a sum of $90 million, the ERP administration ultimately settled on a net surplus of only $10 million (see Table 1). Yet the three western zones were not able to utilise their full entitlements in drawing rights during the period of the agreement; by contrast, practically all West German-issued drawing rights were used by the recipients. The net effect of West German economic aid for Europe thus exceeded planned dimensions and reached $48.35 million (see Table 3).[23]

West Germany thereby demonstrated the attractiveness of its export production, a development which did not meet with unqualified enthusiasm in the Economics Administration. On the other hand, German importers found the British market too expensive to do business there, although they had access to adequate foreign exchange in the form of drawing rights. This development was a main reason for the disproportionate decline of dollar aid to West Germany under the ERP in year two of the plan (32 per cent, compared with the average decline of 20 per cent). It also contributed to the fall of 63 per cent in total foreign aid receipts, the largest of any participant (see Table 2). Total foreign aid thus did not even cover the anticipated burden of aid for Berlin.[24]

France and Austria were the main recipients of West German drawing rights (see Table 4), and Austria was able to use them to compensate for most of the reduction in its dollar aid. In the Federal Republic the effects of the revision of the drawing rights by the Agreement of 1 September 1949 were received with mixed feelings. The head of the Economic Section of the German Delegation to the OEEC, Otmar Emminger, was the most forthright in seeking a reduction in the drawing rights West Germany had to concede. In the context of a short term cost-and-benefit analysis, he felt that the estimates of trade balances needed revision. In his view, the estimates had two shortcomings: they had not taken into account the round of devaluations of important European currencies which had taken place in the meantime, and they had not taken sufficient account of ongoing efforts at liberalising German foreign trade.[25]

The West German Economic Ministry's Department of General Affairs also criticised the fact that 'the Marshall Plan [disburses] the grace of its dollar and drawing rights more or less schematically on the basis of the *current* deficits of the individual European countries... It thus in effect preserves unhealthy imbalances and

Table 2 **Economic Aid within the framework of the ERP (1949–50 $millions)**

	ERP *(1 + 2)* (1)	incl.: conditional aid = drawing rights to give 'European' (2)	drawing rights to take *Marshall Plan* (3)	total foreign aid (1./.2) + 3 = (4)
Western Germany	348.2	163.9	–	184.3[a]
Austria	174.2	2.7	85.8	257.2
Denmark	91.0	7.7	22.6	105.9
France	704.0	34.4	258.0	927.6
Greece	163.5	–	104.3	267.8
Ireland	47.0	–	–	47.0
Iceland	7.3	–	–	7.3
Italy	407.0	24.5	–	382.5
Norway	94.0	5.0	76.8	165.8
Netherlands (including Indonesia)	309.2	20.3	156.5	445.4
Portugal	33.0	1.0	27.2	59.2
Great Britain	962.0[b]	171.0	102.0	893.0
Sweden	48.0	48.0	–	–
Turkey	61.7	8.0	53.3	107.0
Triest	14.0	–	–	14.0
Belgium/Luxembourg	312.5	400.0	–	–87.5
Total	3776.5	886.5	886.5	3776.5

[a] additionally 426 $millions from GARIOA [b] incl. sterling area

Source: Der Vorsitzende des ERP-Arbeitsausschusses, Marshallplan-Information Nr. 26 (23.9.1949) BA, Z14/41.

rewards economic incompetence'.[26] A 'construction flaw' was perceived in the Marshall Plan in that France received an aid total of $21.70 per head of population in the second year of the ERP, Austria $37.20 and the Netherlands as much as $45, whereas West Germany, including GARIOA aid, got just $12 per head. The West German economics administration would undoubtedly have preferred 'if the Marshall Plan in some manner were replaced with or coupled with aid that was supplied on the basis of capital aid, and

Table 3 **West Germany and the 'European' Marshall Plan 1948–49**
(Intra-European Agreement on Payments and Compensation)
(October 1, 1948 – June 30, 1949; in $millions)

a) Drawing rights to be given by West Germany

Receiver	Planned	Realized
Denmark	1.2	1.2
France	53.7	53.7
Greece	4.4	4.4
Netherlands	8.5	8.5
Austria	29.6	29.6
Total	97.4	97.4
Revised Total		96.354

b) Drawing rights to be taken by West Germany

Giver	Planned	Realized		Not realized
Belgium/Luxembourg	21.0	21.0	= 100%	–
Great Britain	52.0	3.684	= 7.1%	48.316
Italy	12.7	12.7	= 100%	–
Netherlands	2.0	2.0	= 100%	–
Norway	8.0	0.0	0%	8.0
Sweden	5.0	0.0	0%	5.0
Turkey	13.5	6.778	= 50.2%	6.722
Total	114.2	46.162	= 40.4%	68.038
Revised total		48.004	= 42.0%	
Economic Aid given by West Germany a) minus b)		48.350		

Source: F. Stedtfeld, Ziehungsrechte (5.1.50) p. 4, BA, B 102/55337 u.
    Aufstellung in Anlage 18 zum Memorandum des Bundesministers
    für den Marshallplan über Nachkriegs-Auslandsschulden v.
    20.9.1951, BA, B 146/234.

not of balance of payments deficits'.[27] The German export trade,
by contrast, pleaded that currency policy considerations should be
restrained in the interests of 'our stricken export industry'.[28] It
pointed to the job creation effect and to the opportunity to invest
profits aquired by export business. Exporters also pointed to 'the

Table 4 **West Germany and the 'European' Marshall Plan 1949–50**
(Intra-European Agreement on Payments and Compensation)
(July 1, 1949 – June 30, 1950, in $millions)

Countries receiving drawing rights	Drawing rights against West Germany (Plan)	Bilateral share (75 %)
France	60.0	45.0
Greece	13.8	10.350
Netherlands	17.5	13.125
Norway	12.6	9.450
Austria	50.0	37.500
Turkey	10.0	7.500
Total planned	163.9	122.925
Total realized	122.214	(100.251)[a]
Drawing rights taken by West Germany (1.12.49–31.5.50)	72.303	
Economic Aid given by West Germany	49.911	

a 82 per cent realized

Source: F. Stedtfeld, Ziehungsrechte (5.1.50) p. 6, BA, B 102/55337 u.
Aufstellung in Anlage 18 zum Memorandum des
Bundesministers für den Marshallplan über Nachkriegs-
Auslandsschulden v. 20.9.1951, BA, B 146/234.

danger that other countries' industries would penetrate these markets'.

Such arguments were not without effect insofar as West German foreign trade policy, in entire accord with the ECA, was directed towards the creation of a unified European economic area in which the German economy could fully realise its potential. A decision on the distribution of industrial locations in Europe was linked to the estimation of surplus capacities in foreign trade. Irrespective of how painful the transfer of resources towards the European deficit countries was for the reconstruction of West Germany, it was more than compensated for by the parallel revision of earlier views on limitating its industrial capacity in favour of other European locations.

The strong demand for German drawing rights also encouraged the supporters of a wide-ranging liberalisation of German foreign trade to 'take the risk and open the doors'.[29] Such a step involved the risk of a balance of payments crisis in the exceptional conditions of the post-war period, but at this point the conditions were favourable under the umbrella of American aid. The Little Marshall Plan was accordingly judged very favourably by the German side: 'Drawing rights are undoubtedly a huge step forward towards a European economic community'.[30]

The commercial conditions under which the re-entry occurred were also determined in large measure by the ERP administration. A decision of the OEEC Council in November 1949 obliged member states to lift quantitative restrictions (quotas) on at least 50 per cent of their total private imports by the end of the year. A further liberalisation, of 60 per cent, was to be achieved by the end of 1950. The 'Liberalisation Codex', which entered into force simultaneously with the European Payments Union (EPU) in September 1950, ultimately envisaged a liberalisation rate of 75 per cent by February 1951. The Federal Republic, as the only non-sovereign member of the OEEC, was destined to push forward along this path, whether it wanted to or not.

Reaction to this forced liberalisation was ambivalent. On the one hand, reprensentatives of sectors such as agriculture and some branches of industry consistently opposed it. They felt they were not yet in a position to keep up with international competition, as a result of the consequences of the war. On the other hand, export industries and most politicians involved in economics, such as the Social Democratic expert on international economics, Fritz Baade, and Economics Minister Ludwig Erhard, saw in this liberalisation the opportunity to make the West German economy competitive again and to secure for it an appropriate share of the world market. They were more disposed to take the risk of adverse balance of payments consequences, since the experience of the 'Little' Marshall Plan had shown that there was strong demand for German investment goods in the neighbouring countries and that the West German export industry was able to cater for much of this demand thanks to its favourable structure. The Economics Administration was, however, convinced that 'educational' tariffs would have to be imposed for an interim period, to have a corrective influence in any area where competition had been distorted. Yet on the question of tariffs Germany once again was unable to prevail against the US intention to promote the dismantling of trade barriers in Europe, and to allow West Germany to make the first moves.

The Paris Agreement of 16 April 1948 on European economic cooperation (OEEC) in the context of the Marshall Plan had broadly set the future West German tariff policy on a path involving the general concession of MFN status, the reduction of tariff rates, and the removal of preferences, discriminatory measures and subventions. A few months later the USA obliged the occupied western zones of Germany to concede MFN status to 13 countries, and then broadened this agreement in August 1949 in the 'Statement of Annecy' to include all countries, irrespective of whether the countries themselves conceded MFN treatment to German exports. On the German side, however, this treaty-fixed obligation was seen as a one-sided servitude, which recalled the impositions of the Versailles treaty.[31] Moreover, the economic consequences of this bias within the liberalisation process had extremely dangerous consequences in early 1951, when Germany ran into sharp balance of payments problems. The president of the Bank Deutscher Länder, the West German central bank, even asked for an additional 100 percent emergency increase of tariffs in order to protect the balance of trade with foreign trade partners.[32]

Given these preconditions, and with persistent American intervention in favour of lower tariffs, the elaboration of new West German tariff rates led in 1950–51 to a break with the protectionist tradition. The Federal Republic adopted a tariff policy that took a middle course between high tariff countries such as Italy, France and Great Britain and the countries with notably low tariffs such as Denmark or the Benelux states. With this present to its trading partners, the Federal Republic entered the General Agreement on Trade and Tariffs (GATT) on 1 October 1951 and thereby reclaimed full sovereignty in tariff and trade policy matters. The Agreement at this point encompassed 34 trading countries, representing 80 per cent of world trade; it formed a loose institutional framework for the systematic dismantling of trade barriers, as the United States in particular wanted. The GATT had already worked out around 55,000 tariff concessions in the three tariff reduction rounds of Geneva, Annecy and Torquay,[33] and the new member could now avail itself of all these as well as of unrestricted MFN status. West Germany was still, despite everything, an important trading country, and its entry into GATT provided a renewed opportunity to tackle entrenched tariff structures and bring about new flexibility. The United States grasped the opportunity to force the Federal Republic to take over the role of the ice-breaker.

The dismantling of import quotas initially dragged the German balance of trade and balance of payments into deficit. The demand for imports was large, and the liberalisation of German exports did not keep pace with it. In 1950 exports were DM 8.362 million, against imports of DM 11.374 million; this did make for equilibrium in the balance of payments. Around 18 per cent of total imports had to be financed through the Marshall Plan. In the context of economic reconstruction this tendency towards deficit was natural, but it also gave rise to the 'German crisis' when the outbreak of the Korean War in late 1950 provoked a stocking up of raw materials. At the end of the year the currency slipped into the red; gold and foreign currency reserves had been exhausted. The Federal Republic had to take up its full allocation of $320 million in the framework of the European Payments Union (EPU), and even then was forced to borrow. The EPU had recently been set up as a multilateral clearing and credit agency for Western European trade; the USA had furnished it a basic stock of Marshall Plan dollars, so that it was able to promote the mutual provision of credit where the clearing of accounts was hampered by inadequate national foreign currency reserves.

The EPU had replaced the mechanism of the second Paris Intra-European Payments and Compensation Agreement in order to establish an autonomous and lasting scheme for a European Clearing Union. The Marshall Plan administration did not succeed in realising its proposal for the formation of a single market based on a single currency, which should have been directed by a European Monetary Authority. This obviously was still out of reach. However, the EPU did provide a system of full inter-European currency transferability providing freedom of inter-European payments on current account, the rapid elimination of quantitative restrictions and maximum possible freedom of commercial transaction. When the EPU was established on 19 September 1950 a new European soft currency block, a clearing system with automatic credit lines, was also established. Germany still did not have much of a say within the managing board of the EPU; nevertheless, the German central bank clearly favoured the EPU as a further step towards a multilateral European trade system and declined a British offer for a German-British payments' agree-

ment on the basis of controlled transferability. German central
bankers did not believe in a reestablishment of the sterling area
and considered the British offer rather as an attempt to sabotage
American plans for the EPU.[34]

The EPU was meant to promote the liberalisation of international commerce for a transitional period until the European currencies became convertible, which in practice took until the end
of 1958. In November 1950 the Federal Republic required a special loan of $180 million in order to prevent the collapse of the
clearing system. As this loan threatened to be swallowed up by the
West German balance of payments, the Bank of the German States
and the federal government took emergency measures. The liberalisation rate of 60 per cent by March 1951 was rescinded, a cash
deposit of half the value in marks of foreign exchange requested
for imports became obligatory, and ultimately the issuing of
import licences was suspended. The German economists did everything possible to prevent Germany's exclusion from the EPU. This
was considered at the time to be the death of the European idea
including the Schuman Plan and was indeed a hard blow for the
German economy.[35] Reaction abroad was unusually sharp.
Warnings abounded about a regression to the days of import discrimination in the Third Reich, dubbed in the English speaking
world after its inventor as 'Schachtianism'. The United States
accepted the interruption of the liberalisation efforts, but seized
the opportunity for wide-ranging intervention in the German market economy.[36]

The balance of payments crisis eased in the second half of 1951.
The same forces that had caused the deficit now ensured that the
Federal Republic could pay for its imports by itself. Raw materials
that had been imported at the beginning of the Korean crisis,
when prices were still low, now left the country as finished products and met rising demand. In 1952 the Federal Republic
achieved its first balance of payments surplus and started on the
road that led it to become the world's second largest trading
nation in the 1960s and 1970s.

The restoration of the Federal Republic's creditworthiness was an
important precondition for its reintegration into the international
economy. This required the settlement of its public and private
foreign debts. Already on 6 March 1951, the federal government
had fundamentally accepted liability for old and new German for-

eign debts. Yet it seemed completely unthinkable that the western rump state could meet the entire debt of the Reich, even if the Federal Republic saw itself as its legal successor. The post-war demands of the occupying powers alone seemed by far to exceed the country's ability to pay, given that it was still enmeshed in a balance of payments crisis of considerable gravity.

The London debt negotiations with the three western powers, which began in 1951, ultimately settled on a transfer of DM 567 million for the first five years and DM 765 million for the following period. The overall amount to be repaid was reduced during the negotiations from DM 29.3 billion to DM 14.5 billion. The United States cut its post-war demands from consignments of the GARIO and ERP programmes from a total of $3.2 billion to $1.2 billion. Great Britain moderated its corresponding demands arising from the UK Contribution Fund from $814 million to $605 million. France, which also claimed to have contributed economic aid to its zone of occupation, waived $4 million of the $16 million debt.[37] Prewar debts were then reduced from DM 8.3 billion to DM 6 billion principal and from DM 4.4 billion to DM 1.4 billion interest arrears. The reparations problem was not covered by the London Debt Agreement, to which fifteen countries were party, but the head of the German delegation, the banker Hermann J. Abs, explicitly concluded – as did the other participants implicitly – that no further demands would be made under the heading 'Reparations'.[38]

The regulation of compensation payments to Israel was unaffected by this. In the Luxembourg Agreement of 1952, the Federal Republic committed itself to 'assimilation assistance' to the State of Israel of DM 3 billion, which would be given over ten years in the form of goods deliveries. The Federal Republic continued to make transfers to Israel after the expiry of the agreement, whether in the form of credit assistance or of other economic aid. It provided an additional DM 450 million to the Jewish Claims Conference for assimilation assistance outside Israel. Beyond that, the Federal Republic paid around DM 24 billion up to 1982 as compensation to Israeli citizens. The total amount of compensation payments for the victims fo the persecution of the Jews, excluding recipients living outside Israel, came to DM 68 billion.[39]

From the perspective of 1951–2 these burdens did not seem light, but only a few years later it was clear that the Federal Republic would not have difficulty in meeting these transfers from the rising foreign exchange receipts of its flourishing foreign trade. For example, the repayment period for post-war debts, which were reduced to $1.8 billion by the London Debt Agreement ratified in February 1953, originally ran to 1988; yet economic recovery allowed the full amount to be repaid ahead of schedule, with large prepayments in 1959 and 1961 and a final payment in 1966.[40] The debt problem, which had severely hampered international relations after the First World War, had been settled in a manner favourable for West Germany's re-entry into the financial and economic system of the western world.

At the start of 1952 the Federal Republic resumed the liberalisation process, and pressed on to the complete abolition of all private quotas on imports from the OEEC area by the end of 1956. The free trade principle also established itself in regard to trade with other western countries. Only products subject to the market regulations of the agricultural sector were excluded. As West German foreign trade grew, its shape also changed. The shift of trade flows from east to west was the most obvious difference. Before the war around 15 per cent of total exports went to Eastern and Southeastern Europe, but this was down to 2 per cent at the beginning of the 1950s. In this respect Germany, of all the European countries, was hardest hit by the division of Europe into two opposing camps. The development of the Federal Republic's trade with the East was hindered not only by its lack of state and political sovereignty; west German industry's traditional export goods were those most affected by the West's embargo regulations (the COCOM list), which concentrated on investment goods of a high standard of technology. Under these conditions it was not possible to raise Eastern and Southeastern Europe's share in West German exports above a level of 5 per cent, although even this meant that the Federal Republic was by far the biggest trader with the Eastern Bloc. Nevertheless, in the 1960s more than 75 per cent of the GDR's trade was with the East (and two-thirds of it still at the eve of the reunification), so that the regional balance of trade in Germany as a whole before the breakdown of the eastern markets in the early 1990s remained essentially unchanged since the pre-war period.

Foreign trade flows shifted correspondingly to the western industrialised countries. They accounted for an average of 85 per cent of the Federal Republic's overall trade in the 1960s. By contrast, developing countries in the same period took only 12.8 per cent of exports and supplied 8.4 per cent of imports. It is therefore remarkable that this provides almost half of the total West German foreign trade surplus. The composition of the volume of trade also changed as a result of the expansion of the 1950s and 1960s; the proportion of food and foodstuffs in total imports fell from 44.1 per cent in 1950 to 26.3 per cent in 1960, 19.1 per cent in 1970 and 12.7 per cent in 1980. The share of manufactured products rose from 12.6 per cent in 1950 to 32.2 per cent (1960), 50 per cent (1970) and 51.2 per cent in 1980. In exports, the share of raw materials fell from 14 per cent in 1950 to 1.9 per cent in 1980; by contrast the export share of manufactured products, already high in 1950 at 64.9 per cent, rose further to 83.4 per cent in 1980. The reintegration of the Federal Republic thus occurred above all in the increased exchange of industrial finished products. In fact the Federal Republic's entire surplus was concentrated in this area, in which the investment goods industry dominated; with a share of 28.5 per cent of total export between 1960 and 1971, this sector made the largest contribution to the trade surplus.

The accession of Germany to the European Economic Community Treaty on 25 March 1957, which entered into force in 1958, was preceded by a controversial decision-making process on the German side. The inner fabric of the treaty made it clear that European policy was based not on a purely economic rationale, but rather on a realistic analysis of political power cutting across calculations of short-term utility, and even across economic principles with a long-term orientation. In the run-up to the signing of the Rome Treaties, this conflict became clearly visible in the German decision-making process and was unambiguously decided in favour of political rather than economic considerations. For the Federal Minister of Economics, the privileges demanded by France, such as the right to Treaty amendment in the transition from the first to the second stage, temporary retention of export aids and import levies, protective clauses in the event of balance-of-payments difficulties, or inclusion of the overseas territories, threatened to 'intensify almost unbearably' the problems for the other members, so that the whole Treaty looked 'unfair and unacceptable.'[41] The Federal Economics Ministry was here following a concept of economic integration that 'will advance in the form of steadily progressing liberalization of movement of goods, services and capital, reduction of tariffs and other protectionist barriers,

that is, on OEEC lines.' According to this view, the 'integration' of
the Six would have in fact become 'an island of disintegration in a
world that had in the meantime become free'. Germany would
then, as Ludwig Erhard put it to the Federal Chancellor in
September 1956, have its freedom of movement cramped and its
vital connections to the other world powers endangered by an
oppressive marriage with protectionist France.

The Foreign Office by contrast did not share this 'plan for economic world conquest by the Federal Economics Minister'.
Instead, it set up against Erhard the primacy of politics, 'since such
a rash forward push into open space must eventually find its limit,
be it an economic crisis or some other upheaval.' All that can last
is 'what is politically organised.' While the Federal Economics
Ministry did not find it acceptable for 'a problem of such economic importance to be handled primarily by another department',
the Foreign Office opposed this by saying that European economic integration was 'at the present stage still in a purely political
sphere and ought therefore to be regarded as a political matter.' It
is scarcely possible to express the primacy of politics inherent in
Germany's economic Euro-policy, and in that of other countries
involved, more clearly than in that statement.

It is difficult to determine whether membership in the EEC
gave a new impulse to the economic development of the Federal
Republic. The argument in favour of this assumption asserts that
Germany benefited from a larger 'domestic' market allowing mass
production with its cost reducing effects, technological progress,
and differentiation of product supplies. At the beginning of the
integration process around 27 per cent of West German exports
went to the six EEC countries. However, just as much went to the
countries of the 'small free trade zone' (EFTA), which stayed outside the community. In 1971, on the eve of the expansion of membership of the Economic Community, the EEC's share of West
German exports had grown to 40 per cent, and after the enlargement in January 1972, the Community absorbed more than 50 per
cent of West German exports. On the whole, the trade-creating
effects of regional consolidation probably made up for and out-
weighed the negative effects of trade diversion.

The progress of co-ordination of economic and social policies
between member states, however, was well below expectations.
Even after April 1973, when the second stage of economic and currency union was announced, the participants' budgetary policies

were determined solely on national criteria. As a result, the medium term guidelines were not met. Measures of tax harmonisation and the liberalisation of capital markets were not taken; if anything there was some backsliding in the coordination of structural, regional and employment policies, as well as in the process of transferring competences to the Community. Nevertheless, tariffs within the Community were dismantled, although certain compensatory levies similar to tariffs were substituted for them in order to balance competitive conditions under taxation. Administrative trade barriers were also dismantled, even though this process seems to have gone into reverse in recent times. As economic conditions become worse, the centrifugal forces of Western European integration are once more strengthened, just as the prosperity of the 1950s contributed much to their weakening. At the same time Germany will have to face the built-in conflict which accompanied her re-entry into the international economy from the very beginning. Should her main concern in European integration be political or economic? This problem has not been solved.

Notes

1. See Bela Balassa, 'Types of Economic Integration', in F. Machlup (ed.) *Economic Integration: Worldwide, Regional, Sectoral*, London 1976, p. 17; Balassa, 'Towards a Theory of Economic Integration', in *Kyklos 14* (1961), pp. 1–17.
2. On the question of the Marshall Plan and Germany, see Charles S. Maier and Günther Bischof (eds), *The Marshall Plan and Germany*, New York/Oxford, 1991; on the question of material aid in particular, W. Abelshauser, 'American Aid and West German Economic Recovery, A Macroeconomic Perspective', in ibid., pp. 367–409.
3. See F. Baade, *Der amerikanische Long-term-Plan und die amerikanische Politik*, Kiel, 1949, p. 3.
4. Ibid., p. 15.
5. Confidential Annual Report, 1948, of the Adviser on the Marshall Plan to the Chairman of the Administrative Council of the Joint UK/US Zone of Occupation (FWG), Frankfurt/Main, 27/1/49, BA, B 146/189, p. 22.
6. More recent evaluations of the economic effects of the Zollverein arrive at much more sceptical conclusions: see Rolf Horst Dumke, *The Political Economy of German Economic Unification: Tariffs, Trade and Politics of the Zollverein Era*, Madison, Wis., University of Wisconsin dis-

sertation, 1976. See also K. Borchardt, *Das Argument des großen Binnenmarktes*, Munich, dissertation, 1956.

7. Confidential Annual Report, p. 23.

8. Auswärtiges Amt (ed.), Verträge der Bundesrepublik Deutschland, Serie A: Multilaterale Verträge, Vol. 1, Bonn 1955, p. 6.

9. See S. Gabriel, 'Der Pariser Zahlungsplan', in *Zeitschrift für das gesamte Kreditwesen 1*, 1948/49, p. 203f.

10. Intra-European Payments and Compensations Agreement, Preamble, BA, Z 14/41.

11. In practice, the funds in the dollar aid current accounts were made available. These were accounts in the respective national currencies in which payments from importers were held and used to purchase US goods from Marshall Plan consignments. This did not alter the fact that these funds gave rise to claims against the resources of the country which had to issue drawing rights.

12. OEEC Faces the Test, in *The Economist*, No. 5481, 11/9/1948, p. 424; see Gabriel, 'Der Pariser Zahlungsplan', p. 204.

13. OEEC Faces the Test, in *The Economist*, No. 5481, p. 425.

14. In other words, foreign exchange to the value of these dollar amounts was made available in the national European currencies each required in order to cover its inter-European trade deficits.

15. An export surplus of $10.2 million was fixed for Bizonia, while a supplementary requirement of $8000.000 was approved for the French zone.

16. In total around 250 bilateral balances had to be considered, but it transpired that only 110 of these required compensatory measures.

17. Gabriel, 'Der Pariser Zahlungsplan', p. 206.

18. Intra-European Payments and Compensations Agreement, Article 1, BA Z 14/41.

19. See for example the remarks on compensation by the German States Bank as per 30 April 1949 (Frankfurt/Main, 31/5/1949) Ba, Z 14/117, pp. 228–32.

20. States' Council of the Unified Economic Areas (VWG), Department of ERP Affairs, M 3–1 Nr. 28/49, Suggestions for the Revision of the 'Little' Marshall Plan, BA, Z 14/41.

21. Switzerland was also interested in participating in the Little Marshall Plan. However it demanded 'free' dollars as recompense for its surplus in inter-European trade, and was not prepared to accept 'conditional' aid as compensation for drawing rights it was to issue to the amount of $200 million. It suited the OEEC and for the USA to require Switzerland to use these restricted ECA dollars for her purchases. Formal Swiss involvement was thus ruled out, although the country was among those used for American 'offshore purchases'. Ibid., pp. 2–5.

22. OEEC Faces the Test, in *The Economist*, 5481, p. 424.

23. The apparently large amount of credits which the Germans were expected to give to their neighbours had nothing to do with the problem of German clearing deficits accumulated during the war. A number of countries which had been occupied by Germany during the war had been forced to make deliveries to the Third Reich in return for credits in German currency. After the war they not unnaturally hoped to be able to use these credits to buy German goods. This problem had to be solved in the context of the London Debt Conference. Shortly after the end of the conference in 1953 Germany allowed step by step that the holders of these so-called 'Sperrmark' could use these claims for investment in Germany.

24. Even taking the GARIOA aid into account, support for Berlin (DM 1.5 billion) absorbed all but DM 500 million of foreign aid; States' Council of the Joint Economic Areas (VWG), Department of ERP Affairs, M 1–1 Nr. 29/49, Distribution of Dollar Aid and inner-European aid for the year 1949/50, BA, Z 14/41.

25. Dr. O. Emminger, minute concerning the reduction of drawing rights, Paris, 11/10/1949, BA, Z 14/117, pp. 77–83.

26. Dr. Günter Keiser, Construction Flaws of the Marshall Plan, 5/11/1949, BA B 146/171.

27. Department Head Dr. G. Keiser (VfW), Joint Rapporteur on 'The Long-Term-Programme and American Policy' at the third general meeting of the Working Group of German Research Institutes, in Munich on 1/2 September 1949, BA, Z 146/171, p. 6.

28. Department Head H. Koelfen, VWG Economic Working Group on Foreign Trade, Trade Treaties Office, to the VfW on 15/8/1949, copy in BA, Z 14/117, p. 137f.

29. Keiser, Construction, p. 8.

30. Ibid., p. 6.

31. See F. Jerchow, 'Außenhandel im Widerstreit. Die Bundesregierung auf dem Weg in das Gatt 1949–1951', in H.A. Winkler (ed.) *Politische Weichenstellungen im Nachkriegsdeutschland 1945–1953*, Göttingen, 1979, p. 256.

32. Vocke to Adenauer, 26 February 1951, in Ludwig-Erhard-Stiftung (ed.), *Die Korea-Krise als ordnungspolitische Herausforderung der deutschen Wirtschaftspolitik*, Stuttgart, New York, 1986, Doc. No. 22.

33. L. Erhard (ed.), *Deutschlands Rückkehr zum Weltmarkt*, Düsseldorf, 1953, p. 210.

34. *FRUS 1950*, IV, 605–612.

35. Vocke to Adenauer, 26 February 1951, in Ludwig-Erhard-Stiftung, p. 275.

36. See W. Abelshauser, 'West German Economic Recovery, 1945–1951: A Reassessment', in The *Three Banks Review*, No 135 (September 1982), pp. 34–53.

37. See *Deutsche Bundesbank (ed.)*, *Deutsches Geld- und Bankwesen in Zahlen 1876–1975*, Frankfurt/Main, 1976, pp. 336–41.

38. See H.J. Abs, 'Das Londoner Schuldenabkommen', in Abs, *Zeitfragen der Geld- und Wirtschaftspolitik*, Frankfurt/Main 1959, pp. 11–42.

39. See Deutsche Bundesbank/BMF, Department for Compensation, p. 342.

40. See Deutsche Bundesbank, pp. 336–41.

41. AA-PA, Büro Staatssekretär, vol. 155. Briefing for Cabinet Meeting of 10 October 1956 (4 Oct 1956) Author: Hartlieb.

HANNS JÜRGEN KÜSTERS

West Germany's Foreign Policy in Western Europe, 1949–58: The Art of the Possible

Introduction

In April 1956, when the famous Spaak report was discussed to open the six ECSC powers' negotiations about the EEC and the Euratom project, Chancellor Adenauer explained to Erhard, then Minister of Economics, the history behind West Germany's foreign policy. 'European integration was the necessary spring-board for us to participate in foreign affairs again', Adenauer wrote. 'European integration was also necessary for the sake of Europe as well as for the sake of ourselves. But, in particular, European integration was necessary because the United States of America took it as the basic starting-point of its European policy at all. Like you, I think, the help of the United States is absolutely necessary for us.'[1]

After the founding of the Federal Republic in September 1949, the Adenauer government pursued three main foreign policy goals: the abolition of the occupation statute, international recognition as a souvereign state in order to become an equal member of the community of states and the solution of the unification question. Their realisation required unconditional orientation towards the western democracies, and this, in fact meant the support of the European integration process.

In the 1950s Bonn's foreign policy was influenced by two fundamental controversies. On the one hand there was the struggle between the Christian Democratic government and the Social Democratic opposition about the priority to be given to Western integration or reunification, and on the other hand there were the

discussions about the right method of integration. The aim here is
to discuss five aspects of West Germany's European policy: the
principles behind and conditions underlying West German foreign policy in the 1950s, the different functions of German
European integration policy, the struggles about conceptions and
methods of integration within the administration, the German
role in the European treaty negotiations on the Schuman plan, the
European Defence Community (EDC) and the Treaties of Rome
and, finally, the German view of the European Free Trade Area
(EFTA) proposal with special reference to British attempts to be
associated with the Common Market.

The argument is that Adenauer fought for the European integration process in order to release the Federal Republic from the
occupation statute and lead it back to an equal position among the
Western European states. His European policy was an instrument
to regain international respect and avoid Soviet control over
Germany. He used integration policy to bring West Germany's
economy back into the world market, to have a security guarantee
against pro-German tendencies towards neutralisation of Germany
and to ensure a military coalition of the Western states with West
Germany against the danger of Soviet expansionism. The
European organisations were a platform for normalising the
German relationship with the West and, in particular, to overcome
German-French rivalries and create a fall-back position to avoid
the incalculable risks of a withdrawal of American forces from the
European continent. After the founding of the European
Communities the Adenauer government used the EEC as a forum
for creation of a European power policy with the aim of a establishing European political union. West German diplomacy tried to
balance national interests in Western Europe. The Chancellor
always hoped to reduce the Franco-British as well as the European-
American tensions, knowing that he never could commit himself
to one side completely because national German interests and his
own European policy approach would not allow him to do so.

Principles and Conditions of West Germany's Foreign Policy

From the very beginning the West German government
carried out a foreign policy strategy which was based on the nega-

tive experiences of the past. In Adenauer's eyes it had to avoid several dangerous possibilities. The option of a neutralised Germany, which would allow a Bismarck-like seesaw policy between Russia and the West, was unacceptable. Any kind of a Rapallo policy was to be avoided. In those years German foreign policy had always to cope with the heritage of the National Socialist foreign policy and to counteract the fear of a new aggression against neighbouring states. There must never again be the temptation of a global German power policy combined with European expansionism leading to war as propagated by the National Socialists. The new German constitutional state had to exemplify those virtues the National Socialists despised: respect for other countries' borders and territorial integrity, clarity about the basic principles of German foreign policy and fulfilment of treaties. The weakness shown by liberal democracies towards totalitarian systems or temptations of appeasement could only be overcome by a strong alliance policy;[2] the menace of the Soviet expansionism should be resisted by the Atlantic defence system, the strategy of isolating the Eastern bloc politically and an embargo policy. The cold war prevented the Federal Republic from playing the role of a mediator between East and West once again.

Adenauer recognised that the Federal Republic – still an occupied state – had not only to root its political structures in the ideas of the Anglo-American democracies. Like the Parliamentary Council that drafted the *Grundgesetz* as an 'anti-Weimar' constitution, Adenauer drafted West German foreign policy as an anti-imperialist anti-National Socialist and, not least, an anti-communist policy with the objective of European integration within the Western Alliance. German foreign policy was meant to become a reliable factor in international politics.

Even before the Federal Republic came into existence, the first chancellor had anticipated the change from the allied war coalition to the East-West confrontation and its far-reaching consequences as a basic condition for Germany's foreign policy.[3] As a *Realpolitiker* the Chancellor knew that a sovereign West German state would only receive international recognition if its leading politician declared his support for Western policy. Many critics scolded him as an opportunist. The alternative would have been the policy of opposition or attitude of denial to the Western powers for which the SPD leader, Schumacher, argued; this would have led to a complete deadlock in relations with the allied powers.

Adenauer wanted West Germany to become a full member of NATO as soon as possible to counter all tendencies toward a neutral or pro-Soviet foreign policy. The Germans had to normalise their bilateral rivalries with the Western countries, in particular with France and Great Britain. They had to improve relationships with the Jewish people and later on, if possible, with the Russians and the Poles. Moreover, the chances to settle the German-French rivalry had never been so favourable because France itself depended economically and militarily on the support of the West and the United States. But, at first, the Federal government had to prove its ability to become an independent state by making permanent gestures of Western solidarity.

In September 1949, the main hinderance was the statute of occupation which the three Western allies imposed on the newly elected Federal government. This prohibited an independent national foreign policy. The Adenauer administration was only allowed to act freely in OEEC affairs[4] and to negotiate on internal German traffic and trade relations. According to a commitment at the Foreign Ministers Conference in Paris in June 1949, the four allied powers wanted East and West Germans to settle the problems resulting from the Berlin blockade. Other contacts with the Soviet occupied zone or Eastern European state were generally conducted by the High Commissioners, who behaved like an *areopag* on the Petersberg.[5] Enlarging West Germany's international authority would in fact mean that the occupation statute would need to be revised in order to get rid of restrictions and enable West Germany to become a sovereign state. If West Germany was once again to be an equal member of the international community, the Western powers would inevitably be forced to risk a certain independence on the part of the Federal government in handling domestic and foreign affairs.[6]

Each step toward a more independent German policy was recognised in London, Paris and Washington as an incalculable step towards the reconstruction of the German Reich, which was not in the interest of any allied power in East or West at that time. Fears of a development of an unstable democracy in West Germany, the possible emergence of neo-nationalist movements and the expectation that the Germans would not resign themselves to their fate as a divided country produced a feeling of uncertainty on the allied side. The negotiations about the Bonn treaty, signed in May 1952, were the logical consequence of the half-hearted step to transfer more political self-determination to the Germans without giving them full sovereignty. A remnant of the control rights remained with the Allies, especially concerning the questions of reunification and the negotiations about a peace treaty with unified Germany.

From the first days of its existence the Adenauer administration claimed to be the only legitimate and freely elected representative of the whole German people.[7] The so-called '*Alleinvertretungsanspruch*' (claim exclusively to represent the German people) was always seen as a political axiom and possessed, in fact, no legal foundation.[8] The three Western powers supported this principle for political reasons, in order to prevent the Soviet Union presenting the GDR as the single legal German state and achieving its international recognition.[9] Adenauer did not harbour the illusion of a quick settlement among the four allied powers on Germany and the conclusion of a peace treaty.[10] He always feared the revival of the Potsdam coalition. In the worst case Germany would be treated as a defeated and occupied area and would have to accept a *Carthaginian peace* dictated by the allied powers of the Second World War. Like the other Western states, Adenauer was only ready to agree to German reunification on condition that Western integration should take place.

Following the Western formula of free elections, the constitution of a National Assembly and an independent all-German government were elements of the basic democratic approach to the self-determination of the German people. At the same time this was the safest method by which the Western allies could defend the division of Germany for many years and postpone any agreement with the Soviets. Both the German states practised the strategy of isolation from each other. But the GDR was at a disadvantage because Bonn could constantly point out that the Pankow regime was not elected freely. In 1953 there may have been some idea in Churchill's mind to neutralise mid-Europe and to make arrangements for a package deal with the Russians.[11] However, the Kremlin did not believe the offer to be genuine.[12] Neutralisation was, perhaps, acceptable for the SPD opposition but not for the Western hegemonial power. The Eden plan, the Western conception of reunification, demanding free elections in all parts of Germany and being connected in 1955 with security guarantees for a demilitarised zone in mid-Europe,[13] was completely unacceptable to the Soviet Union: the plan also demanded the elimination of Soviet power in Germany and possibly in the Western satellite states.

But in 1955, when the Federal Republic normalised its relationship with the Soviet Union and established diplomatic contacts, the informal strategy to isolate the GDR was no longer workable. The Hallstein doctrine was the only political instrument of the Federal government to avoid the international wave of recognition of the GDR.[14] Until 1958 the Western deliberations on the reunification question had been focused upon security guarantees for the Soviets on the assumption that it would be possible to pay Moscow an acceptable price for giving up the GDR, but in fact there was no real chance of negotiations. Given the unyielding Soviet attitude, the American Foreign Secretary John Foster Dulles preferred the continuance of the postponement policy, and he was supported by the British, the French and Adenauer himself.

Different Functions of West Germany's European Integration Policy

European integration embodied a fundamental political determination to achieve a Western détente policy which would permanently eliminate the German-French antagonism. It was an attempt at a *rapprochement*, a policy of understanding which would solve the bilateral problems which had seemed to be insoluble for more than a century. Without a new style of German-French relationship there could be no consensus in Western Europe, and this consensus was in turn a necessary prerequisite for any kind of integration. After achieving sovereignty, Germany would be an equal and important economic partner with a corresponding increase in political influence. Of course politicians like Adenauer always had it in mind the prospect that in the future German foreign policy might gain in international weight and establish a balance of power policy in cooperation with the other Western European states. Hence Western integration was both the route for escape from international isolation and the framework for future foreign German policy.

Likewise integration had an economic function. In order to achieve a certain internal stabilisation West Germany needed to recover from the disastrous economic consequences of the last war.[15] The Federal Republic was cut off from the *Ostgebiete* (Eastern areas), its former export markets and source of raw material imports. The country depended on international trade and capital transfer to build up her industries. The Marshall plan, integration in the OEEC and the currency reform of 1948 were important pre-requisites for the modernisation of the German economy and its orientation towards the Western hemisphere.[16] Adenauer thought pragmatically that the interdependence of the industrial democracies in Western world would lead neighbouring countries to have confidence in West Germany.[17] Reconstruction and more prosperity, better terms of trade and a currency mechanism that worked; these factors would make good the loss of old trade relations with the Eastern parts of Germany. Thus the Bonn government had no other choice but to align its trade policy to the West.[18] Through European integration West German industrialists got quickly back into the world market, the export rate increased, the dollar gap closed, and industrial products regained their former symbol of quality, 'Made in Germany'.[19]

Nevertheless, the recovery of German industries depended on conditions prescribed by the United States. Washington was the paymaster-general of the Marshall Plan and had a strong interest in ensuring that German industries within OEEC,[20] especially these in the Ruhr area, should be within the Western dominated sphere of influence. Rapid economic development in West Germany served as catalyst to dissolve the anti-liberal principles then dominating the European market: protectionism, foreign exchange restrictions and a lack of convertibility. The Germans had to pay a price for that preferential treatment. The Americans expected an uncompromising observance of the Western embargo policy towards Eastern Europe[21] and looked with suspicious eyes on Bonn's attempts to maintain economic ties with the GDR. The embargo policy was actually the reverse side of the Marshall Plan coin; the American integration programme was a strategic welfare policy in favour of the Western European states but, much more importantly, it was also a strategic counter-welfare programme towards the Eastern communist states. The Adenauer administration supported this programme from 1950 onwards.[22]

However, the Chancellor's philosophy of European integration was not based only on the conception of economic entanglement.[23] He also looked for further political connections between the nation-states in order to overcome the danger of nationalism. Adenauer wanted a policy of Western integration which would connect Germany with the West and the West with Germany in order to override nationalistic movements. He tried to abolish the existing political and military discriminatory barriers: the limited sovereignty of the Western allied treaty with Germany and the non-membership of NATO. His kind of European-Atlantic internationalism contained elements of American liberal free trade thinking, but stressed as well the common interests of the European societies and occidental culture. Integration and cooperation between the industrial centres of Western Europe seemed to him a necessary step for the modernisation of obsolescent industries. 'If we take the leadership in European questions', he declared to the executive board of the CDU in September 1952, 'we have a good chance to impress the stamp of a Christian ideology on the making of Europe'.[24] In Adenauer's view it was always necessary to strengthen the idea of Christianity as a bulwark against the ideological influences of Soviet socialism among Western socialist parties.

Finally, in Adenauer's view, western integration always had the function of a fall-back position in security and defence policy. He never doubted that the Federal Republic would only be recognised as a state if it had an army able to defend the people. His first contacts with German generals can be traced back to the sessions of the Parliamentary Council at the end of 1948.[25] The Chancellor did not deny the necessity of German soldiers[26], but he never saw them as being under the authority of a national army. They should be a part of a European or Atlantic defence alliance in which the Germans would have the right of participation. Whenever the security of the Federal Republic was threatened, the Western democracies should be involved and forced to react as if this was an attack on their own country.[27] Western integration was from that perspective a certain kind of security burden-sharing supporting West Germany's forward position against the Iron Curtain.

German Conceptions and Methods of European Integration

Within the German government there was a great administrative controversy about the correct method of European integration. From 1949 to 1958 the *Auswärtiges Amt* (Foreign Ministry) and the Ministry of Economics quarreled about spheres of competence and different integration methods.[28] Conflicts arose from the reduced competences of West Germany in foreign affairs, but were also caused by the lack of a Foreign Office until March 1951 and the slow establishing of the foreign trade department. Adenauer had transferred authority for economic integration policy to Erhard's Ministry, but in the following years the *Auswärtiges Amt* laid claim to these. Instead of shaping new forms of administrative cooperation, both ministries struggled for political and diplomatic representation in European organisations. Only in 1958 was an understanding reached and the Ministry of Economics received authority to conduct EEC policy.

The conflict about methods of integration was of the same fundamental importance. In 1950, Bonn took part in multilateral negotiations on the Schuman Plan without any clear conception of West German policy. The debate about the functional or the constitutional approach towards integration during the coming years was the result of a paradoxical situation. The *Auswärtiges Amt*, with State Secretary Walter Hallstein and the head of the European section Carl Friedrich Ophüls, supported a constitutional form of integration. They wanted to set up strong supranational institutions endowed with political authority and a binding common decision-making process to produce European community legislation.[29] Sectoral integration seemed to them an intermediate stage on the way to a Federal European state.

On the other hand, Erhard emphatically rejected the partial integration idea reflected in the coal and steel community. In his eyes supranational institutions obstructed the international exchange of goods. Economic experts and business managers also warned of the consequences of a European sector integration. In 1953, the academic advisory board of the Ministry of Economics consequently recommended that partial integration would be the wrong way to achieve a European common market with a customs union, free capital exchange and convertibility.[30] The instrument of regional liberalisation of West European trade would lead to regional protectionism. Erhard also refused the Beyen plan for a European customs union[31] or the common market idea being discussed in the Schuman Plan department of the Ministry of Economics, although Article 24 of the GATT treaty foresaw it as a legal instrument of liberalisation. As a defender of the state of global free trade existing before the First World War, the apostle of the market economy was afraid of the protectionist effects on

non-member states of the ECSC.[32] He spoke in favour of a functional integrational approach with inter-governmental arrangements for tariff reductions and the increase of trade volume as
concluded in the OEEC.[33] Its member states did not suffer from
the interventions of supranational institutions like the High
Authority or the EEC Commission later on.

The Chancellor took a pragmatic line. He was never interested
in any particular approach; the academic debates within the
administration about constitutional or functional models of integration did not matter to him. The substance of what was agreed
among the Western states was decisive. It depended on the willingness of the nation-states to go ahead step by step. The politicians
were to look for political compromises and the right balance of
national interests. Therefore, he never excluded a European state
from membership in the European Communities *per se*. In confidential conversations with Western prime ministers and foreign
secretaries he always stressed the importance of Great Britain's
participation,[34] knowing that the Federal Republic could not
afford to rely only on the United States or the Fourth French
Republic in Europe. All three Western allied powers had responsibilities towards Germany as a whole.

The Federal Republic's Role in Western European Negotiations

The idea of a supranational High Authority for the
Western European coal and steel industries, presented by the
French Foreign Minister Schuman on 9 May 1950, could be traced
back to discussions within the OEEC on new industrial structures.[35] The need to solve these problems on a European level
could not be denied. Only a few weeks earlier, negotiations with
Italy and the Benelux countries on first steps towards a common
customs union (Fritalux)[36] had failed because of the French
refusal to let the Germans participate within measurable time.[37]
The real surprise was not the proposal to harmonise the coal and
steel sectors, but the institutional construction and the fact that
French diplomacy took the initiative.[38] It indicated a change in the
unyielding French attitude against West Germany's integration
into the West.[39] In respect to American and British inclinations to
permit the West Germans more political freedom, Schuman's

announcement, one day before the London conference between Acheson and Bevin started[40], was a clever tactical step to relieve the French from Anglo-American pressure to review their German policy. Further, the propaganda of the people's front movement in the GDR was forcing the Western powers to act; they were expecting a powerful offensive from the East. This was one aspect of what the US High Commissioner John McCloy called, the 'struggle for the soul of Faust'.[41]

Schuman's offer met Adenauer's Western policy halfway. In the autumn of 1949, the Chancellor mentioned in official declarations the four aims of his foreign policy: a German-French understanding as a first step towards European integration, the cessation of the policy of dismantling German industries, the necessity of a security guarantee and rearmament, and a reconciliation with the Jewish people. In March 1950, he proposed in two interviews a German-French customs union with a common parliament, comparing it with the first steps towards German integration in middle of the last century when the German *Zollverein* had been founded.[42] The Chancellor accepted the Schuman Plan for several reasons. Sector integration seemed to be the right starting point for bringing in the Germans as equal partners at the negotiating table and for opening a new type of bilateral relationship, and it helped to abolish the allied controls over the Ruhr area.[43] But it also seemed to be a suitable instrument which connected the economic problems of Western Europe with the interests of the United States to build a common front against Soviet expansionism in Europe. Finally, the Schuman Plan was a new approach to integration, and promised to provide something more serious than the resolutions of the Council of Europe. However, the Plan also meant that Adenauer had to accept supranational controls over German industries[44] and was confronted with the problem of de-cartelisation.

The establishment of the National People's Police in the GDR was a welcome opportunity for Adenauer to demonstrate the menace of communist expansion towards Western Europe. Even in April 1950, three months before the Korean war broke out, the Chancellor requested security guarantees[45] from the allied powers in case of a social revolution or a surprise attack on the Federal Republic. He offered a German defence contribution which would create ties with the West. The Americans recognised the necessity of German rearmament and gave the Chancellor the chance to open negotiations over West Germany's membership of the Western military alliance.[46] The very complicated negotiations over the plan proposed by the French Prime Minister Pleven and the possible alternative of Germany's integration in NATO plunged Western diplomacy into a total dilemma. The United States wanted Bonn on its side in the Cold War without necessarily allowing the Germans to command their own army.[47]

The British, and even more so the French, reacted reluctantly.[48] Both governments feared a national West Germany army and looked for European solutions on the basis of the Defense Community in order to have German soldiers under their control. They also demanded security guarantees if the Germans should be rearmed. Therefore West Germany had to be discriminated against; it could become a member of the EDC but not of NATO. It was no accident that, at the same time as the EDC treaty was being negotiated in 1951–52, the French Commissariat for Atomic Energy (CEA) prepared plans for building more reactors to produce plutonium 239 for military use.[49] France wanted to become a nuclear partner of the Anglo-American atomic powers, possessing a superior weapon by the time the Germans would be rearmed.[50]

At the end of 1950 it became clear that there was a connection between the revision of the occupation statute, the sovereignty of the Federal Republic, German rearmament and economic and military integration. The Germans had no difficulty in accepting the transformation of sovereign rights to supranational institutions, for which they were struggling in negotiations with the three Western Powers prior to the Bonn treaty of May 1952.[51] But even before signing the treaty it was clear, in the light of the resistance and the unstable political majorities in France, that it would be very difficult to pass the EDC treaty through the French National Assembly. In mid-1952 principal supporters of the EDC like Schuman lost influence, but started a diplomatic attempt to rescue the project by proposing the creation of a European Political Community (EPC). Schuman's proposal to put the EDC and the ECSC under the roof of the EPC[52] was a tactical step to win over the Gaullists.[53] Binding the Germans politically to the West and transfering parliamentary rights of control over German rearmament to a supranational political organisation was meant to convince opponents and facilitate the ratification of the EDC treaty. Furthermore, it strengthened the democratic rights of the EDC-Assembly and put the European army under parliamentary control. To parry criticism by the British government, the EPC project needed the support of Adenauer and a stand-still agreement with the British to counteract their attacks in the Council of Europe.[54]

In Adenauer's perception the draft of the EPC constitution, worked out by the von Brentano committee in March 1953, was a basic document to take priniciple decisions on further integration steps.[55] The Germans played the role of mediator. Bonn pushed the process of political integration as far as possible without forgetting that ratification of the EDC treaty would be the key for equality, partnership and sovereignty on the part of the West Germans. In that view the EPC project was a tactical means to get the EDC and the treaty on Germany ratified. The EPC was the long-term goal, only really adumbrated then, but useful if several commitments could be agreed as a result of it. In the first place the success of the EPC depended on the ECD treaty, and in the second place it needed the right economic integration concept which would abolish protectionism and solve financial problems. Bonn oscillated between the inclination to make a compromise with the French to rescue the EDC and the desire to overcome the partial integration approach by supporting the Benelux proposal of a customs union as nucleus of a common market.

In August 1954, Western European diplomats were prepared to react in case the EDC failed to pass the French National Assembly. This was at first sight a setback for Adenauer's integration policy, but it did not produce the dilemma that has been described in the past. The Chancellor used his new role as someone whose demands had to be fulfilled. The alternative solutions, integrating the Germans into NATO, had already been discussed some months before.[56] The occupation regime was abolished, the Federal Republic received full sovereignty and improved her position in the European Community. In return Adenauer declared the renunciation of ABC weapons production.[57] The three Western powers retained the rights and responsibilities heretofore exercised or held by them relating to Berlin and Germany as a whole, including the reunification of Germany and a peace settlement.[58] That meant a certain degree of control remained with the allied powers and reassured the Bonn government that they would support the aim of reunification later on. The revised London and Paris agreements which come into effect in May 1995 are a deal which reflected political opportunism and legal necessity, and which allowed Germany's Western allies to avoid giving up the common obligations as occupying powers which they shared with the Soviet Union.

German policy on Europe had always to reckon with a double dependence. The longer the integration process went on, the deeper the division of the German nation, the less the degree of integration and the less the advantages of Western cooperation became. West Germany was in a dilemma in that the political elite wanted to push integration forward and at the same time was forced to take the initiative in the question of reunification. The Geneva Summit diplomacy in July 1955[59] and the Kremlin's invitation of Adenauer to Moscow[60] seemed to verify the thesis that critics were wrong when they argued that, after the ratification of the Paris treaty the Soviets would lose interest in negotiating with the Western powers. But actually the critics were right. The Soviets retaliated against the integration of West Germany into NATO with their own theory of two separate and sovereign states in Germany. Moscow had missed the chance for the neutralisation of Germany and the strengthening of social revolutionary forces in France and Italy.

Adenauer would not have changed his Western integration policy until the Western powers had achieved a real agreement with the Soviet Union on the reunification of a Germany bound to the West. He explained the obstructive Soviet tactics at the Four Power conference of foreign ministers as being a clear sign of an intransigent attitude which could only be countered by power politics and Western integration. In December 1955, after the failure of the Four Power conferences, Adenauer declared to Dulles that the spirit of Geneva was a miracle. The Chancellor was relieved by the negative result of the negotiations for he had feared an East-West compromise on disarmament at the price of Germany's neutralisation. 'The German government is ready to join the common market as well as the atomic energy pool'[61], he emphasised and expected American efforts to convince the French that a clear vote was necessary to progress towards the European Community.

Although he had supported the Messina resolution of June 1955 with mixed feelings because economic integration could mean to give up the aim of a political union[62], Adenauer supported the opening of the Brussels negotiations in 1956. But in September of that year, he also warned against the establishment of bureaucratic institutions, perfectly organised on the supranational level, which Great Britain would feel unable to join.[63] The door should be kept open for the British.[64] When the United States considered a withdrawal of troops from Europe and the ghost of neo-isolationism appeared, the Chancellor contemplated an EDC revival if Washington should carry out the Radford plan.

While the Euratom project made progress[65], common market negotiations were blocked by the conditions presented by the French government in September 1956. Monnet pushed Adenauer to give up the linkage between the atomic organisation and the EEC project in order to sign the Euratom treaty. But the Chancellor followed his counsellors Etzel, Carstens and von der Groeben and held up the agreement. Otherwise, the *Auswärtiges Amt* feared, the French would not accept the Common Market[66] and German industry would not accept Euratom alone. Erhard suggested the postponement of the Brussels negotiations and the examination of the British Free Trade Area proposal launched in the OEEC as a counter-strategy to the common market approach of the Six.[67]

Nevertheless, the successful outcome of the EEC negotiations was an historical accident, initiatied by Nasser's Suez crisis in November 1956. The failure of the Anglo-French adventure increased the pressure on the Mollet government and led to a breakthrough in the Brussels negotiations.[68] It tipped the balance for the French government's decision in principle to join the EEC project.[69] The defeat in Near East and the consequences of this for French influence in the world pushed into the background the doubts which had previously been entertained about participation the common market. Success in the negotiations was, above all, dependent on the acknowledgement of leading French politicians and diplomats that the EEC would be the best way to modernise their own economy, combined with the advantage of gaining a comfortable instrument with which to control the German economy.

The Adenauer administration had to cope with many internal difficulties, in particular with Erhard's opposition, which the Chancellor could not solve. But he was strong enough to make the enormous financial compromises[70] which allowed the French to sign the Treaties of Rome. He preferred economic entanglement within the Six to an uncertain intergovernmental cooperation with the OEEC member states. He saw economic integration as a step forward to a more important political integration. Furthermore,

EEC and Euratom improved the German-French relationship on a bilateral and European basis and strengthened the Western Alliance against the danger of communism. Bonn diplomats knew that the EEC was an excellent platform from which the West Germans could play the role of an equal and respected member in the European power concert.[71] But what about the British?

The Six and British European policy

Twice Great Britain was invited to join the European Community[72]; in 1950, when the Schuman Plan was discussed, and in 1955 after the Messina conference. But the British government was never committed to the idea of a European Union. London fought against the plan because of its incalculable consequences for the balance of power in Europe and the special relationship with America. For economic reasons the British wanted to maintain their special relations with the Commonwealth, and for military and security reasons they wanted to avoid a possible choice between their Atlantic and their European partners. That did not mean that there was no British 'European' conception of political cooperation on the intergovernmental level to find some ways of economic cooperation such as the OEEC or by association with other European organisations. But these plans did not correspond at that time to the interests and insights of the six founding states of the EC.

In 1950, the French began to attempt to bring the British government to discuss the Schuman Plan. It may be that Monnet expected more difficulties if the Attlee government were really to take part in the exploratory conversations. It may also be that the Paris government provoked a negative answer in order to negotiate an agreement among the Six alone.[73] But there is no doubt that the withdrawal from the Brussels negotiations in November 1955 was a fundamental mistake of British diplomacy[74] which they could not soon correct. A few months later and sooner than expected, London was confronted with the alternative of being isolated from the rest of Western Europe economically or of making sacrifices in the field of foreign trade in order to come to arrangements with the ECSE countries.[75] Surely, considering French protectionism, the British diplomats were absolutely right in doubting that the customs union and the common market would ever become reality.[76] But the British counter-strategy, proposing an industrial Free Trade Area that excluded agriculture products only, upset the French bureaucracy which did not find it easy in any case to go along with the anti-protectionist philosophy of the Spaak report. London hoped for Erhard's support and over-estimated the political influence of his foreign trade conception.

British diplomats never expected the U-turn by the French. They suggested that the Six would never agree on the common market and that even if they did, the French protectionists would not agree; and if the French protectionists did not agree then the common market would not function. This was a completely wrong assumption. In fact, the disastrous economic situation and the need for modernisation caused the French government reluct-antly to change its attitude. In view of the guarantees the French were granted in the EEC treaty, it was agreed that the Fourth Republic's economic and monetary problems could not be solved within the context of a European Industrial Free Trade Area alone.[77]

The diplomats of the *Auswärtiges Amt* were inclined to German-French cooperation and expected more difficulties if other OEEC countries participated beyond those which agreed to the Treaty of Rome. The interests of the Six and those of the rest of the OEEC member states differed too greatly, particulary on the issue of agri-culture. Britain wanted to exclude the very aspects of the Free Trade Area that the Mollet government was especially keen to see included. Through the automatic opening up of a Free Trade Area the French economy would have lost the same guarantees for the transitional period that the government had laboriously wrest-ed from the other five partners in Brussels. Besides, the British did not envisage an easing of the financial burdens brought on by France's colonial problems.[78]

However, it was not least the British government's vacillating posture that meant the plan for a Free Trade Area was never a viable alternative to the idea of comprehensive integration. The Macmillan government gave the free trade project its full support only after the Suez adventure had failed.[79] Paris could hardly understand this British opportunism. If the plan for a Free Trade Area was ever considered by the London government to be a gen-uine substitute for the common market, aimed at winning over France and, perhaps, Adenauer through the influence of Erhard, the project had been condemned before it even started. It took no account at all of the main interest of the ECSE members to give up the approach of sector integration in favour of a customs union and a common market as the prerequiste for a political union.

The institutional reforms proposed in the British *Grand Design* which officially intended to connect all European organisations was a clear tactical manoeuvre against the setup of new supranational institutions.[80] It could be foreseen that the three communities, ECSE, EEC and Euratom, would become the power centre of the European continent, not the OEEC or the Western European Union. The real intention of the British, to hinder the Rome Treaty, failed. At the beginning of 1957 London changed its tactics and tried to associate with the Six.[81]

The offer of the EEC states to negotiate on a European Free Trade Area left the British hopeful that they would be able to influence the parliamentary debates on the ratification of the Rome Treaties. It was possible that the Treaties might fail again in the French Assembly, and the British government might be offered another opportunity to take the initiative once again as it did after the refusal of the EDC treaty.[82] The Foreign Office observed suspiciously that the common market could be dominated by the French and the Germans who would get the upper hand and soon determine continental policy. If it had not been for the promise of Great Britain to retain its troops in Europe, then Macmillan would have attacked the French because of their tactics to bring the French Union into the common market.[83] The Prime Minister was said to be ready to offer British support in developing the French atomic bomb in case of a failure of the Rome Treaties in the National Assembly; only a few months later there were some discussions on German-French military cooperation[84] in order to counteract the British nuclear dominance in Western Europe.

So far as is known today, Adenauer was the only German chancellor who tried hard to end the formula of discriminating against West Germany's nuclear status by substituting for it a national, a German-French or the option of a NATO nuclear force.[85] Bonn's Foreign Minister von Brentano advocated the opinion that the common market would be the hard core of the EEC, which had come first. The Free Trade Area proposal would not have existed if there had been no common market. If it failed, then the British plan would fail too. Every step back from the Rome Treaty reduced the substance of the European Community and became a danger for Western Europe.[86] On the one hand the *Auswärtiges*

Amt wanted to accept French demands for the same escape clauses and the same guarantees and rights they got in the EEC treaty; indeed, von Brentano distrusted the British and suspected they would not agree to a fair compromise. On the other hand German diplomacy could not afford to follow the French strategy of attacking the British by presenting maximum demands.[87] Erhard fought for the liberal free trade concept in the OEEC council[88] in order to hinder the EEC treaty, which seemed to him economic nonsense. Even before the treaties were signed, state secretary Hallstein stressed in the German parliament that the government supported the EEC and the European Free Trade Area.[89] In other words, the projects should not fail because of West Germany's veto.

The Federal government pursued a twofold strategy. The EEC and Euratom would not be substantially questioned. Consequently, Bonn had to struggle for less discrimination among all the OEEC member states. The Germans looked for technical compromises and got into a dilemma because of French and British interests. These internal conflicts made the Germans susceptible to both sides, because their vote could strengthen the British as well as the French position. Members of the British cabinet forced the Prime Minister to offer different options and to take the initiative in Western European policy, particularly as the breakdown of the Free Trade Area negotiations was expected. Early deliberations on the foundation of the EFTA began in mid-1957.[90] In October 1957, when the OEEC council of ministers appointed an intergovernmental committee with the British paymaster-general Reginald Maudling as chairman, Prime Minister Macmillan gave him the following advice: hold a common front of the 11 OEEC member states, counter the phalanx of the Six and pull the Germans onto the British side, since their negotiating position would be strong after the elections in September.[91] But the Maudling committee had little opportunity to find political compromises for a Free Trade Area between the Six and the Seven.[92]

The decisive question was: should the Free Trade Area only reduce the customs barriers and quotas and be fitted only with the absolutely necessary institutional authority? Or, should the Free Trade Area contain most of the common market rules? In that case the OEEC would change its character into that of a customs union like the strict EEC system, with temporary escape clauses for the intermediate period. The alternative was the weakening of the

EEC by adopting the less obliging rules of the OEEC. On 1 January 1958, when the EEC treaty came into effect, the French government started to fight back against the Free Trade Area. Paris demanded the enlargement of the British Commonwealth preferential system to cover the other OEEC member states.[93] This demand was completely unacceptable to the British.[94]

A Franco-German accord on the nature of the free trade zone was indispensable. In effect, the negotiations of the Maudling committee were shifted to the EEC. The Federal government searched for compromises between the French and the British;[95] in Bonn there was great sympathy with the French argument that Great Britain would have a double trade advantage if the Commonwealth system was not enlarged to cover Western Europe. Macmillan hoped for much from France, knowing that the Fourth Republic was politically and economically at the end of the road and would perhaps agree to compromise. But the Prime Minister also recognised that the French could explode the free trade project if they wished. Adenauer tried to avoid the danger of a second division of Western Europe. In April 1958 he stressed in conversations with Macmillan the political importance of the Free Trade Area and British participation in order to associate the OEEC with the Common Market.[96] Erhard pointed out the technical possibilities of solutions for a commitment, while von Brentano preferred pragmatic agreements between the Six and a few countries of the OEEC, being particularly interested in further steps towards European economic integration. This inconsistency both strengthened and weakened the German negotiating position.

In the spring of 1958 Adenauer doubted de Gaulle's attitude towards European integration, fearing that the French constitutional crisis could postpone the establishment of the EEC institutions and the common market. But the Chancellor knew that de Gaulle was the only personality in France able to prevent a civil war.[97] Adenauer was careful to act in a certain accordance with Great Britain. The Chancellor rejected British plans for disengagement in Europe and the reduction of British troops on the continent because of the incalculable consequences such a move would have for the Western alliance. Macmillan, when he visited Paris at the end of June 1958, hoped for a change in de Gaulle's unyielding attitude over the Free Trade Area question, but he was disappointed. His argument that Britain would not suffer from a common market which was only the prolongation of the continental barrier did not impress de Gaulle, and his announcement of a possible trade war in Europe was ignored by the French Prime Minister.[98]

After their meeting in Colombey-les-deux-Eglises mid-September 1958, Adenauer was sure that de Gaulle supported the EEC. The General, meanwhile, had decided to follow the *pacta sunt servanda* policy and use the Rome Treaty and its escape clauses to accomplish the absolutely necessary recovery and modernisation of the French economy.[99] The Chancellor criticised the British disengagement policy, but evaded de Gaulle who tried to commit him to an anti-British course. De Gaulle would only agree to the Free Trade Area if it was shaped according to the rules of the Common Market; otherwise, it would be a danger for the French economy and perhaps a threat to French existence. In British eyes the Free Trade Area in the style of the EEC meant giving up liberal trade principles in Europe. At the beginning of October, Adenauer told Macmillan that de Gaulle had agreed that the Free Trade Zone should come into effect by the 1 January 1959.[100] But de Gaulle's proposal of a nuclear triumvirate[101] made the Chancellor sceptical of de Gaulle's reliability, for he had not previously mentioned his plans to Adenauer.

The French and British both made plans to break up the negotiations not later than the end of November. 'If the French make no move we should break off the negotiation', Macmillan wrote in his diary on 31 October 1958.[102] The Prime Minister believed that de Gaulle wanted the British out of the continent.[103] In fact, the French declared the failure of the Free Trade Area negotiations in mid-November 1958. Maudling agreed at once. The Germans made a last attempt to get an agreement with the French about follow-up negotiations, but the Federal government did not want to make too many concessions to the French position, acknowledging that the French counter-strategy enabled the realisation of the far-reaching EEC integration programme. Adenauer supported de Gaulle's position for he expected more political and economic stability in Western Europe from the common market approach, but he also hoped there might be a slim chance to make a compromise with the British over the OEEC. De Gaulle was the only statesman of the allied powers who unconditionally supported West Germany's isolation policy towards the GDR at that time, and stood by Adenauer when Khrushchev precipitated the Berlin crisis with his ultimatum in November 1958.[104] Macmillan was convinced that the Germans had sold their soul to the French and built an unholy alliance against Britain.[105]

The break up of the negotiations had advantages for all participants. France could get on with the reform of its economy, Great Britain kept its special Commonwealth relations but was forced to negotiate with the OEEC members about the Free Trade Area Organisation. The EC Commission could build up the common market,[106] and the Federal Republic was certain that European integration would continue. But the British question remained unsolved.

Conclusions

From 1949 to 1955 negotiations with the Western powers were the only way for the Federal Republic of Germany to get rid of the occupation statute and become a sovereign and equal partner in the Western world. Without strong ties to the Western states there could be no freedom of action for the Federal government. Adenauer recognized the necessity of European integration as a new course in German foreign policy for the sake of the political and economic development of the Federal Republic, for the sake of Europe – in order to reduce the fears of aggression – and for the sake of a common front against communism. The price for Germany's Western integration was Adenauer's demand of a security guarantee against military attacks by the Soviet Union and full membership in EDC and NATO. Integration had the function of a fall-back position if American troops were to leave the continent.

On a long-term basis, integration offered the ideal platform for the Bonn government to get back to the position of a European power equal to Great Britain and France. It would only be a question of time until the economic potential of German industry led to more political influence. The EEC institutions were the right place for the Western European partners to keep the Germans under a certain degree of control. There were also in the German government important politicians and diplomats who saw the building of a federal European Union as the main way to secure peace in Europe. They hoped for a chance to transfer the concepts of market economy and federalism currently operating within the German state to the European level. The approach of a federal, not an intergovernmental, European Union with a market economy was supported by the United States as being in its own interest. In this perspective Adenauer was right in emphasising that European integration was necessary, because the United States took it as the starting-point of its entire European policy. The West Germans practised the art of the possible to construct their foreign policy as western-oriented, solid, calculable and always backed up by all the three allied powers. Thereafter, in the framework of the European Community, they tried to practise a new kind of controlled power politics among the Western European states.

Notes

1. Letter, Adenauer to Erhard, 13 April 1956, Foundation Chancellor Adenauer House (Stiftung Bundeskanzler-Adenauer-Haus), Bad Honnef-Rhöndorf (StBKAH), III/23.
2. H.-P. Schwarz, 'Die westdeutsche Außenpolitik – Historische Lektionen und politische Generationen', in W. Scheel (ed.), *Nach dreißig Jahren: Die Bundesrepublik Deutschland – Vergangenheit, Gegenwart, Zukunft*, Stuttgart, 1979, pp. 145–73.
3. Letter, Adenauer to Weitz, 31 October 1945, enclosure: My opinion about the international situation. K. Adenauer, *Erinnerungen 1945–1953*, Stuttgart, 1965, pp. 39–40.
4. On 4 October 1949 the Federal Cabinet decided to become a member of the OEEC and agreed formally to the ERP. *Die Kabinettsprotokolle der Bundesregierung*, vol. 1, 1949, U. Enders and K. Reiser (eds), Boppard, 1982, pp. 97–8.
5. *Adenauer und die Hohen Kommissare, 1949–1952*, series Akten zur Auswärtigen Politik der Bundesrepublik Deutschland, ed. H.-P. Schwarz in connection with R. Pommerin, 2 vols, München, 1989–1990.
6. H.-P. Schwarz, 'Entscheidung für den Westen – Freiheit, Wiederaufbau, Souveränität, Sicherheit und Wiedervereinigung als Strukturelemente westdeutscher Außenpolitik 1949–1955', in M. Funke (ed.), *Entscheidung für den Westen: Vom Besatzungsstatut zur Souveränität der Bundesrepublik 1949–1955*, Bonn, 1988, pp. 9–37.
7. On 20 September 1949 Adenauer firstly proclaimed it in his governmental declaration and reiterated the demand to the Allied High Commission. Letter, Adenauer to McCloy, 26 October 1949, Political Archive of the Auswärtiges Amt, Bonn (PAAA), Political Department 2, 1709.
8. Letter, François-Poncet to Adenauer, 23 September 1950, enclosure: Formula of Definition of the Legal Status of the Federal

Republic and Interpretative Protocol. *Die Kabinettsprotokolle der Bundesregierung*, vol. 3, 1950 Wortprotokolle (verbatims), U. Enders and K. Reiser (eds), Boppard, 1986, pp. 149–50.

9. For British reactions see D. Childs, 'British Labour and Ulbricht's State: The Fight for Recognition', in A. M. Birke and G. Heydemann with the assistance of H. Wentker (eds), *Großbritannien und Ostdeutschland seit 1918. Britain and East Germany since 1918*, Prince Albert Studies, vol. 9, Munich, London, 1992, pp. 95–106. B. Becker, *Die DDR und Großbritannien 1945/49 bis 1973: Politische, wirtschaftliche und kulturelle Kontakte im Zeichen der Nichtanerkennungspolitik*, Bochum, 1991, pp. 63–150.

10. R. Morsey, *Die Deutschlandpolitik Adenauers: Alte Thesen und neue Fakten*, Rheinisch-Westfälische Akademie der Wissenschaften, Vorträge G 308, Opladen, 1991.

11. J. W. Young, 'Churchill's bid for peace with Moscow, 1954', *History*, vol. 73, no. 237, 1988, pp. 425–48; R. Steininger, 'Ein vereintes, unabhängiges Deutschland? Winston Churchill, der Kalte Krieg und die deutsche Frage im Jahre 1953', *Militärgeschichtliche Mitteilungen*, no. 36, 1984, pp. 105–44.

12. V. M. Zubok, *Soviet Intelligence and the Cold War: The 'Small' Committee of Information, 1952–53*, Working paper no. 4, Cold War International History Project, The Woodrow Wilson Center (ed.), Washington, D. C., 1992.

13. Memorandum from the Assistant Secretary of State for European Affairs (Merchant) to the Secretary of State, 15 June 1955, *Foreign Relations of the United States* (FRUS), 1955–1957, vol. V, Austrian State Treaty, Summit and Foreign Ministers Meetings, 1955, Washington, D. C., 1988, pp. 228–30; H.-J. Rupieper, *Der besetzte Verbündete: Die amerikanische Deutschlandpolitik 1949–1955*, Opladen, 1991, pp. 433–46.

14. Verbatim Record of a Conference of the Ambassadors of the Federal Republic of Germany at Bonn, 8–10 December 1955, Federal Archive (Bundesarchiv), Coblence (BA), Herbert Blankenhorn papers 351, 41a; W. G. Grewe, *Rückblenden 1976–1951*, Frankfurt/Main, 1979, pp. 251–62.

15. W. Bührer and H.-J. Schröder, 'Germany's Economic Revival in the 1950's: The Foreign Policy Perspective', in E. di Nolfo (ed.), *Power in Europe? II Great Britain, France, Germany and Italy and the Origins of the EEC 1952–1957*, Berlin, 1992, pp. 174–96.

16. C. S. Maier with the assistance of G. Bischof (eds), *The Marshall Plan and Germany: West German Development within the Framework of the European Recovery Program*, New York, Oxford, 1991; H.-J.Schröder (ed.), *Marshallplan und westdeutscher Wiederaufstieg: Positionen – Kontroversen*, Stuttgart, 1990.

17. Adenauer, Declaration, 30 March 1953, Bundesrat, Archive,

Committee on Foreign Relations, Protocol of the 33th session, 28/53.

18. R. Neebe, 'Optionen westdeutscher Außenwirtschaftspolitik 1949–1953', in L. Herbst, W. Bührer and H. Sowade (eds), *Vom Marshallplan zur EWG: Die Eingliederung der Bundesrepublik Deutschland in die westliche Welt*, Munich, 1990, pp. 163–202. G. Mai, 'Osthandel und Westintegration 1947–1957: Europa, die USA und die Entstehung einer hegemonialen Partnerschaft', ibid., pp. 203–25.

19. C. Buchheim, *Die Wiedereingliederung Westdeutschlands in die Weltwirtschaft 1945–1958*, Munich, 1990.

20. I. D. Turner (ed.), *Reconstruction in Post-War Germany: British Occupation Policy and the Western Zones 1945–55*, Oxford, 1989.

21. T. E. Førland, 'An Act of Economic Warfare? The Dispute over NATO's Embargo Resolution, 1950–1951', *The International History Review*, vol. 12, no. 3, 1990, pp. 490–513, and T. E. Førland, '"Selling Firearms to the Indians": Eisenhower's Export Control Policy', *Diplomatic History*, vol. 15, no. 2, 1991, pp. 221–44.

22. Letter, Adenauer to the Allied High Commission, McCloy, enclosure: Memorandum, 5810/0703/50, 2 February 1950. PAAA, Political Department 2, 1305; Record of the 75th meeting of the Council for the Occupation Statute and Foreign Affairs of the Deutscher Bundestag, 1st Session 1949, enclosure: 1, Report of H. Kroll on the actual East trade situation, 12 March 1952, Parliament Archive, Bonn.

23. H.-P. Schwarz, 'Adenauer und Europa', *Vierteljahrshefte für Zeitgeschichte*, vol. 27, no. 4, 1979, pp. 471–523.

24. Adenauer, Declaration to the board of the CDU, 5 September 1952, in *Adenauer: 'Es mußte alles neu gemacht werden.' Die Protokolle des CDU-Bundesvorstandes 1950–1953*, ed. G. Buchstab, Stuttgart, 1986, p. 132.

25. M. Messerschmidt, C. Greiner and N. Wiggershaus, 'West Germany's Strategic Position and her Role in Defence Policy as seen by the German Military 1945–1949', in J. Becker and F. Knipping (eds), *Power in Europe? Great Britain, France, Italy and Germany in a Postwar World, 1945–1950*, Berlin, 1986, pp. 353–69.

26. K.A. Maier, 'Die internationalen Auseinandersetzungen um die Westintegration der Bundesrepublik Deutschland und um ihre Bewaffnung im Rahmen der Europäischen Verteidigungsgemeinschaft', in *Anfänge westdeutscher Sicherheitspolitik 1945–1956*, vol. 2, Die EVG-Phase, Militärgeschichtliches Forschungsamt (ed.), Munich, 1990, pp. 1–234.

27. Telegram, Robertson (Wahnerheide) to Foreign Oficce, German section, no. 669, contains the translation of Adenauer's letter to Robertson, 28 April 1950, Public Record Office, London (PRO), Foreign Office, General Correspondence (FO) 371, 85624.

28. See the author's contribution, 'Der Streit um Kompetenzen und Konzeptionen deutscher Europapolitik 1949–1958', in L. Herbst et al. (eds), _Vom Marshallplan zur EWG_, pp. 335–70.

29. Hallstein, Memorandum 'Answers to the Ideas of the Minister of Economics about the Problem of Cooperation or Integration', 30 March 1955, Ludwig Erhard Foundation, (Ludwig-Erhard-Stiftung), Bonn (LES), Ludwig Erhard papers, I. 4) 46.

30. Report about the question of European integration, 1 May 1953, _Wissenschaftlicher Beirat beim Bundesminister für Wirtschaft: Sammelband der Gutachten von 1948–1972_, ed. Bundesministerium für Wirtschaft, Göttingen, 1972, pp. 177–92; and Report about the question of a Common Market, 11 October 1955, ibid., pp. 199–211.

31. R.T. Griffiths and A.S. Milward, 'The Beyen Plan and the European Political Community', in W. Maihofer (ed.), _Noi si mura_, European University Institute, Florence, 1986, pp. 595–621.

32. W.R. Smyser, _The Economy of United Germany: Collossus at the Crossroads_, New York, 1992, pp. 129–48; U. Lappenküper, '"Ich bin wirklich ein guter Europäer": Ludwig Erhards Europapolitik 1949–1966', _Francia_, vol. 18, no. 3, 1991, pp. 85–121; D. Koerfer, _Kampf ums Kanzleramt: Erhard und Adenauer_, Stuttgart, 1987.

33. Erhard, Memorandum 'Thoughts about the Problem of Cooperation or Integration', private study, March 1955. LES, I. 4) 46.

34. Memorandum of Conversation Adenauer-Pella, Bühlerhöhe, 18 January 1955, StBKAH, III/68.

35. G. Bossuat, _La France, l'aide américaine et la construction européenne 1944–1954_, Paris, 1992, pp. 707–94; J. Gillingham, _Coal, steel, and the Rebirth of Europe, 1945–1955: The Germans and French from Ruhr Conflict to Economic Community_, Cambridge, 1991; K. Schwabe (ed.), _Die Anfänge des Schuman-Plans 1950/51, The Beginnings of the Schuman-Plan_, Baden-Baden, 1988.

36. R.T. Griffiths and F.M.B. Lynch, 'L'échec de la 'Petite Europe': les négociations Fritalux/Finebel, 1949–1950', _Revue Historique_, no. 274, 1986, pp. 159–93.

37. P. Gerbet, _Le relèvement 1944–1949_, Paris, 1991, pp. 309–30.

38. R. Poidevin, 'Die europapolitischen Initiativen Frankreichs des Jahres 1950 – aus einer Zwangslage geboren?', in L. Herbst et al. (eds), _Vom Marshallplan zur EWG_, pp. 257–62.

39. J.W. Young, _France, the Cold War and the Western Alliance, 1944–49: French Foreign Policy and Post-War Europe_, New York, 1990, pp. 205–11, 228–31.

40. Exchange of letters Schuman-Adenauer, 7 and 8 May 1950, _Adenauer, Briefe 1949–1951_, series Adenauer Rhöndorfer Ausgabe, R. Morsey and H.-P. Schwarz (eds), Berlin, 1985, pp. 208–11.

41. Summary Record of a Meeting of the United States Ambassadors at

Paris, 21–22 October 1949, *FRUS 1949*, vol. IV. Western Europe, Washington, D.C., 1975, p. 485.

42. Interview, Adenauer with Kingsbury Smith, 21 March 1950, Information to the Press No. 347/50, Press and Information Office of the Federal Government (Presse- und Informationsamt der Bundesregierung), Bonn, Press Archive, F 25.

43. C. Lüders, *Das Ruhrkontrollsystem: Entstehung und Entwicklung im Rahmen der Westintegration Westdeutschlands 1947–1953*, Frankfurt/ Main, 1988.

44. C. Goschler, C. Buchheim and W. Bührer, 'Der Schumanplan als Instrument französischer Stahlpolitik', *Vierteljahrshefte für Zeitgeschichte*, vol. 37, no. 2, 1988, pp. 171–206; W. Bührer, 'Die französische Ruhrpolitik und das Comeback der westdeutschen Schwerindustriellen 1945–1952', in P. Hüttenberger and H. Molitor (eds), *Franzosen und Deutsche am Rhein 1789–1918–1945*, Essen, 1989, pp. 27–46.

45. H.-P. Schwarz, *Adenauer: Der Aufstieg: 1876–1952*, Stuttgart, 1986, pp. 727–74.

46. Adenauer, *Erinnerungen 1945–1953*, pp. 355–9, K. Adenauer, 'Warum Wiederbewaffnung? – Das Sicherheitsmemorandum vom 29. August 1950', in W. von Raven (ed.), *Armee gegen den Krieg: Wert und Wirkung der Bundeswehr*, Stuttgart-Degerloch, 1966, pp. 13–16.

47. I.M. Wall, *The United States and the Making of Postwar France, 1945–1954*, Cambridge, 1991, pp. 188–232; C. Greiner, 'The Defense of Western Europe and the Rearmament of West Germany, 1947–1950', in O. Riste (ed.), *Western Security: The Formative Years: European and Atlantic Defense 1947–1963*, New York, 1985, pp. 150–77; N. Wiggershaus, 'The Decision for a West German Defense Contribution', ibid., pp. 198–214.

48. S. Dockrill, 'Britain and the Settlement of the West German Rearmament Question in 1954', in M. Dockrill and J.W. Young (eds), *British Foreign Policy, 1945–56*, London, 1989, pp. 149–72; S. Dockrill, 'The Evolution of Britain's Policy towards a European Army 1950–54,' *The Journal of Strategic Studies*, vol. 12, no. 1, 1989, pp. 38–62; H.J. Yasamee, 'A Chair in the Smoking Room: The German Question in 1950', *FCO Historical Branch, Occasional Papers*, no. 3, ed. Foreign and Commonwealth Office, London, 1989, pp. 26–35.

49. J. Bariéty, 'La décision de réarmer l'Allemagne, l'échec de la Communauté Européenne de Défense et les accords de Paris du 23 octobre 1954 vus du côté français', *Revue Belge de Philologie et d'Histoire*, 71 (1993) Fasc. 2: Histoire Médiévale, Moderne et Contemporaine, pp. 354–83; B.Goldschmidt in *L'aventure de la bombe: De Gaulle et la dissuasion nucléaire (1958–1969)*, Paris, 1985, pp. 28–30; G.-H. Soutou, 'Die Nuklearpolitik der Vierten Republik', *Vierteljahrshefte für Zeitgeschichte*, vol. 37, no. 4, 1989, p. 606.

50. G.-H. Soutou, 'La politique nucléaire de Pierre Mendés France', *Relations internationales*, no. 59, 1989, pp. 317–30.

51. Grewe, *Rückblenden*, pp. 127–56.

52. P. Fischer, 'Die Bundesrepublik und das Projekt einer Europäischen Politischen Gemeinschaft', in L. Herbst et al. (eds), *Vom Marshallplan zur EWG*, pp. 279–99; R. Cordozo, 'The Project for a Political Community (1952–54)', in R. Pryce (ed.), *The Dynamics of European Union*, London, 1987, pp. 49–77.

53. See the author's contribution 'Zwischen Vormarsch und Schlaganfall – Das Projekt der Europäischen Politischen Gemeinschaft und die Haltung der Bundesrepublik Deutschland 1951–1954', in G. Trausch (ed.), *Die Europäische Integration vom Schumanplan bis zu den Verträgen von Rom*, Baden-Baden, 1993, pp. 181–2.

54. *Documents on British Policy Overseas (DBPO)*, series II, vol. I, The Schuman Plan, the Council of Europe and Western Integration May 1950–December 1952, R. Bullen and M.E. Pelly (eds), assisted by H.J. Yasamee and G. Bennett, London, 1986, chapter IV, pp. 741–1011; J.W. Young, 'Churchill's "No" to Europe: The "Rejection" of European Union by Churchill's Post-War Government, 1951–1952', *The Historical Journal*, vol. 28, no. 4, 1985, pp. 923–37.

55. Adenauer, Informal talk with the Press, 10 March 1953, *Adenauer, Teegespräche 1950–1954*, series Adenauer Rhöndorfer Ausgabe, R. Morsey and H.-P. Schwarz (eds), Berlin, 1984, pp. 417–8. Adenauer to the board of the CDU, 11 March 1953. 'Es mußte alles neu gemacht werden.', p. 425.

56. P. Guillen, 'La France et l'intégration de la RFA dans l'OTAN', *Guerres Mondiales et Conflits Contemporains*, no. 159, 1990, pp. 73–91.

57. Neuviéme Séance à Neuf (Plénière), London, 2 October 1954, *Documents Diplomatiques Français 1954*, Annexes (21 Juillet–31 Décembre), ed. Ministère des Relations Extérieures, Paris, 1987, p. 205; Verbatim records of the 9th Plenary meeting. PRO, FO 1086, 176.

58. G.-H. Soutou, 'La France, l'Allemagne et les accords de Paris', *Relations internationales* no. 52, 1987, pp. 451–70.

59. K. Gotto, 'Die Sicherheits- und Deutschlandfrage in Adenauers Politik 1954/55', in B. Thoß and H.-E. Volkmann (eds), *Zwischen Kaltem Krieg und Entspannung: Sicherheits- und Deutschlandpolitik der Bundesrepublik im Mächtesystem der Jahre 1953–1956*, Boppard, 1988, pp. 137–51; D. Carlton, 'Großbritannien und die Gipfeldiplomatie 1953–1955', ibid., pp. 51–69.

60. H.-P. Schwarz, *Adenauer: Der Staatsmann: 1952–1967*, Stuttgart, 1991, pp. 207–22.

61. Letter, Adenauer to Dulles, 12 Decembre 1955; StBKAH, III/54.

62. Memorandum of Conversation between Adenauer and his counsellors, 25 May 1955; BA, Blankenhorn papers 351, 41b.

63. Memorandum of Conversation Adenauer-Gaitskell, 19 September 1956. StBKAH, III/68; K. Adenauer, *Erinnerungen 1955–1959*, Stuttgart, 1967, pp. 219–22; Adenauer, 'Speech to the Grandes Conférences Catholiques at Brussels', 26 September 1956, *Konrad Adenauer, Reden 1917–1967: Eine Auswahl*, H.-P.Schwarz (ed.), Stuttgart, 1975, pp. 327–32.

64. K. Schwabe, 'Adenauer und England', in L. Kettenacker, M. Schlenke and H. Seier (eds), *Studien zur Geschichte Englands und der deutsch-britischen Beziehungen: Festschrift für Paul Kluke*, Munich, 1981, pp. 353–74.

65. P. Weilemann, *Die Anfänge der Europäischen Nukleargemeinschaft: Zur Gründungsgeschichte von Euratom 1955–1957*, Baden-Baden, 1983; M. Eckert, 'Kernenergie und Westintegration: Die Zähmung des west-deutschen Nuklearnationalismus', in L. Herbst et al. (eds), *Vom Marshallplan zur EWG*, pp. 313–34.

66. P. Guillen, 'Europe as a Cure for French Impotence? The Guy Mollet Government and the Negotiation of the Treaties of Rome', in E. di Nolfo (ed.), *Power in Europe? II*, pp. 505–16.

67. Erhard, Memorandum 'Draft of a European Program', 29 October 1956, BA, Franz Etzel papers 254, 84.

68. See the author's study *Fondements de la Communauté Économique Européenne*, Luxembourg, Brussels, 1990.

69. R. Girault, 'France entre l'Europe et l'Afrique', in E. Serra (ed.), *Il Rilancio dell'Europa e i Trattati di Roma*, Milan, 1989, pp. 351–78.

70. For the financial details see the author's study *Fondements*, pp. 266–8.

71. F. Knipping, '"Firm with the West!" Elements of the International Orientation of West Germany in the Mid-1950s', in E. di Nolfo (ed.), *Power in Europe? II*, pp. 517–29.

72. C.A. Wurm, 'Großbritannien und die Anfänge der europäischen Integration 1945–1951: Ein Überblick', in G. Schmidt (ed.), *Großbritannien und Europa – Großbritannien in Europa: Sicherheitsbelange und Wirtschaftsfragen in der britischen Europapolitik nach dem Zweiten Weltkrieg*, Bochum, 1989, pp. 57–88.

73. *DBPO*, series II, vol. I, chapter 1, pp. 1–155.

74. Sceptical to this view J.W. Young, '"The parting of the Ways"? Britain, the Messina Conference and the Spaak Committee, June–December 1955', in Dockrill and Young (eds), *British Foreign Policy, 1945–56*, pp. 197–224; S. Burgess and G. Edwards, 'The Six plus One: British policy-making and the question of European economic integration, 1955', *International Affairs*, vol. 64, no. 4, 1988, pp. 393–413.

75. *The Memoirs of Lord Gladwyn*, London, 1972, pp. 294–5; A. Horne, *Macmillan 1894–1956*, vol. I of the Official Biography, London, 1988, p. 386.

76. R. Lamb, *The Failure of the Eden Government*, London, 1987, pp. 73–101.

77. Plan G, version of 29 September 1956, H. Macmillan, *Riding the Storm 1956–1959*, London, 1971, pp. 753–4.

78. Girault, *France entre l'Europe et l'Afrique*, pp. 351–78.

79. Macmillan and Thorneycroft, Declarations, 26 November 1956, House of Commons, Debates (Hansard), vol. 561, col. 35–54, 154–64.

80. *The Memoirs of Lord Gladwyn*, p. 292.

81. Macmillan, *Riding the Storm*, p. 432–3; P.H. Spaak, *Memoiren eines Europäers*, Hamburg, 1969, pp. 315–16.

82. Macmillan ibid., p. 436.

83. Macmillan Diaries, 9 March 1957; A. Horne, *Macmillan 1957–1986*, vol. II of the Official Biography, London, 1989, pp. 32, 637.

84. F.J. Strauß, *Die Erinnerungen*, Berlin, 1989, pp. 313–34; C. Barbier, 'Les négociations franco-germano-italiennes en vue de l'établisse-ment d'une coopération militaire nucléaire au cours des années 1956–1958', *Relations internationales*, no. 104, 1990, pp. 81–113; E. Conze, 'La coopération franco-germano-italienne dans le domaine nucléaire dans les années 1957–1958: un point de vue allemand', ibid., pp. 115–32.

85. H.-P. Schwarz, 'Adenauer, le nucléaire, et la France', *Revue d'histoire diplomatique*, no. 106, 1992, pp. 297–311. Military aspects of the West German nuclear policy are discussed by J. Steinhoff and R. Pommerin, *Strategiewechsel: Bundesrepublik und Nuklearstrategie in der Ära Adenauer-Kennedy*, Baden-Baden, 1992.

86. Von Brentano, Declaration, 5 July 1957. Verhandlungen des Deutschen Bundestages (Debates), 2nd session 1953, Stenographische Berichte (Verbatims), vol. 38, pp. 13331–4; Memorandum of Conversation Dulles-von Brentano, 5 March 1957, *FRUS 1955–1957*, vol. IV Western European Security and Integration, Washington, D.C., 1986, pp. 531–3.

87. Memorandum of Conversation Dulles-Adenauer, von Brentano, 4 May 1957, *FRUS 1955–1957*, vol. XXVI Central and Southeastern Europe, Washington, D.C., 1992, pp. 239–40.

88. Erhard, Declaration to the Council of the OEEC, 12 February 1957, in *Ludwig Erhard, Gedanken aus fünf Jahrzehnten: Reden und Schriften*, ed. K. Hohmann, Düsseldorf, 1988, pp. 486–9.

89. Hallstein, Declaration, 21 March 1957, *Verhandlungen des Deutschen Bundestages*, vol. 35, pp. 11327–34.

90. Macmillan, *Riding the Storm*, pp. 435–6.

91. Macmillan, Memorandum, 13 July 1957, Horne, *Macmillan*, vol. II, p. 31.

92. J.C. Snoy et d'Oppuers, 'Les etapes de la Cooperation Européenne et les Négociations Relatives à une Zone de Libre-Échange',

Chronique de Politique Etrangère, vol. 12, 1959, pp. 569–623; P.Uri, 'La Zone de Libre-Échange', *Revue d'économie politique: Le Marché Commun et ses problèmes*, vol. 1, 1958, pp. 310–23.

93. J.F. Deniau, *L'Europe interdite*, Paris, 1977, pp. 96–9.

94. R. Maudling, *Memoirs*, London, 1978, p. 72.

95. A. Müller-Armack, *Auf dem Wege nach Europa: Erinnerungen und Ausblicke*, Stuttgart, Tübingen, 1971, pp. 206–10.

96. Protocol of the Third Meeting Adenauer-Macmillan, 18 April 1958, BA, Blankenhorn papers 351, 87.

97. Record of Conversation Macmillan-von Brentano on 7 June 1958, Washington, D.C., 8 June 1958, PRO, Premier Minister's Office (PREM) 11, 2345.

98. Compte Rendu des Entretiens Macmillan-de Gaulle, 29 and 30 June 1958, *Documents Diplomatiques Français 1958*, tome I (1ᵉʳ Janvier–30 Juin), Paris, 1992, pp. 862–74; Exchange of letters Macmillan-de Gaulle, 30 June and 5 July 1958, Macmillan, *Riding the Storm*, pp. 449–51, Charles de Gaulle, *Lettres, Notes et Carnets, Juin 1958–Décembre 1960*, Paris, 1985, pp. 42–3.

99. Note pour les Affaires Étrangères, 13 August 1958, Charles de Gaulle, *Lettres, Notes et Carnets*, p. 73.

100. Record of Visit of the Prime Minister to Bonn, October 8–9, 1958, PRO, PREM 11, 2328.

101. Letter de Gaulle to Eisenhower and Macmillan enclosing the Memorandum, 17 September 1958, Charles de Gaulle, *Lettres, Notes et Carnets*, pp. 82–4, 87; M. Vaïsse, 'Aux origines du mémorandum de septembre 1958', *Relations internationales*, no. 58, 1989, pp. 253–68; Also 'Memoranda of conversations between de Gaulle and Dulles at Paris, 5 July 1958', *FRUS 1958–1960*, vol. VII Part 2 Western Europe, Washington, D.C., 1993, pp. 53–64.

102. Macmillan, *Riding the Storm*, p. 455; P. Gore-Booth, *With Great Truth and Respect*, London, 1974, p. 252.

103. Macmillan Diaries, 31 October 1958; Horne, *Macmillan*, vol. II, pp. 111, 644.

104. Schwarz, *Adenauer: Der Staatsmann*, pp. 502–26; M. Trachtenberg, *History and Strategy*, Princeton, 1991, pp. 169–234.

105. Note, Macmillan to Lloyd, 28 November 1958, H. Macmillan, *Pointing the Way 1959–1961*, London, 1972, p. 48; Maudling, *Memoirs*, p. 69.

106. H. von der Groeben, *Combat pour l'Europe: La construction de la Communauté européenne, 1958–1966*, Brussels, 1985.

WERNER BÜHRER

German Industry and European Integration in the 1950s

According to Fritz Berg, President of the Federation of German Industry (Bundesverband der Deutschen Industrie or BDI), achieving a united Europe counted among the most important goals of German industrialists. Since politicians still seemed to be captivated by ideas of prestige and national sovereignty, he even claimed some sort of European pioneering role in this respect for German industry.[1] Four years later, in September 1954, Wilhelm Beutler, general manager of the Federation, while rejecting any hegemonic ambitions, confirmed this declaration by stressing the seriousness and honesty of German endeavours towards European unity. He conceded, however, that in the meanwhile European 'enthusiasm' had been replaced by 'realism'.[2] Although one may doubt whether there had been such enthusiasm at the beginning of the integration process, attitudes had obviously changed as West Germany gained more independence.

In 1949, when the Federal Republic of Germany was founded, some major decisions on post-war Germany's international relations and its role in Europe had already been taken by the occupying powers. Among these, the decision to incorporate the western part of Germany into the framework of a comprehensive European recovery programme was particularly important. This meant that, despite some *discussion* in West German political and economic circles on the perspectives and implications of European integration, the *decision* to take part in these efforts had been made in Paris, London, and especially in Washington. This should be kept in mind although the Federal Government, for example by the accession to the Organisation for European Economic Co-operation (OEEC) at the end of October 1949 or by the approval of the Schuman Plan, subsequently 'ratified' these decisions. Moreover, since participation in common reconstruction efforts seemed to be the only chance for West Germany to recover in due time, German officials and industrialists most likely would have made the same decisions even without Allied interference.

Compared with the other participants, however, the Germans took particular interest in European cooperation and integration. It is true that they were looking for goods in short supply, markets and funds as were the French or the Italians. But they were just as much interested in achieving *Gleichberechtigung* – treatment on equal terms. This, for instance, would have meant that all Allied restrictions such as the limits on steel production, the foreign trade controls and decartelisation would have to be abolished. This also implied that the government should be able to decide foreign policy matters on its own. In short, seen from the German point of view, European integration seemed to be by far the best and most effective means to regain sovereignty.

To achieve this goal the Federal Republic was ready to fulfil Allied – especially American and French – expectations and requirements to an extent it certainly would have rejected under 'normal' conditions. This was one of the reasons why German attitudes towards European integration became more rigid and criticism increased during the 1950s; step by step, its political and economic elites became more self-confident and less inclined to adapt to schemes that seemed to hamper their ambitions. This was especially true for German industry. Its outlook on European integration changed between the end of the 1940s and the end of the 1950s from almost full support, first to cautious reluctance and then to pragmatic participation.

This process – the formulation and modification of integration conceptions and policies by German industry, its motives and expectations, and the attempts to influence, with the help of powerful businessmen and trade associations, the integration policy of the government – is the subject of the following article. In the first section the article outlines the relative strength of the various branches of industry in the post-war period and the interest group structures. Subsequently it focuses on the more general aspects of industry's attitudes towards cooperation and integration, and on the ways and means of active participation in the building up of

European connections and in the work of European institutions. The fourth section concentrates on the main steps of European integration and the efforts of important industrial associations to put through their ideas and goals, and tries to evaluate the role of German industry in the integration of Western Europe.

Structural changes and the organisation of German business

How important were the various sectors of industry in post-war Germany, and did differences in economic strength have any impact on the influence of the different sectors over their industry-wide associations? During the Second World War the influence of the various sectors depended on the extent to which they contributed to the war economy. Although the production of consumer goods remained at a relatively high level, those industries involved in armaments production ranked at the head of the intra-industrial hierarchy. After the war, these sectors understandably became the main targets of Allied dismantling and control measures. Moreover, despite some evidence that 'wartime investment had increased the industrial capital stock by more than the extent of wartime damage', individual industries such as coal-mining, steel, electricity generation and transportation 'had been seriously affected by wartime destruction and post-war disintegration'.[3] And until late summer 1947 it was by no means clear whether the German economy would be restored in its capacity as one of the biggest industrial 'workshops' in Europe or would become instead a supplier of raw materials such as coal.

The mere fact that coal and steel were vital to economic reconstruction was therefore not enough to give those industries a privileged position. In the case of coal mining, the reconstruction period seemed to be nothing more than a short respite in the decline of this formerly so powerful industry.[4] In contrast to the coal sector the iron and steel industry was able to establish during the 1950s, for at least two decades, a position not so far from its pre-war rank. Nevertheless, the so-called Investment Aid Act (Investitionshilfegesetz) of 1952, which obliged the other sectors to support investments in the energy sector, the railways and the coal and steel industries,[5] was one of the last great victories of Ruhr heavy industry over finishing and consumer goods industries.

Leading sectors of the 1950s and the following decades became the chemical industry, mechanical engineering, motor manufacturing and electrical engineering.[6] The following tables may give an impression of the rapid growth of production in these branches and the growing shares of employment and sales.

Table 1 **Index of industrial production, 1950–65**

Year	Industry (Total)	Mining	Basic raw materials	Capital goods	Consumer goods	Food products	Energy	Construction
1950	100	100	100	100	100	100	100	100
1955	176	128	176	216	167	158	172	188
1960	248	132	254	323	235	219	245	260
1865	327	135	348	423	304	286	351	365

Table 2 **Employees and sales in individual sectors, 1950–65**

Year	Totals		Mining %		Basic raw materials %		Capital goods %		Consumer goods %		Food products %	
	Empl. 1000	Sales Mio. DM	Empl.	Sales	Empl.	Sales	Empl.	Sales	Empl.	Sales	Empl.	Sales
1950	4.935	82.061	11.6	5.5	22.4	27.4	29.0	22.3	27.3	24.8	6.8	18.1
1955	6.815	171.568	9.5	4.8	21.1	29.9	33.4	28.9	26.3	19.3	6.1	14.3
1960	8.081	266.373	7.6	4.3	21.0	30.3	37.6	31.8	24.1	17.6	6.0	13.0
1965	8.460	374.612	4.9	3.6	22.3	31.8	42.9	38.8	23.8	19.4	6.4	14.9

Source: Winkel, *Wirtschaft*, p. 98 and 100.

Did these structural changes find expression in the system of industrial federations and in the power hierarchy of the various industrial associations? On the face ot it, the former organisational pattern – regional, social policy and economic policy organisations – and even the traditional hierarchy were soon reestablished. 'Thus, of the national organisations in the business sphere, the Federation of German Industry may very well rank first in prestige, financial strength, and influence.' The BDI is composed of federally structured associations of the various branches of industry – thirty-four in 1949 and thirty-nine in 1964. The coal and steel associations formally joined the BDI in 1953. In 1961, according to a BDI official, '98 per cent of all West German industrialists are represented through the BDI'.[7] Fritz Berg, the owner of a medium-sized metal manufacturing firm, was elected president, and the BDI's political influence resulted not least from his close personal contacts with Chancellor Konrad Adenauer.[8] On the other hand, these relationships occasionally gave Adenauer the possibility to manipulate the Federation for his own purposes. W. Alexander Menne (chemical industry) and Otto A. H. Vogel (textile industry and president of the Augsburg Chamber of Industry and Commerce) were elected vice-presidents. The presidential board of the BDI consisted of Alexander von Engelberg (gravel industry), Otto A. Friedrich (rubber), Franz Linsenhoff (construction), Gustav Möllenberg (machine tools) and Hermann Reusch (steel).[9]

Some historians, for example Volker Berghahn, argue 'that the informal balance of power was clearly tilted towards heavy industry, and it was to be some time before a change occured in this respect'.[10] In particular, Reusch's role as some sort of 'grey eminence' of the BDI seems to furnish some evidence in favour of this interpretation. I do not share this view, however, and the Federation's position concerning European integration speaks particularly against there being a predominant position for heavy industry. Besides this, the number of votes possessed by the individual associations in the Membership Assembly did not allow heavy industry to control the BDI's affairs. In 1954, for example, the coal industry had fifteen and the steel industry eight votes. In contrast, the chemical industry disposed of eight votes, mechanical engineering thirteen, electrical engineering nine and textiles eleven votes out of a total of 113 votes.[11] In any case, the associations of all these industries, with the exception of coal, played an important role in BDI politics.

The second 'pillar' was formed by the employers' associations headed by the Federation of German Employers' Associations (Bundesvereinigung der Deutschen Arbeitgeberverbände, or BDA). They were engaged mainly in labour and social policies. As stated by Braunthal, the BDA ranked between the BDI and the Diet of German Industry and Commerce (Deutscher Industrie- und Handelstag, or DIHT), the umbrella organisation of about eighty regional chambers of commerce. In the field of European integration, however, the DIHT far surpassed the employers associations in importance. According to Berghahn, the DIHT, 'its heterogeneity notwithstanding, was by and large out-ward-looking and liberal-capitalist', whereas the BDI 'represented the conservative traditions of large-scale industry, but also mir-rored the old tensions between its various branches...'[12] However, as far as European integration was concerned, the BDI, too, opened up new paths.

Types and characteristics of European attitudes

During the First World War prominent industrialists, for example Emil Kirdorf, Hugo Stinnes and August Thyssen, and var-ious associations counted among the most nationalistic and expan-sionistic circles of the German *Reich*.[13] After the defeat, other businessmen like Max M. Warburg, Carl Melchior, Emil Georg von Stauß, Wilhelm Cuno, Richard Merton, Carl Bosch and Felix Deutsch, representing banking, shipping, metal, chemical and electrical industries, rejected old-fashioned *Machtpolitik* in favour of a new, cooperative economic foreign policy.[14] Later, after the Treaty of Versailles had been signed, even such hard-boiled heavy industry representatives as Stinnes changed course and searched for cooperative solutions – for instance to the Franco-German coal problem.[15] The various international cartels, too, although their 'de-nationalising' effects should not be overestimated,[16] might have contributed to the emergence of some sort of internationalis-tic mentality.

This did not of course mean that nationalism had lost its attrac-tion, as the experience of the Third Reich showed. Did German businessmen learn something from this experience? The American political scientist Gabriel A. Almond, on the basis of some fifty interviews during the summer 1954, came to the conclusion 'that the learning has been incomplete, the lessons are undigested, and present responses to the political situation are based upon simple power calculations and situational adjustments'. Since there were 'no realistic grounds for hopes of vindication or revenge', the revival of an 'adventurous nationalism' seemed highly improbable. What was apparent, however, among all groups of the population was a demand, varied in degree, 'for more independence in the conduct of foreign policy'.[17] According to Almond and other researchers, heavy industry elites were particularly predisposed to such nationalist trends. It is not without its ironic aspects, therefore, that coal and steel after the war had to play the pioneering role in the integration of Europe.

Almond distinguished three different streams of pro-European attitudes among German businessmen:

> In the first place, there is a genuine European current based upon one or a combination of religious, cultural, economic, and political considerations. Secondly, there is a phenomenon which may be appropriately characterized as an 'escape into Europe'. And, finally, there is a kind of 'crypto-nationalist' Europeanism, a belief that German economic and political dominance may be attained through European integration. These attitudes occur most typically in combination, but it is possible to distinguish among individuals according to the type of attitudes that predominates in the thinking of each.[18]

In his study on the BDI, Braunthal came to similar conclusions:

> Many businessmen evidently support integration because they favor the economic and political strengthening of the European continent and the doing away with the narrow focus on nationalism. Others apparently see integration as giving Germany a dominant role in a supranational union. Whatever the motivation, industrialists have unquestionably broadened their horizons.[19]

In reality, however, it is quite difficult to decide which of these motives might have been predominant as far as certain industrialists were concerned. Günter Henle of Klöckner steel works, for example, was an ardent supporter of Franco-German reconciliation and avowed opponent of traditional power politics. Yet during the Schuman Plan negotiations, when the Ruhr *Verbundwirtschaft*, i.e. the efficient and cost saving exchange of fuels and supplies within *one* company, was attacked by the French and the Americans, he, too, was afraid to loose this structural advantage – one of the steel industry's, and therefore Germany's, trump cards.[20] Hermann Reusch by contrast, who in 1950 counted among the critics of the Schuman Plan, later worked to obtain a fair judgement on the ECSC.[21] And, of course, it was and is not unusual, for German industry in particular, for European attitudes to be based on national or even sector and company interests. Perhaps it is more useful to distinguish not between different types of Europeanism, but between different characteristics or components of pro-European thinking.

One strong characteristic of German Europeanism was its strong anti-communist motivation. As BDI president Berg once put it, German industry was closely attached to the western world; western civilisation was the source of its resistance against the 'Asiatic flood'. Only European unity therefore would guarantee the power to withstand the 'Eastern storm'.[22] Typical, too, was the fact the Germans, businessmen and politicians alike, were compelled to a larger extent than other Western Europeans to subscribe to European integration and to use European 'packaging' in order to achieve their specific national goals.

Another essential of the industry's conception of European unity was the reconciliation with France. In particular Günter Henle of Klöckner steel works, who was one of the more prominent 'political' industrialists, and not only because of his Christian Democratic Party membership and his seat in the Bundestag, became a committed advocate of Franco-German rapprochement. In an analysis of November 1949 he stated that the situations of both countries, as a consequence of the 'massive landslide...in Germany since 1945', had come to resemble each other. The Federal Republic wished to cling to the West because it saw itself 'today threatened, exposed and defenceless', and was therefore 'itself gripped by the demand for *sécurité*' that had been dominant in France 'as strongly ever since 1918'. Pointing to the fact of the Iron Curtain, he set German relationships in a wider context, stressing that 'yesterday's world had vanished, with all its ambitious goals and aspirations'. Old rivalries had become 'suicidal and senseless'. The Federal Republic, he asserted, had no new objectives of 'future power politics in the West' and was aware that 'in the age of the atom bomb old-style power politics can no longer exist'. By contrast with the 1920s, it was clear from the circumstances of the Cold War that 'the idea of sovereignty had to give place to higher requirements', when the common welfare and the existence of Europe was at stake.

And, alluding to widespread fears in France, he explicitly stressed that there was no wish to 'swallow up' Germany's neighbour since this was well beyond German strength, even if such a belief in German capabilities might be flattering. Ideas such as 'predominance', so Henle concluded, had now become outdated; whoever really wanted to be in Europe ought to get rid of 'sentiments of this kind'.[23] This analysis, in particular the appraisal of some sort of 'special Franco-German relationship', was representative of the decisive circles in West German industry, and it corresponded precisely with the convictions of Chancellor Konrad Adenauer. Since German industry, and heavy industry in particular, had a long tradition of cooperation with the French, this accord should not be taken as proof that Adenauer succesfully manipulated German businessmen and their associations.

Finally, the absence of any thinking of Europe as a 'Third Force', at least as far as the prominent industrialists were concerned, should be mentioned. Close contacts to the United States as the dominating Western power were considered to be very important. This attitude resulted from security needs as well as economic considerations.[24] Surprisingly, the possibility of conflicts between these two political options seems to have been ignored.

Institutionalised participation in European politics

Already during the inaugural meeting of the BDI's predecessor organisation in October 1949 several spokesmen declared their belief in European cooperation. To them, this cooperation was the only chance to save western civilisation. Hermann Reusch, managing director of one of the six leading West German steel works, the Gutehoffnungshütte, who, as mentioned before, became one of the most influential persons in the BDI, emphasised moreover the important role of the Federal Republic in general and of a powerful German industry in particular. According to him, any European community would be impossible without German participation.[25]

To demonstrate its European conviction to the public, the Federation founded a special committee on European questions in December 1950. Berg was elected as chairman.[26] After this impressive overture, however, the committee disappeared from the public scene almost completely. In 1953 its name was changed into 'Committee on International Relations' – to signal its 'expanded field of activity', as the semi-official history of the BDI put it.[27]

Of course, the presidential and the executive boards talked frequently about integration questions, and within the BDI executive staff the international relations branch was responsible for integration issues. But not until 1957 did the DIHT install a department of European economic integration; in 1958 two committees on European problems were established in order to cope with the increasing number of tasks after the foundation of the European Economic Community (EEC).[28] Before that time European problems had been discussed by the *Hauptausschuß*, the Foreign Economic Policy or the Tarifs Committee of the DIHT. The various branch associations proceeded similarly. To deal with the problems arising out of the Schuman Plan negotiations, the steel association, for instance, installed several working groups and a coordinating committee for the technical subcommittees.[29] As far as the BDA was concerned, integration matters fell under the competence of the International Social Policy Department and the Committee on EEC Social Policy.[30]

Besides this, the European activities of the individual associations were made public in detail. Each annual report, for example, included a special chapter summing up the work of the past year. During the annual sessions of the membership assemblies, too, the problems and prospects of integration, played an important role. In October 1952 the BDI held a 'Europe Day' at Trier with Paul-Henri Spaak, Ludwig Erhard and Georges Villiers, president of the *Conseil National du Patronat Français*, addressing the audience. The Federation wanted this congress to be understood as an appeal to the political leaders to overcome still existing reservations and to intensify integration efforts – and as a demonstration of the high level of cooperation that already had been reached by European industry.[31]

Another field of European activity was the engagement of national associations and individual businessmen in various transnational and international organisations. The first of these 'clubs' joined by the Federation of German Industry was the Council of European Industrial Federations (CIFE), established in

September 1949 with headquarters in Paris as a consultative body to the OEEC. Berg became member of the steering committee even before the BDI's foundation, and soon a liaison office was set up to deal with the routine work of the Council. The Federation used this organisation as a platform to re-establish contacts with the industrial associations of the Western European countries.[32] In 1957 Berg was elected President of the CIFE.[33]

Within its framework, again at French prompting, a new 'club' was formed in September 1952, the Union of Industries of the Schuman Plan countries. This organisation grouped 'the national associations of the six countries into a tight body, meeting far more frequently than the parent organisation, largely independent of it, and determined to gain recognition as the sole ECSC employer organisation'.[34] The Union allowed the member associations to coordinate their economic policies and to influence the activities of the High Authority of ECSC. Therefore the BDI was quite satisfied with the Union. 'During the short time of its existence', the 1952–53 BDI annual report said, 'a close cooperation has developed enabling the Union to resolve even difficult problems in a spirit of friendly understanding'.[35]

The various branch associations also succeeded in setting up transnational organisations. While the steel associations of the six countries formed in 1952 a rather informal *Club des Sidérurgistes*, the coal associations in the same year established a much more formal organisation, the West European Coal Producers' Study Committee.[36] It might have been the steel associations' fear of being suspected of cartel ambitions that explains their refusal to found a well organised 'club'. The German branch associations participated in the activities of these transnational groups as they did in the case of, for example, the Liaison Committee of European Metallurgical Industries, the Common Office of Scrap Consumers, or, later on, in the *Organisme de Liaison des Industries Métalliques Européennes* or the *Sécréariat International des Groupements Professionnels des Industries Chimiques des Pays de la Communauté Economique Européenne*.[37] The DIHT concentrated its efforts during the first half of the 1950s on the International Chamber of Commerce.[38] In the field of social policy, too, cooperation was institutionalised, and the Federation of German Employers contributed to the work of the respective organisations.[39]

In 1958, after the European Economic Community had been established, the Union of Industries of the Schuman Plan

Countries gave way to a new Union of Industries of the European
Community. Although this organisation was regarded as a proper
instrument to press for the achievement of economic principles
and structures similar to those in the Federal Republic, BDI spokesmen left no doubt that they looked upon the EEC as a starting
point for an all-European integration.[40] Thus, from the BDI's point
of view, it would have been wrong to concentrate organisational
efforts almost exclusively on the Community. Correspondingly the
Federation opposed the establishment of a strong Union machinery in order to protect the autonomy of the national associations.[41]
The BDI, however, did not play a dominant role within these various European industrial associations, nor did the BDA or DIHT; it
was the French *Patronat* that held the leadership.[42] This might have
been one reason why, in addition to these multilateral cooperation
efforts, bilateral contacts with the industrial organisations of
France, Italy, the Netherlands, the United Kingdom or the United
States remained important for the BDI as well as for the BDA and
the DIHT. Furthermore, several national associations maintained
liaison offices in Brussels in order to maintain close and permanent
contacts with European institutions.[43]

But the representatives of the associations and individual industrialists also demonstrated their pro-European attitudes and commitments in another way. They supported, personally and
financially, 'private' pressure-groups such as the *Europa-Union* or
more academic 'clubs' such as the European League for Economic
Co-operation (ELEC) or the *Comité Européen pour le Progrès
Économique et Social* (CEPES).[44] While the industrialists were in a
minority position in the pressure-groups – but nevertheless tried
to exploit them for different purposes – [45] they played a dominant
role in ELEC and CEPES. In 1953, for example, Berg, BDI general
manager Beutler, Otto A. Friedrich and W. Alexander Menne of
the presidential board were members of the German group of
CEPES. The BDI planned to give DM 35,000 to support the activities of the group in 1953–54. To avoid duplicating work and, more
important, duplicating funding, the Federation demanded the
cooperation or even fusion of ELEC and CEPES.[46] Although it is
difficult to evaluate the importance of all these activities from the
BDI's point of view, surely the *Europa-Union* or CEPES were less
important than the European 'clubs' of industrial associations. But
as a platform to establish or intensify transnational contacts they
undoubtedly were quite useful.

All these ways of influencing the integration process described hitherto represent more or less indirect forms of participation. There was, of course, direct participation as well. Members of several branch associations – steel, coal, non-ferrous metals, chemicals and textiles – engaged themselves in the work of the technical committees of the OEEC. Not all of the German businessmen or association officials appreciated the efforts of these committees. The general manager of the textiles association, for example, felt embarrassed to pass on the official OEEC documents because he regarded them as being of poor quality.[47] Whereas participation in the OEEC was restricted to the period after its foundation, the BDI, the Iron and Steel Association and the semi-governmental *Deutsche Kohlenbergbauleitung* (DKBL) had a voice in the drafting of the ECSC treaty. Berg and Reusch represented the Federation on one of the advisory commissions that had been set up to support the German delegation during the negotiations in Paris, but did not often attend meetings. Reusch resigned in September 1950 in order to protest against the Allied decartelisation policy, but what might have been meant as an appeal to his colleagues to reject the ECSC project failed.[48] In short, as far as the Schuman Plan was concerned, the influence of the steel association and the DKBL clearly exceeded that of the BDI.

In January 1956, when the negotiations on the common market and Euratom started, the associations tried to intervene. The BDI established an ad hoc presidential board to establish contact with members of the German delegation 'sympathetic to the BDI's objectives'. But once again the Federation was discontented with the degree of its influence. According to Braunthal, Berg 'was reported to have protested personally to Adenauer that industrial associations in other EEC countries were being consulted more frequently than the BDI had been in Germany'.[49] Paradoxically, similar associations in other West European countries made the same complaints to their respective governments about the supposedly greater influence of German industry.

After the various treaties had come into force, the associations were busy trying to 'infiltrate' the individual boards and committees of the European organisations. Franz Etzel and Fritz Hellwig, who successively held one of the German seats in the High Authority of the ECSC, were closely allied to industrial circles. Rudolf Regul and Hermann Dehnen of the DKBL and Wilhelm Salewski, former general manager of the steel association, became leading officials of the ECSC bureaucracy. Berg and, from 1957 to 1967 Hans-Günther Sohl, president of the BDI between 1973 and 1976, represented German industry in the Consultative Committee.[50] Finally, two of the eight business seats in the German group of the Economic and Social Committee of the EEC went to the BDI and one to the BDA.[51] In the 1960s Beutler played a very active role in this committee.

To sum up, by using both direct and indirect methods, the German industrial associations contributed to the process of European integration. So which conceptions of cooperation and integration did they prefer, and to what extent did they succeed in realising their ideas and goals?

Integration conceptions and policies

The OEEC was the first international organisation after the Second World War to give the Germans the chance to learn what it meant to participate in a joint, cooperative European programme. It soon became apparent that this meant something different than the type of 'cooperation' practised during the war.[52] In the beginning, West German interests were represented by the Military Governors of the three Western zones. German advisers were admitted and were allowed to attend the negotiations, but they had to take their seats in the second or third row and were not permitted to speak for themselves. When the Federal Republic officially joined the OEEC in the autumn of 1949, it was the first time since the war that Germany was able to become a member of an international organisation on equal terms – at least formally. The Western powers considered this step to be some kind of test of West Germany's ability and willingness to adapt to modern standards of behaviour in international relations.[53]

Industry in general in West Germany welcomed the Marshall Plan and the OEEC. The reasons, leaving *Gleichberechtigung* out of consideration, are easy to understand: since the OEEC dealt with problems concerning economic integration it seemed to be the proper platform for West Germany, which lacked political power but had the economic potential that would be required in order to reconstruct Europe in due time. Moreover, the ERP was seen as a chance to revive traditional forms of cooperation between national industries including international cartels, as Salewski of the steel association explained in an immediate reaction to Secretary of State George C. Marshall's famous speech at Harvard University.[54] And, finally, the OEEC type of cooperation did not greatly restrict the members' freedom of movement.

Though some historians explicitly or implicitly deny any decisive contribution on the part of the OEEC to the process of European integration,[55] the organisation – in particular by its efforts to liberalise trade and, with the help of the European Payments Union (EPU), to multilateralise payments – actually did play an important role. German industry in principle supported these efforts because the Federal Republic depended more than ever on liberal foreign trade structures. This did not mean that each association agreed with the liberalisation programme – steel, textiles and even the chemical industry raised some objections – but this criticism was directed mainly against the pace of liberalisation and supposed discrimination against the Germans.[56] Most industrialists and association officials were well aware of the urgency – and the advantages – of trade liberalisation. Despite some objections in detail a large majority within the DIHT, for example, took a positive position on liberalisation since it seemed to be the first step towards an 'integrated European *Wirtschaftsraum*'.[57] After the Federal Government stopped liberalisation in February 1951, the BDI was counted among the first to come out in favour of re-liberalisation.[58]

In contrast to this, as far as the division of Marshall aid and the coordination of industrial investments were concerned, there was a general and growing discontent in Germany. BDI staff members accused the OEEC of misdirection and other OEEC countries of parochialism and misuse of Marshall aid, insinuating that this aid might be used more effectively in West Germany.[59] The 'investment policy' of the organisation, particularly in the steel sector, was repeatedly attacked by representatives of the German steel industry.[60] Sometimes it seemed that in West Germany only measures and policies to the country's own advantage were regarded as *European*.

But, in spite of some harsh criticism, the BDI in particular valued the OEEC very highly. The BDI's annual report of 1954–55 praised the Paris organisation as the 'most successful instrument of European economic integration...working without supranational powers'.[61] The DIHT was less enthusiastic: while stressing the remarkable progress in economic cooperation, the 1957–58 annu-

al report at the same time emphasised the limits of the liberalisation policy of the OEEC.[62] Nevertheless, the DIHT also held the
Paris organisation in esteem. In addition to the reasons mentioned
above, the impressive development of the Federal Republic within
the OEEC since 1952 might be another explanation. From not initially being allowed to make independent decisions and subject to
embarrassing examinations during the balance of payments crisis
in 1950–51, Germany became the largest and most consistent creditor of the European Payments Union.[63] Thus, and because interference with national politics was kept at a tolerable level, the
OEEC type of European integration had many supporters among
German industrialists.

The fact that the High Authority would have supranational powers explains why the European Coal and Steel Community was less
popular than the OEEC. Thus, after a number of mostly positive
immediate reactions,[64] more and more critical comments were to
be heard. The Iron and Steel Association raised a number of
objections against the 'dirigistic' elements of the French plan, and
against 'harmonisation' of production factors and prices and of
labour costs: '"pro-European" sentiment was widely mingled with
anti-supranational demands, indicating that for many businessmen integration meant little more than the removal of Allied controls'. It should not be left unmentioned, however, that several
steel industrialists, in spite of some criticism, spoke in favour of the
Schuman Plan.[65] The Federation of German Industry did not
oppose the French initiative in public, but Berg and his colleagues
took a rather critical view of the negotiations. The prospect of
replacing the highly unpopular Allied Ruhr Authority by the Coal
and Steel Community was welcomed, but at the same time,
'German weaknesses due to war losses, damage and reparations
were mentioned incessantly in order to buttress the argument of
sacrifice'.[66] Therefore the BDI stressed in particular that the treaty
should take into account the 'economic realities' and, of course,
should ensure that the activities of businessmen and their associations should not be restricted.[67] The BDA was interested principally in the social provisions of the treaty. As it soon became obvious
that the ECSC's powers in this field would be quite small, the
BDA's anxiety eased.[68]

It was the Korean War and the following boom that decisively
influenced the attitudes of most German industrialists towards the
Schuman Plan. Suddenly it seemed possible to get rid of all the

Allied restrictions without accepting new schemes of control, even if such control might no longer be unilateral, as in the past five years. As mentioned above, Hermann Reusch of *Gutehoffnungshütte*, a member of the BDI's presidential board, took the lead in attacking the Schuman Plan. He became annoyed at the thought of Germany accepting economic disadvantages for political reasons, even though the country was economically stronger than its competitors.[69] But he and others who agreed with him did not succeed in building up a powerful front against the coal and steel pool. Ludwig Erhard, Minister for Economics, and Franz Blücher, Minister for the Marshall Plan, though showing some sympathy with the critics, did not dare to support them openly.

It seems remarkable that neither the steel association nor the coal interests backed the opponents of the ECSC. Obviously they knew very well that there was hardly any realistic alternative to the Schuman Plan, in spite of their considerable dissatisfaction with the decartelisation and deconcentration clauses of the ECSC.[70] Was this, to use Almond's terms, some sort of 'escape into Europe' – or was it a sign of growing, honest 'Europeanism' within German heavy industry? Or should this be taken as evidence that 'those branches of industry, such as coal, which equate supranational action with their own survival', differ from the general pattern?[71] As far as industrialists like Günter Henle of Klöckner steel works were concerned, European cooperation and integration was felt to be inevitable for political and economic reasons. Others, like the senior officials of the iron and steel association, adapted pragmatically to the new political conditions in Western Europe. In any case, 'declining' industries seem to be more open to integration efforts than 'strong' ones.

The BDI, however, adhered to its criticism, while the coal and steel leaders remained reluctantly supporters. After the ECSC treaty had been signed, but before its ratification, the Federation switched over to the offensive and, in the spring of 1952, publicly declared that economic integration in the future should not be accomplished by sectoral approach but by trade liberalisation and broader 'horizontal' arrangements which would aim at the harmonisation of the economic policies of the participating countries.[72] Harmonisation measures, in other words, had to be restricted to those fields, in which the Germans expected advantages. And 'harmonisation', without doubt, meant that the other participants had to adjust themselves to the German practice. Objections that were raised during the common market negotiations, that sectoral integration might distort the individual national economies, did not play a decisive role. Despite spectacular activities like the *Europa-Tag* in October 1952, scepticism and criticism within the BDI increased. In May 1953, after the European Defence Community treaty and the so-called Contractual Agreements with the Western Powers had been signed, Berg stated that the time of occupation had come to an end: 'We start a new period of our political and economic life as a self-responsible state.'[73] Although it took another two years until the Federal Republic achieved formal sovereignty, Berg's statement was typical of a new German self-confidence which was demonstrated not only in economic but in political circles as well.

After 1945, most initiatives and plans to integrate Europe had been characterised by the intention to control Germany. Now, from the German point of view, any further restriction or supervision had to be avoided. Taking into account Germany's dependence on foreign trade, the BDI and DIHT tried to adjust future methods of cooperation to the needs of the West German economy. They urgently demanded, for example, the harmonisation of the trade and economic policies of the NATO member states[74] – again understood as harmonisation on German terms. Supranational sectoral integration was no longer seen as a proper means to protect German interests. Therefore the failure of the European Defence Community was regarded as a striking proof of the unsuitability of the sectoral approach. In contrast to Chancellor Konrad Adenauer, the BDI demonstrated coolness at this setback: it was not integration as a whole, but only one possible method that had failed.[75] During the preparatory discussions for the Messina conference the BDI consequently declared that the process of integration should not be continued by abandoning sovereign rights. Now, after the Paris treaties had been ratified, the OEEC type of integration was praised by the BDI as the only possible way in the future.[76]

In any case, the readiness to participate in European projects declined after May 1955. This became particularly clear when nuclear energy cooperation was discussed. Some members of the German government, especially the Minister for Atomic Energy, Franz-Josef Strauß, strongly supported by the BDI and several associations and firms, opposed the foundation of an European atomic community. They favoured bilateral arrangements with the United States or the United Kingdom in order to obtain what seemed necessary to build up national nuclear energy capabilities. It was American disapproval, assisted by individual Western European governments, that convinced Adenauer at least of the necessity to join the European scheme.[77] French insistence on Euratom, however, made pressure in favour of a common market easier for the German government.

Although the Federal Republic was still not in a position to take the political lead in integration efforts, the Germans succeeded in gaining acceptance for their market economy principles. The BDI therefore commented favourably on the common market negotiations.[78] In particular the reduction of supranational powers of the new community, as compared to the ECSC, and the overall approach met with general consent. The projected common trade policy was also approved, not least because of the strengthening of the community's 'bargaining power'. Trade policy was therefore no problem to the BDI. Criticism concentrated on the insufficient harmonisation of economic policies, the possibility of turning away from the German-type *Ordnungspolitik* and eventual problems resulting from the coexistence of EEC and ECSC, but none of the BDI representatives and officials would have run the risk of failure due to opposition from German industry.[79] The BDA raised objections against a possible harmonisation of social costs and labour law to the disadvantage of the German side and demanded that each member state should be responsible for its social policy.[80]

While stressing general consent to the common market programme of the Adenauer government, the DIHT criticized the traffic policy and tariff provisions of the projected treaty and the special rules in favour of agriculture. Since all participants had to make certain sacrifices in the interest of international cooperation, however, the DIHT supported the common market and Euratom.[81] Did the industrial associations have any influence on the negotiations at all? According to Hanns Jürgen Küsters, the role of the industrial associations – and trade unions – was not very important.[82] One should not, however, jump to conclusions from the fact that there seemed to be little direct participation on behalf of the associations. Their positions were by no means unknown to the officials of the ministries involved, and the close contacts between Berg and Adenauer have already been mentioned.

What were the attitudes of the steel and of the coal associations? The steel association, until then not among the principal critics, attacked sector integration severely in a statement of February 1956. Only full-scale economic integration was seen as a proper means to avoid undesirable trends and to effect a real economic fusion of the individual economies of the participating countries.[83] The mining association shared this view, although its opinion about the ECSC was less negative. In particular, according to a memorandum of February 1956, the association expected that market economy principles should be implemented much more strongly.[84] Thus, under changed circumstances, both associations took a more critical view of the ESCS than they had done before.

To sum up, German industry supported the common market and, very reluctantly, Euratom, not least because of the flexibility of the EEC treaty which seemed to make possible necessary 'improvements' of the EEC. The projected common trade policy and common tariffs were welcomed, assuming a non-protectionist policy and relatively low tariffs. This pragmatic outlook on EEC and Euratom was of course far from Adenauer's enthusiastic prognosis that the economic power of 'little Europe' would have an impact on world affairs.[85] Whereas the Chancellor also believed in the political effects of the EEC, the BDI, for example, was less optimistic. But the Federation's main interest was elsewhere: by analysing the production costs and competitive situation of German industry, the BDI came to the conclusion that 'a certain confidence and optimism in joining the Common Market was quite justified'.[86] Nevertheless, there can be no doubt that the process of protracted bargaining over interests was not liked by the German industrialists. And it was also obvious that from their point of view the EEC was not the end, because the Europe of the Six might endanger the economic community created by the OEEC and lead to a division of Western Europe into two trade blocs. To understand these fears, one has to remember the percentage shares in the Federal Republic's overall foreign trade: in 1957, 26 per cent of German exports and imports were with the Six and 23 per cent with the Seven.[87] Thus German industry was interested in any proposal or measure directed against the threatened economic division of Western Europe.

As is known, during the negotiations about the common market and Euratom the British government had proposed the foundation of a free trade area composed of the Six and the rest of the

OEEC members. Agriculture was to be excluded from the free trade provisions. As Miriam Camps put it, 'the adoption of free trade in industrial products with important competitors like the Six would mean a major change in British trade policy, which for nearly twenty-five years had been highly protectionist',[88] so this initiative should not be seen merely as an attempt to torpedo the common market project. Ludwig Erhard, German Minister for Economics, welcomed the British proposal enthusiastically, as did German industry. Erhard's consent seemed to have been mistaken by the British as the consent of the whole German government. But Chancellor Adenauer, despite some promises to Macmillan, did not support the British initiative wholeheartedly.[89]

The OEEC then began to discuss the plan. A special working group came to the conclusion that a free trade area of the kind proposed was technically possible. During a meeting of the OEEC Council in February 1957, Erhard praised the free trade project as an 'important, not to say the most important political and economic initiative to integrate Europe for years'.[90] Whereas Paul-Henri Spaak in the name of the Six stressed the priority of the common market project, the German minister spoke of the two plans as belonging together.

After the Treaties of Rome had been signed, the climate of the negotiations on the free trade area proposal gradually worsened. The BDI nevertheless continued to support the project because, as a BDI official emphasised, 'the Germans wanted the free trade area, they had to support it and should do all they can to solve the problems'.[91] Moreover, the Federation saw it as its great task to act as a mediator between French and British interests.[92] There were, however, warnings not to get involved too deeply in the Franco-British conflict because this might endanger the existence of the OEEC and EPU which had proved to be 'the most successful European institutions so far'.[93] The DIHT shared the BDI's position. A free trade area seemed to be the best means to support the efforts of the EEC: 'The area of European integration has to be extended as far as possible'.[94] Both associations maintained their point of view even after the breakdown of the free trade negotiations in November 1958.[95] In a letter to Adenauer BDI president Berg worried about the possibility of trade conflicts in Western Europe and encouraged the Chancellor to continue the negotiations. Adenauer, however, as Berg stated with a tone of resignation, obviously wanted to avoid putting any pressure on the French.[96]

Nevertheless, from German industry's point of view towards the end of the 1950s, there was a need to break out of 'European narrowness' and join the Atlantic Community.[97] The attempts to expand trade into the so-called developing countries and the achievement of convertibility of the most important European currencies were directed to this same goal.[98] In short, Western Europe was getting too small for the 'economic giant' West Germany. The integration into European schemes without being able to dominate them economically and politically caused dissatisfaction. But since money cannot buy everything, the Germans had to accept their new role in international relations – and they did.

This interpretation may be illustrated by a statement of an economic association official in 1960. According to him, there were no longer any ambitions of power politics in Germany as well as in Western Europe. In spite of the extraordinary boom during the 1950s, he considered Europe's traditional powerful position to be lost. What was his point of view regarding the new European hierarchy? The glory of spiritual leadership he conceded to Rome. Political leadership he ascribed to Paris, because after the recent past any German ambitions in this field would be impossible for a long time, if not forever. Economic leadership, however, he claimed for the Federal Republic.[99] European integration, despite some discontent within German industry, started to become 'irreversible'.

Recapitulating the first half of the EEC's transition period, a BDI publication underlined that the Federation had supported the establishment of the EEC from the beginning. Obviously the BDI had come to realise that 'bigger markets encourage technical progress and economic development in general'. Although the authors of the report denied the possibility of verifying the effects of integration precisely, they left no doubt that 'the economic boom of the last few years can be put down to the EEC to a considerable extent'.[100] German industry therefore remained interested in the continuation of the integration process according to the principles of the EEC treaty, i.e. without supranational elements. The German industrialists, one could say, had become 'pragmatic Europeans'.

Notes

1. Speech by Berg during the foundation of the 'Europa-Ausschuß' of the BDI, 18 December 1950, BDI-Altregistratur (BDIA), Aufsätze Präs. Berg ab 1950.

2. Beutler, 'Die politische Bedeutung wirtschaftlicher Zusammenarbeit' in *Vortragsreihe des Deutschen Industrieinstituts* No. 38, 20 September 1954.

3. Klaus Hinrich Hennings, 'West Germany', in Andrea Boltho (ed.), *The European Economy: Growth and Crisis*, Oxford, 1982, pp. 472–501 (p. 477). See also Werner Abelshauser, *Wirtschaft in Westdeutschland 1945–1948. Rekonstruktion und Wachstumsbedingungen in der amerikanischen und britischen Zone*, Stuttgart, 1975; Alan Kramer, *The West German Economy, 1945–1955*, New York/Oxford 1991.

4. See Werner Abelshauser, *Der Ruhrkohlenbergbau seit 1945. Wiederaufbau, Krise, Anpassung*, Munich 1984; Mark Roseman, *Recasting the Ruhr, 1945–1948: Manpower, Economic Recovery and Labour Relations*, New York/Oxford, 1992.

5. See Heiner R. Adamsen, *Investitionshilfe für die Ruhr. Wiederaufbau, Verbände und soziale Marktwirtschaft 1948–1952*, Wuppertal, 1981; Kramer, *The West German Economy*, p. 171.

6. See Harald Winkel, *Die Wirtschaft im geteilten Deutschland 1945–1970*, Wiesbaden, 1974, pp. 96–104; Gerold Ambrosius, 'Wirtschaftlicher Strukturwandel und Technikentwicklung' in Axel Schildt and Arnold Sywottek (eds), *Modernisierung im Wiederaufbau. Die westdeutsche Gesellschaft der 50er Jahre*, Bonn, 1993, pp. 107–28.

7. Quoted in Gerard Braunthal, *The Federation of German Industry in Politics*, Ithaca, N.Y., 1965, p. 31. On industrial associations see also Hans-Peter Ullmann, *Interessenverbände in Deutschland*, Frankfurt am Main, 1988; Werner Bührer, 'Unternehmerverbände', in Wolfgang Benz (ed.), *Geschichte der Bundesrepublik Deutschland*, bd. 2, Wirtschaft, Frankfurt am Main, 1989, pp. 140–68.

8. See Arnulf Baring, *Außenpolitik in Adenauers Kanzlerdemokratie. Westdeutsche Innenpolitik im Zeichen der Europäischen Verteidigungsgemeinschaft*, vol. 2, Munich, 1971 (paperback edition), pp. 53–7.

9. See BDI (ed.), *Fünf Jahre BDI. Aufbau und Arbeitsziele des industriellen Spitzenverbandes*, Bergisch Gladbach, 1954, p. 44.

10. Volker R. Berghahn, *The Americanisation of West German Industry 1945–1973*, Leamington Spa/ New York, 1986, p. 66; also Ullmann, *Interessenverbände*, pp. 243–4.

11. 'List of number of votes of the member associations', 28 April 1954, Archives of the IHK Augsburg (AIHKA), NL Vogel, BDI Allgemein, 1 December 1953–31 December 1954. Braunthal, *The Federation of German Industry*, p. 36, nevertheless thinks that the 'weighting of the vote could lead to oligarchic control by the heavy industry of the Rhine-Ruhr-complex'.

12. See Braunthal, *The Federation of German Industry*, pp. 26–9; Berghahn, *Americanisation*, pp. 66–8.

13. See Fritz Ficher, *Griff nach der Weltmacht. Die Kriegszielpolitik des kaiserlichen Deutschland 1914/18*, Kronberg/Ts., 1977 (paperback reprint).

14. See Leo Haupts, *Deutsche Friedenspolitik 1918–19. Eine Alternative zur Machtpolitik des Ersten Weltkrieges*, Düsseldorf, 1976; critical of this view is Peter Grupp, *Deutsche Außenpolitik im Schatten von Versailles 1918–1920. Zur Politik des Auswärtigen Amts vom Ende des Ersten Weltkriegs und der Novemberrevolution bis zum Inkrafttreten des Versailler Vertrags*, Paderborn, 1988, esp. pp. 43–9.

15. See Peter Wulf, *Hugo Stinnes. Wirtschaft und Politik 1918–1924*, Stuttgart, 1979.

16. See Clemens A. Wurm, 'Politik und Wirtschaft in den internationalen Beziehungen. Internationale Kartelle, Außenpolitik und weltwirtschaftliche Beziehungen 1919–1939: Einführung' and Ulrich Nocken, 'International Cartels and Foreign Policy: The Formation of the International Steel Cartel 1924–1926' in Clemens A. Wurm (ed.), *International Cartels and Foreign Policy: Studies on the Interwar Period*, Wiesbaden, 1989, pp. 1–31 and 33–82.

17. Gabriel A. Almond, 'The Politics of German Business' in Hans Speier and W. Phillips Davison (eds), *West German Leadership and Foreign Policy*, Evanston/White Plains, 1957, pp. 195–241 (223–4).

18. Almond, 'The politics of German Business', p. 232–3.

19. Braunthal, *Federation*, p. 288.

20. See Werner Bührer, *Ruhrstahl und Europa. Die Wirtschaftsvereinigung Eisen- und Stahlindustrie und die Anfänge der europäischen Integration 1945–1952*, Munich, 1986, esp. pp. 132–5 and 198–9.

21. See Werner Bührer, 'Die Montanunion – ein Fehlschlag? Deutsche Lehren aus der EGKS und die Gründung der EWG' in Gilbert Trausch (ed.), *The European Integration from the Schuman-Plan to the Treaties of Rome*, Baden-Baden, 1993, pp. 75–90.

22. 'Report on the Membership Assembly of the BDI', 28 March 1950, in *Drucksache* Nr. 4, p. 18.

23. 'Gedanken zu einer deutsch-französischen Aussprache', 22 November 1949, Klöckner Archives, NL Henle, Europäische Bewegung/ Der Deutsche Rat/ Exekutiv-Komitee/ 1.6.–1.12.1949.

24. See Werner Bührer, 'Der BDI und die Außenpolitik der Bundesrepublik in den fünfziger Jahren' in *Vierteljahreshefte für Zeitgeschichte*, vol. 40, 1992, pp. 241–61, esp. pp. 251–3.

25. 'Report on the Foundation of the Commission for Economic Questions of the Industrial Associations', p. 6. See also 'Gemeinsame Willensbildung', in *Handelsblatt*, 21 October 1949.

26. Speech by Berg on the occassion of the foundation of the *Europa-Ausschuß*, 18 December 1950, BDI Archives (BDIA), Aufsätze Präs. Berg ab 1950.

27. *Der Weg zum industriellen Spitzenverband*, Darmstadt, 1958, p. 350.

28. DIHT, *Tätigkeitsbericht für das Geschäftsjahr 1957/58*, p. 53 and *Tätigkeitsbericht 1958/59*, p. 325.

29. Wirtschaftsvereinigung Eisen- und Stahlindustrie, *Tätigkeitsbericht Juni 1950*, p. 5.

30. See Hans-Wolfgang Platzer, *Unternehmensverbände in der EG – ihre nationale und transnationale Organisation und Politik*, Kehl am Rhein/Straßburg, 1984, p. 258.

31. See BDI, 'Europa-Tag in Trier 30–31 October 1952' in *Drucksache Nr 18*.

32. See *Fünf Jahre BDI*, p. 172–3; Platzer, *Unternehmensverbände*, p. 37–40; Ernst B. Haas, *The Uniting of Europe: Political, Social and Economic Forces 1950–1957*, London, 1958, p. 324.

33. *Jahresbericht des BDI 1957/58*, p. 23.

34. Haas, *The Uniting of Europe*, p. 324.

35. *Jahresbericht des BDI 1952/53*, p. 25

36. See Hans Dichgans, *Montanunion. Menschen und Institutionen*, Düsseldorf/Vienna, 1980, pp. 136–9; Haas, *The Uniting of Europe*, pp. 325–7.

37. Haas, *The Uniting of Europe*, pp. 327–30; Platzer, *Unternehmensverbände*, pp. 199–220.

38. See, for example, DIHT, *Tätigkeitsbericht 1954/55*, pp. 230–2; Walther Herrmann, 'Internationale Bestrebungen der Unternehmerverbände' in *Europa-Archiv*, vol. 7, 1952, pp. 5247–8.

39. See Platzer, *Unternehmensverbände*, pp. 257–62.

40. See Braunthal, *Federation*, p. 326.

41. See Platzer, *Unternehmensverbände*, pp. 57–8.

42. See Sönke Reimers, 'The "Union des Industries de la Communaute Européenne" (UNICE) between the Common Market and a European Free Trade Area' in *Historians of Contemporary Europe Newsletter*, Vol. 7, No. 3–4, December 1992, pp. 147–55.

43. As far as the BDI is concerned see Platzer, *Unternehmensverbände*, p. 58.

44. As regards ELEC see Michel Dumoulin and Anne-Myriam Dutrieue, *La Ligue européenne de coopération économique (1946–1981). Une groupe d'étude et de pression dans la construction européenne*, Bern/Paris, 1993; on CEPES see Anne-Myriam Dutrieue, 'La CEPES, un mouvement patronal européen (1952–1967)' in Michel Doumulin, René Girault and Gilbert Trausch (eds), *L'Europe du Patronat. De la guerre froid aux années soixante*, Bern et al., 1993, pp. 213–30.

45. See Wilfried Loth, 'Die Europa-Bewegung in den Anfangsjahren der Bundesrepublik' in Ludolf Herbst, Werner Bührer and Hanno Sowade (eds), *Vom Marshallplan zur EWG. Die Eingliederung der Bundesrepublik Deutschland in die westliche Welt*, Munich, 1990, pp. 63–77, esp. p. 74.

46. BDI to members of the presidential board, 11 July 1953, AIHKA, NL Vogel, BDI-Außenhandelsausschuß, Juli 1951–September 1953.

47. Textiles association to Vogel, 26 July 1950, AIHKA, NL Vogel, Marshallplan/Pariser Verhandlungen, April 1949–October 1950. See in general Werner Bührer, 'Die deutsche Industrie und der Marshallplan 1947–1952' in Comité pour l'Histoire Économique et Financière de la France (ed.), *Le Plan Marshall et le relèvement économique de l'Europe*, Paris, 1993, pp. 449–65, esp. 457–60.

48. See Bührer, *Ruhrstahl*, pp. 179–85.

49. Braunthal, *Federation*, pp. 321–2.

50. See Dichgans, *Montanunion*, pp. 188–90.

51. See Braunthal, *The Federation of German Industry*, pp. 322–3.

52. See, for example, John R. Gillingham, *Industry and Politics in the Third Reich: Ruhr Coal, Hitler and Europe*, Wiesbaden, 1985.

53. The problems of the incorporation of West Germany into the ERP and OEEC are described by Werner Bührer, Auftakt in Paris. Der Marshallplan und die deutsche Rückkehr auf die internationale Bühne 1948/49' in *Vierteljahreshefte für Zeitgeschichte*, vol. 36, 1988, pp. 529–56.

54. See Bührer, *Ruhrstahl*, pp. 85–8.

55. See Alan S. Milward, *The Reconstruction of Western Europe 1945–51*, London, 1984, esp. pp. 168–211; Wilfried Loth, *Der Weg nach Europa. Geschichte der europäischen Integration 1939–1957*, Göttingen, 1990, esp. pp. 66–8.

56. See Werner Bührer, 'Erzwungene oder freiwillige Liberalisierung? Die USA, die OEEC und die westdeutsche Außenhandelspolitik 1949–1952' in Herbst, Bührer and Sowade (eds), *Vom Marshallplan zur EWG*, pp. 139–62, esp. p. 154.

57. Statement by Carl-Gisbert Schultze-Schlutius, general manager of the Hamburg Chamber of Commerce at a DIHT *Hauptausschuß* conference, 26 January 1951, verbatim report, p. 58, in DIHT Archives, Bonn, Hauptausschuß, Sitzungen 1951; furthermore see 'Report on the 5th session of the foreign economy experts' working group', 27 October 1950, ibid., 300–12 Außenwirtschaftsreferenten, Sitzungen bis 1953.

58. See 'Memorandum regarding re-liberalization', 25 July 1951, Bundesarchiv-Koblenz (BA), B 146, 858.

59. See 'Report on the BDI conference at Bad Dürkheim', 28 March 1950, p. 9.

60. See, for example, 'Report on the session of the OEEC steel committee', 2–3 March 1949 and 9–10 March 1950, Archiv der Wirtschaftsvereinigung Stahl, Düsseldorf, 0308, Eisen- und Stahlkomitee der OEEC, 9.3.1949–30.9.1950. In general, see Jan van den Heuvel, 'Co-ordination of industrial investments' in *At Work for Europe: An Account of the Activities of the Organisation for European Economic Co-operation*, Paris, 1956, pp. 79–83.

61. *Jahresbericht des BDI 1954/55*, p. 18.

62. DIHT, *Tätigkeitsbericht 1957/58*, p. 42.
63. See Jacob J. Kaplan and Günther Schleiminger, *The European Payments Union: Financial Diplomacy in the 1950s*, Oxford, 1989, pp. 245–65.
64. See Bührer, *Ruhrstahl*, pp. 170–2.
65. Haas, *The Uniting of Europe*, p. 165; positive comments are mentioned by Bührer, *Ruhrstahl*, pp. 178–9. See furthermore John Gillingham, 'Solving the Ruhr Problem: German Heavy Industry and the Schuman Plan' in Klaus Schwabe (ed.), *The Beginnings of the Schuman-Plan*, Baden-Baden, 1988, pp. 399–436, esp. 413–22.
66. Haas, *The Uniting of Europe*, p. 163.
67. *Geschäftsbericht des BDI 1950/51*, p. 12.
68. See Werner Bührer, 'Die "Europäisierung" des Arbeitsrechts aus unternehmerischer Sicht 1950–1990' in *Archiv für Sozialgeschichte*, vol. 31, 1991, pp. 297–311, esp. pp. 301–3.
69. Wellhausen to Reusch, 25 August 1950, Haniel Archiv, NL H. Reusch, 40010146/44.
70. See Bührer, *Ruhrstahl*, pp. 185–206; Gillingham, 'Solving the Ruhr Problem', pp. 422–32.
71. Haas, *The uniting of Europe*, p. 176.
72. 'Declaration of the BDI regarding sectoral integration', 26 March 1952, BA, NL Blücher, 103.
73. 'Meeting of the BDI', 17–19 May 1953, p. 15.
74. See, for example, *Jahresbericht des BDI 1952/53*, p. 16.
75. See *Jahresbericht des BDI 1954/55*, p. 23.
76. 'Meeting of the presidential board', 8 June 1955, BDIA, Sitzungsprotokolle 1955/56.
77. See Foreign Relations of the United States, 1955–57, vol. IV, pp. 335ff.; Christian Deubner, *Die Atompolitik der westdeutschen Industrie und die Gründung von Euratom*, Frankfurt am Main/New York, 1977; Michael Eckert, 'Die Anfänge der Atompolitik in der Bundesrepublik Deutschland' in *Vierteljahrshefte für Zeitgeschichte*, vol. 37, 1989, pp. 115–43.
78. See 'Meeting of the presidential board', 23 May 1956, BDIA, Sitzungsprotokolle 1955/56.
79. See *Jahresbericht des BDI 1956/57*, pp. 33–42; Platzer, *Unternehmensverbände*, pp. 49–55.
80. See Bührer, '"Europäisierung" des Arbeitsrechts', pp. 303–4.
81. See DIHT, *Tätigkeitsbericht 1956/57*, p. 25.
82. Hanns Jürgen Küsters, *Die Gründung der Europäischen Wirtschaftsgemeinschaft*, Baden-Baden, 1982, pp. 275–6.
83. See 'Provisional statement regarding European economic integration', February 1956, Archiv der Wirtchaftsvereinigung Stahl, Düsseldorf, NL Salewski.
84. See 'Memorandum concerning full-scale European integration', 14 February 1956, BA, B 116, 7296.

85. ' Kanzler-Tee', 22 February 1957, in *Adenauer. Teegespräche 1955–1958*, Berlin, 1986, p. 181.

86. *Jahresbericht des BDI 1957/58*, p. 27.

87. See Braunthal, *The Federation of German Industry*, p. 303.

88. Miriam Camps, *Britain and the European Community 1955–1963*, Princeton, 1964, p. 100; see also Küsters, *Gründung*, p. 280–94.

89. See Daniel Koerfer, *Kampf ums Kanzleramt. Erhard und Adenauer*, Stuttgart, 1987, pp. 201–5.

90. OEEC, Council, Minutes of the 355th Meeting, 12–13 February 1957, BA, B 146, 867.

91. 'Meeting of the presidential board', 26 February 1958, BDIA, Sitzungsprotokolle 1958/59.

92. 'Meeting of the presidential board', 29 March 1958.

93. 'Meeting of the presidential board', 29 April 1958.

94. 'Statement concerning questions of the free trade area', 4 December 1957, in DIHT, *Tätigkeitsbericht 1957/58*, pp.437–9.

95. See Camps, *Britain*, pp. 153–72.

96. See 'Meeting of the presidential board', 9 December 1958, BDIA, Sitzungsprotokolle 1958/59.

97. 'General Assembly of the BDI', 23 June 1959, BDIA, Sitzungsprotokolle 1959.

98. See, for example, *Jahresbericht des BDI 1957/58*, pp. 37–41, and *Jahresbericht des BDI 1958/59*, pp. 74–80; DIHT, *Tätigkeitsbericht 1958/59*, p. 36–7.

99. 'Meeting of staff members of industrial associations', 8 April 1960, BDIA, Sitzungsprotokolle 1960.

100. BDI (ed.), *Die deutsche Industrie im Gemeinsamen Markt. Bericht über die bisherigen Auswirkungen der Europäischen Wirtschaftsgemeinschaft 1958–1963*, Bergisch-Gladbach, 1965, pp. 3–6.

KLAUS SCHWABE

The United States and European Integration : 1947 – 1957[1]

I

Since the recent upheaval in Eastern Europe and the unification of Germany the problem of approaching European union
has become both more complicated and more urgent. According to
Chancellor Helmut Kohl, German unification and progress in further integrating the European Communities are 'two sides of the
same coin', and he promised that the new Germany would continue
to contribute to the development of ever stronger ties that would
hold the European communities together and would prevent
Germany and the other European member states from returning to
a nationalist foreign policy. At the same time the newly independent
East European nations are demanding an early admission to the
European Community. Thus both the strengthening of the structure of the EC and the enlargement of its membership are on the
agenda. It goes without saying that these two goals are potentially
contradictory: accepting new East European members may call for
allowances to be made for their particular economic problems and
thus for more flexible conditions of entry and membership, while
on the other hand, a tighter structure of the European communities
may make the accession of new members more difficult.

One of the arguments of this paper will be that the problem of
the scope of membership and the degree of integration of the EC
is as old as the history of European integration efforts since the
end of the Second World War. It was one of the major problems
with which the United States was confronted in developing a poli-

115

cy in support of some kind of European union. Even today America may feel the need to take a stand on the issue of how many members the European community should have and to what degree the 'fortress' of Europe should draw more closely together. Viewed from the American angle, the only difference between the immediate post-war era and the present time seems to be that the economic problems arising from Europe's integration loom larger today than they did at the time of the Marshall Plan.

From the moment this plan for reviving Europe's economy was launched the United States committed itself to the goal of some sort of European integration. It continued to uphold this position to the bitter end, that is up to the failure of the European Defence Community in 1954. My *first task* is to present the reasons behind this policy, which certainly need explaining. Having committed itself to the goal of European unity the United States faced two more equally important questions. On the one hand, there was the question as to the means, the leverage, which the United States was willing to employ in order to ensure that the task of European integration was actually accomplished by the Europeans. This will be the *second question* briefly to be touched on in this paper. On the other hand, in promoting European integration America had to get a clear idea as to the internal structure of an integrated Europe, i.e. an idea of the range of its membership and of its organisational or constitutional make-up. It had to decide which was better: a large membership within a wider Europe or a tight structure within the core of Europe consisting of only a restricted number of members. Generally the problem of the *structure* of a European union, as seen through American eyes, will be the *third and major question* that this paper will have to address.

II

Why did America support European integration so soon after World War Two? This was actually an option that antedated even the Marshall Plan. Once Hitler's Germany was defeated, many officials in the State Department and in the diplomatic field recognized that European cooperation simply imposed itself as a necessity in view of the havoc created by the Second World War. Thus, immediately after the end of hostilities, the US government took various initiatives in order to bring about some economic cooperation among the nations of Europe. The United States urged all-European organisational efforts. The Economic Commission of Europe (ECE), which was founded in March 1947, was at least in part the result of American pressure. The ECE acted under the authority of the United Nations. It is noteworthy that this first American attempt at integrating Europe's economy was expressly designed to overcome incipient East-West tensions and to prevent Europe from splitting into an Eastern and a Western half.[2]

The Marshall Plan, however, was implemented outside the framework of the United Nations. By 1947 the American government and public had begun to disassociate itself from the Rooseveltian universalist stance and began instead to consider regional alternatives. Obviously, this was the result of the Cold War, which was already in full swing when the Marshall Plan was launched. A new motive appeared behind America's willingness to help rebuilding Europe's economy along cooperative lines: American assistance was declared necessary not only in order to re-establish prosperity in Europe but at the same time also in order to remove the material and social roots of political extremism, whether left-wing or right-wing, which threatened to overcome the European nations. In this new context European unity assumed the role of not only facilitating the material reconstruction of the Old World, but also of laying the spiritual foundations for politically healthy democratic communities. European unity was perceived as a new inspiring ideal that promised to cure Europe's citizens of the despondency and the cynicism to which they had become susceptible under the impact of the postwar miseries. Ultimately, the American public and government hoped, an economically healthy Europe would be a force psychologically and ideologically strong enough to counteract Soviet propaganda, perhaps even strong enough to attract East Europeans to the West.[3]

But there was yet another reason why the American public and government advocated European integration with increasing vigour. This was because Germany's contribution to the reconstruction of Europe on the one hand seemed indispensible, while, on the other hand, it raised the spectre of an industrially restored Germany that would again attempt to gain economic and ultimately political predominance in Europe. The only way to avoid this seemed to attempt to harness and to control Germany's industrial capacity within a strong European framework.[4]

This view was shared by prominent members of the American

Congress. A sort of starry-eyed idealism inspired the American law makers and opinion leaders at that time; there was a hope that America's historical experience could somehow be repeated by the war-torn Europeans. At any event, since early 1947, Congressional pressure to get the Europeans to integrate was a political fact of life that the American executive had to reckon with.[5] The Truman administration itself shared the hopes and motives to which Congress and the American public had given expression in promoting the idea of European integration, and had committed itself to the objective of European integration as an essential, even though long-term, aim of the Marshall Plan. It was convinced that the European Recovery Program (ERP) had to be a multilateral and a cooperative endeavour on the part of the Europeans.[6] Even more than the public the administration was aware of the need for integration, which was considered to be an indispensable prerequisite to the economic reconstruction of Germany. This former enemy country presented particularly formidable obstacles to economic recovery because it was divided into airtight zones of occupation, ceilings had been imposed on its steel production, and reparation claims by former enemies like France had to be met. The State Department in particular recognised that plans for the reconstruction of Germany had to be devised in such a way as not to antagonise Germany's neighbours any further, but to dovetail with the requirements of the reconstruction of Europe at large. All this could best – if not solely – be achieved by creating a European roof, by integrating Europe into one economic unit.[7]

But what if the Europeans for their part refused to unite in the way the United States advocated? What if the Soviet Union, its East European satellites, or the communist parties all over Europe tried to boycott or to undermine this effort to coordinate Europe's reconstruction effort? Would the United States try to break this kind of resistance, and if so, how? Such queries raise the problem of the means America was prepared to use in order to implement its program of European reconstruction and integration, which is the second question, to be discussed in this paper.

III

In this respect, the State Department was less than happy about Congressional and public attitudes. Americans seemed to believe that the Europeans could be pressured by the United States into forming a union overnight. The State Department did not share that illusion. It recommended reticence in interfering in the domestic affairs of recipients of Marshall Aid, even when control of the aid allocations by the respective countries was at stake.[8] It was all the more aware of the difficulties, if not of the impossibility, of forcing some sort of unity on unwilling Europeans. A European shotgun marriage, the department felt, simply would not work; it would be counterproductive as it would provide grist to the mill of communist propaganda that was charging the United States with heavy-handed imperialism in Europe. It was the Department's unwavering conviction, therefore, that European integration, if it was to take roots and was to last, had to be devised in Europe and not in Washington. All America could offer was 'friendly aid' or counsel.[9]

The Department remained faithful to that view over the years in the face of considerable Congressional pressure to establish a linkage between American aid and European integration, and to make American aid depend on progress in European integration.[10] In the final analysis one could argue that the State Department's reluctance to put more than rhetorical pressure on the Europeans may even have contributed to the setbacks that the process of European integration suffered in the mid-1950s.

IV

This reluctance to appear as a teacher who would teach the Europeans good European integrationist manners had something to do with the way the American government viewed the problem of the structure of European integration. This paper has thus reached the *third* and most complicated *problem* which helps us to understand America's European policies in the era of the Marshall Plan.

Even in early 1947, when America's official policy with respect to European unification had not yet matured, policy-makers within the State Department were aware of the different choices facing the Europeans in devising a common organisation. There was first the alternative some planners within the Department would have preferred – the formation of a sort of a supranational organisation which would be able to enforce European decisions even in the face of opposition from one of its constituent members. A supranational structure would permit majority decisions among the Europeans and exclude the possibility of a national veto. All this, obviously, would infringe upon the members' sovereignty. At the other end of the range of choices there was a merely cooperative set-up in which the member nations would just consult with each other, but would act only (if at all) once a unanimous consensus had been reached. In that case the principle of national sovereignty would have been up-held.[11]

It cannot be stressed enough that initially in 1947 the State Department, although it favoured the supranational approach in principle, actually settled for much less – a loose cooperative arrangement as the organisational framework for Europe's reconstruction. The Department compromised because it was anxious to win over as many European countries as possible to a common reconstruction effort, not only the Western Europeans but also the neutrals like Sweden and Austria, all of Germany and even Eastern Europe.[12] In particular, the desire to gain Eastern European adherence was inspired by the hope that those countries' participation in a common European reconstruction program would loosen the Soviet grip that held them in bondage. If, on the other hand, communist Europe chose to boycott the American sponsored reconstruction effort, the State Department wanted to make sure that this stance remained exceptional in the all-European context. An overly strong European roof was likely to have the opposite effect in that it would restrict the number of potential participants, as it was likely to antagonise all those European countries that did not belong to the inner circle of America's traditional European allies like France, Belgium, and Britain, and preferred a neutralist position in the contest between East and West.[13]

This rationale explains the extremely cautious language the American Secretary of State George Marshall chose in his famous speech of June 5, 1947, which on the face of it offered American aid to all Europeans including the Soviets. As for European integration, Marshall did not go further than to stress the need of a 'joint' European programme agreed to by the Europeans 'as to the requirements of the situation' as a condition of American assistance.[14] But in spite of this guarded language, the Truman administration hoped tacitly that the process of integration by virtue of its own momentum would in the long run lead to a strong, maybe even supranational European organisation.[15] These initial hopes were dashed in the two years that followed Marshall's speech. It is true that with some American prodding the Europeans succeeded in agreeing on a series of cooperative organisations: in April 1948 the OEEC – Organisation for European Economic Cooperation – was established, which was in charge of administering the American aid, followed in May 1949 by the Council of Europe, designed by its statutes to be no more than a mere debating society for issues of European interest. On the military side, the Brussels pact was concluded between the countries of Western Europe in March 1948, and a year later in April 1949 NATO was founded. All of these organisations, however, were conventional cooperative undertakings that in no way restrained the sovereign rights of their members and were far from the innovative supranational approach the American government favoured.

American policy-makers were disappointed with these meagre results of their endeavours to integrate Europe. They were all the more disillusioned as in the meantime the motives that underlay their support of a closer European union had become even stronger. In May 1949 the West German republic had been founded. That part of Germany had just begun to experience what was later called the German economic miracle; to the State Department an economic giant seemed to be on the rise, and the question arose as to how the capacities of that rising giant could be committed to the West once and for all. In 1949 this was not yet a problem, because the new West German republic was still subject to tight controls exercised by the Allied High Commission. But, as the Department rightly foresaw, in some not too distant future these controls would have to be abandoned. One day West Germany would gain sovereignty and be in a position to decide her foreign allegiances autonomously.

If then Germany remained segregated from the rest of Europe, as it had been after its defeat, what guarantees did the West have to make sure that Germany would cast its lot with the Western world? Was it not possible, Department experts asked, that Germany would embark on a policy of independence from all of its neighbours and the superpowers, trying to play off the East against the West? Would not Germany in making use of such opportunities try to establish itself again as the dominant power in Europe? The American government knew one means to prevent such a disquieting development, which was to build up a strong political

European organisation, a federation endowed with genuinely
supranational powers. Such an organisation would indeed be able
to harness Germany's power to the West for the foreseeable
future; it would contain Germany as much as it would contain the
Soviet Union, making it impossible for Germany to break away
from its commitments with the West, even if it felt that it could
gain major objectives – such as reunification – through negotiations with the Soviet Union.[16]

But a supranational integration, though hoped for, was not
forthcoming. The neutrals were opposed to it, and so was
America's closest ally during this century, Great Britain. Partly in
order to maintain its ties with the Commonwealth, partly for reasons of prestige in aspiring to a leadership position in Europe's
reconstruction efforts, partly also in order to discourage foreign
interference with its socialist economy, Britain refused to join any
organisation that wielded supranational authority and thus
restricted Britain's sovereignty and special position as a world
power. British influence had kept the newly founded European
organisations free of supranational powers. Britain had simply
threatened not to join such organisations, and this threat muted
all European criticism, as a Europe without British leadership
seemed unthinkable.[17] At the same time, the British government
was opposed to a merely continental European union, which, it
feared, would be detrimental to British export interests and generally would challenge London's claim to leadership in Europe.[18]

Throughout the two first years of the Marshall Plan the
American government shared the British view as to Britain's leadership role in Europe. It was for this reason that America accepted
a British suggestion to send George Kennan, the director of the
prestigious Policy Planning Staff of the State Department, to
London in the summer of 1949 in order to exchange views on possible options for some sort of European integration, in particular
options that would facilitate British leadership in an integrated
Europe.[19] This move made it necessary for the State Department
to clarify its own attitude as to the desirable scope and structure of
an integrated Europe. Kennan and the Policy Planning Staff were
assigned that task.

Kennan consulted a whole array of intellectual luminaries for
discussions, in the course of which Britain's position vis-à-vis
Europe, Germany's role on the continent, Anglo-American relations and other related topics were pondered at length while the

spectre of another Soviet-German 'Rapallo' was copiously and elo-
quently conjured up.[20] The result was a paper that deserves to be
looked at more closely for three reasons: firstly, it was the first
occasion that American government officials undertook an in-
depth analysis of the problem of European integration and
America's attitude towards it, secondly it prepared the way for a
momentous change in America's policy in this question, and thirdly it has acquired a new significance in the light of our present
time.

The Policy Planning Staff's position paper dated July 7, 1949 is
in many ways a remarkable document.[21] At a time when the Paris
Four Power Conference on Germany had just ended in failure and
the division of Germany and the European continent, as it
seemed, had become an accomplished fact, Kennan and his staff
reminded American policy-makers that this division of Europe
would not last forever and that therefore all steps designed to
bring about a closer European union were bound to be provisional.[22] The American government, the paper continued, had every
interest in maintaining this fluid state of affairs in Eastern Europe,
as it had never accepted the latter's separation from the rest of
Europe as permanent. It was in part for this reason that the paper
strongly recommended that Great Britain stay out of any closer
European union, because the Eastern European nations were not
prepared to share Anglo-Saxon ideas of self-government once they
had cast off the Soviet yoke.

There were additional reasons why Britain's membership in any
closer European association was considered inadvisable. For valid
reasons, Britain itself was strongly opposed to joining irrevocably
any stronger – let alone supranational – European organisation. A
supranational European organisation thus was only possible if
British hesitations over European integration did not represent
the 'ceiling' beyond which a European union could not advance;
in other words, if Britain remained outside such a union.[23] Last
but not least, British interests – Britain's Commonwealth commitments, access to the North American markets, the stabilisation of
the pound – pointed toward a closer Atlantic union with Canada
and the United States rather than with the European continent.
While Britain itself would stay outside the process, European –
continental – integration as such remained an important objective, not so much for economic as for political reasons. These
political reasons centred around Germany and its future role in

Europe, which was to Kennan then more than ever the major concern, as his opposite numbers in the British Foreign Office noted.[24]

Fixated on Germany, Kennan and the Political Planning Staff advocated speedy progress in European supranational integration because a tight and possibly supranational organisation would promote a closer Franco-German understanding, a key aim of America's European policy, and would tie Germany to the West and thereby would help to 'contain' (original language) Germany and prevent it from again becoming a domineering force in Europe.[25] A fundamental prerequisite to a closer union of the European continent, the paper stressed, was the continued US military commitment in Europe within the framework of the Atlantic alliance. American leadership in that alliance would replace merging sovereignties on the military level.[26] The Policy Planning Staff thus envisaged two stages of European integration: a short-term stage which called for progress in both the formation of a trans-Atlantic partnership of the Anglo-Saxon nations, and the development of supranational structures in a Western European continental union, with both processes protected by the military umbrella provided by NATO. A second stage foreseen in a distant future would require the merger of Eastern Europe with the Western European continental union, with Britain again remaining outside this 'third force' between the superpowers.[27] As to the Eastern European countries Kennan did not expect objections to supranational European structures on their part, as almost all of these peoples looked 'back on unhappy and frustrating experience in national framework'. Thus Kennan failed to perceive a conflict between what he called 'breadth' and 'depth' in a united Europe, i.e. the number of its members and the degree of its integration, provided Great Britain did not join it.[28]

This was a somewhat complicated scheme, which Kennan first discussed with the new Secretary of State Dean Acheson and then, with the latter's blessing, submitted to French and British officials during the following weeks.[29] It proved to be unacceptable to both the French and the British. French officials dreaded a situation in which France was left alone with Germany on the continent.[30] The British reaction was somewhat calmer but basically no less negative than the French; while suggesting that Great Britain stay away from a closer continental European union, Kennan had implied that the leader of the Commonwealth was too weak to exercise effective leadership in Europe and that its own interests prevented it from playing an active role in Eastern Europe. Hence Britain would remain unattractive to Eastern Europeans and thus would ultimately hinder an extension of a united Europe into the East once Soviet rule in that area had collapsed. To Kennan's opposite numbers in London all this seemed far-fetched and, as one may safely assume, certainly did not correspond with their own notions about the role of their country as a leader in the world as well as in Europe.[31]

Kennan may have gained an exaggerated personal impression of the negative response that his paper evoked at the Foreign Office.[32] What really struck him was the discovery that his ideas seemed to be unacceptable to the State Department as well – a perfect situation in which he could indulge in his habit of revelling in the role of a maverick.[33] American officials continued to discuss possibilities of setting up a European organisation that would be acceptable to Britain, but at the same time would be strong enough and sufficiently supranational to contain West Germany, but this turned out to be an attempt to square the circle. Personally, Kennan got involved in a heated argument with Charles Bohlen, then the second man at the US embassy in Paris, who maintained that the unification of Europe without Britain was impossible and that France without British support would rather seek neutrality in the Cold War than be aligned alone with Germany on the continent.[34] Kennan retorted that Great Britain was no help to France as it was too weak economically and militarily as to be able in the long run to balance the weight of Germany in Europe. This could be done and was done only by the United States. It was the task of France to prevent the Germans from making their way against the Western powers. The French should not continue to be preoccupied with what others could do to save them, but 'strike out', 'with such other continental countries as they can gather around them, to make Europeans out of the Germans while there is still time'.[35]

Meanwhile, Secretary of State Acheson had not given up the idea of European integration along supranational lines. In fact, without Kennan's becoming aware of it, these weeks in the autumn of 1949 were to be the moment of his ultimate triumph. The new Secretary of State did espouse the one idea that had figured so prominently in the paper of the Policy Planning Staff just cited – the idea of a purely continental but at the same time supranation-

al European union that accepted what so far had been unthinkable, Britain's remaining outside of such a union. In the face of
strong opposition from several senior American diplomats,
Acheson insisted on October 24, 1949 that he did not 'wish to see
... progress ... on the road to integration (including Western
Germany) ... retarded by British reluctance...'.[36] 'France and
France alone', he urged, 'can take the decisive leadership in integrating Western Germany into Western Europe...'[37]

Acheson had thus changed America's policy with regard to the
process of European integration in a most significant way, a
change that has continued to influence European integration
through to the present. At that turning point the American government decided that it was more urgent to have a tighter even
though a smaller supranational European organisation capable of
containing Germany, rather than to gain British adherence to
such an organisation and thereby widen its membership: structural cohesiveness from now on counted for more than breadth of
membership.

What gave additional significance to this change were repeated
attempts by Acheson to win the French government over to this
new policy. At one point he took advantage of the fact that the
question of reducing the removal of plants in Germany had
become acute. Within this context Acheson sent a letter to the
French foreign minister Robert Schuman on October 30, 1949
and implored his French counterpart to 'move rapidly' in the
German question in order to forestall a resurgence in Germany of
extremist right-wing elements, as had been the case in the twen-
ties. 'No country', he continued, 'has a greater stake than France
in the answer [to the German question]... Now is the time for
French initiative and leadership of the type required to integrate
the German Federal Republic promptly and decisively into
Western Europe... Because of their dislike and fear of
Communism and of the Soviet Union the Germans are psychologically and politically ripe to take measures for genuine integration
with Western Europe. Unless advantage is taken of this political
opportunity, we may again face a Germany aligned with the Soviet
Union or feeling itself able to ask for bids'.[38]

There were a couple of months of procrastination until France
was ready to accept the role which the United States had offered.
Partly for motives of their own, partly undoubtedly remembering
the American representations a few months earlier, the French

government under the influence of Jean Monnet and Robert Schuman proposed a sectoral merger of the economies of France and West Germany on May 9, 1950, exactly five years after the defeat of Hitler. This meant that the coal and steel industries of both countries would fall under the control of a supranational authority that was independent of the national governments of the two countries. Any European country that felt it could accept this supranational structure was invited to join. In the end, the structure included West Germany – as it was not yet sovereign it had nothing to lose – Italy and the Benelux countries, but not Great Britain; in other words it was a Continental union. In spite of lingering fears of European protectionism, the United States did not hesitate to lend all-out support to this revolutionary proposal. Political imperatives overruled economic interests.[39]

This promising development was jeopardised after only eight weeks by the outbreak of the Korean war. Europe, and West Germany in particular, felt threatened by communist subversion and an ensuing Soviet invasion following the Korean model. German troops, the American Joint Chiefs of Staff demanded, had to be raised in order to help to deter Soviet aggression. From then on American interest in European integration was diverted from the Schuman plan to German rearmament. France had roundly rejected the mere idea of creating a new German army. The alternative which the French minister of defence René Pleven proposed in October 1950 amounted to sectoral military integration in Europe, i. e. a European army with nationally mixed forces, a common defence minister and a common budget.

At first American political and military experts, their pro-European feelings notwithstanding, refused even to entertain this proposition as it seemed totally impracticable.[40] After the French had modified their proposal and given assurances that the European Defence Community (EDC) they advocated would be firmly integrated into NATO and would not discriminate against the Germans, the American government gradually brought itself to accept the EDC. Eisenhower, then NATO commander in Europe, and McCloy, the American High Commissioner in Germany, had been instrumental in persuading the Truman administration to adopt this new policy. Since June 1951 the EDC came more and more to be regarded as the cornerstone of European supranational integration, which would continue what the Schuman Plan had begun. A political organisation for a united

Europe, it was hoped, would be established and serve as the basis for the EDC and thus bring the process of European integration to fruition.[41]

As it turned out, however, the EDC nearly wrecked this development. One of its flaws had been that Britain of course would not even consider membership in it. This frightened many French politicians who feared that France alone would have to cope with Germany's future military power, EDC or not. French military experts secretly lobbied for integrating German forces into NATO rather than into an EDC. Generally, pro-European parties lost during the French election of 1951 and henceforth enjoyed less influence within the cabinets. Schuman was forced to resign from his position as French foreign minister. It is true that in May 1952 the EDC treaty had finally been signed after endless negotiations, but it still had to be ratified by the national parliaments and it remained doubtful whether the French National Assembly could muster a majority in support of it.[42]

In this situation the Truman and the Eisenhower administrations mobilised all American prestige and influence in order to ensure a ratification by the French parliament of the EDC treaty, a ratification, moreover, without modifications that would have eliminated its supranational features.[43] Against all odds the United States maintained this position because it did not want to compromise the supranational principle by openly abandoning it, and because it refused to disown Adenauer, the staunchest European, who had staked his political prestige on a success of the EDC and whose domestic base had grown dangerously brittle.[44] Perhaps America used too much rhetorical 'agonising' pressure instead of employing real leverage in order to ensure the ratification of the EDC. However, all efforts turned out to be of no avail. On August 30, 1954 the French National Assembly rejected the EDC. This meant that plans for a political union for Europe lapsed as well. America's policy of integrating Germany into Europe was a shambles.

The British picked up the pieces and put them together. They proposed a widening of the Brussels pact and its transformation into a Western European Union. West Germany was to be member both of the WEU and NATO, the WEU being designed to control and, if necessary, to limit Germany's armaments. This new arrangement did not contain any supranational provisions, and it was for this reason that Britain could join it without misgivings.

America had no other option than to accept. In many ways this seemed to be the end of America's integration policy in Europe. The supranational ideal was discredited; the United States had lost much of its previous leverage and prestige as Europe was no longer dependent on American economic assistance and, under the auspices of detente, no longer felt immediately threatened by the Soviet Union. What we know of European integration today – the common market and the Brussels European Commission – was the result of European initiatives, Dutch and French in particular, rather than American nudges. In its final phase, the relaunching of Europe of 1955–56 actually bore anti-American undertones. To some extent, this reflected the crisis of confidence in European-American relations, which had its origins in American plans to reduce its conventional military presence in Europe and culminated in the Suez crisis of late October–early November 1956, when the United States deserted Great Britain and France while these two countries were trying to regain military control over the Suez canal. Not only did the American government denounce the Western European military intervention against Nasser's Egypt, it seemed also to collude with the Soviet Union in this issue.

In this crisis Adenauer considered it vitally necessary to play the European card, in other words to demonstrate the solidarity of Western Europe as opposed to the two superpowers. According to him, this meant in practice that the governments involved in negotiations for a European Common Market (EEC) and an atomic energy board (EURATOM) ought no longer to haggle over details, but should subordinate economic differences to the political need to strengthen the position of Western Europe in world politics.[45] As for France, the Suez crisis strengthened the resolution of its government to bring the EEC negotiations to a successful conclusion. Although the French negotiators, with this purpose in mind, had already decided to offer concessions before the crisis, they still found it easier to defend them to the French public by pointing to America's 'betrayal' of West European interests in the Eastern Mediterranean and the need to build up a common European front against the overbearing superpowers.[46]

The United States for its part had supported both the EEC and the Euratom all along. Again it subordinated its fears of European protectionism to its hopes for European integration by way of a common market; again it regarded Germany's ties to that common market as a palliative against a resurging German nationalism; again it considered an economic community in Europe as a first step leading to its political unification; again it preferred a smaller but more tightly knit European organism to a larger but weaker organisation. This time, however, it strongly criticised Great Britain for not wanting to support this organisation. To what extent American influences had an impact on the negotiations that led to the Treaty of Rome in March 1957 is a question that cannot yet be answered on the basis of the available records.[47]

V

This latest stand which America took in support of the common market bears witness to a remarkable consistency in United States policy with regard to the structure of a European union. Since the launching of the Marshall Plan American policy-makers were consistent in their belief that Europe had to overcome its national rivalries and to set up an overarching supranational organisation, which in a distant future might develop into a European United States. Whether Republicans or Democrats, they were consistent in subordinating economic considerations to this overriding political aim. They continued to be impressed with the key importance of a Franco-German reconciliation, and since late 1949 were willing to support the supranational integration of only a part of Western Europe provided that France and Germany were members of it. They never abandoned that stance. They unreservedly supported the Schuman Plan and the EDC, and later on the Common Market, because these organisations promised to meet these requirements.

At the same time and with regard to the means which America could select in order to speed up that process, they had no illusions about the fact that any system of European integration that the United States tried to impose on the Europeans would have no future. For this reason the American government quite consciously adopted a more gradualist approach, accepting Britain's staying away from the core of Europe and putting up with the delays in the process of European integration. They banked on a long term success: once a nucleus of European integration was formed which encompassed France and West Germany, they hoped that the rest of Europe would ultimately join it. In 1954 they were content that at least the basis of Franco-German understanding could be salvaged from the wreckage of the EDC. When, in 1956, European integration again appeared on the agenda American policy-makers reverted to its original policy of supporting the European nucleus forming a common market. Again the Americans relied on the intrinsic momentum of the process of European integration, which held out the hope of attracting all of Europe in the not too distant future.

Notes

1. The following is an expanded, documented and updated version of an article published by the author six years ago. Klaus Schwabe, 'Die Vereinigten Staaten und die Einigung Europas 1945–1952' in O. Franz (ed.), *Europas Mitte*, Göttingen, 1987, pp. 166–82.

2. See Klaus Schwabe, 'Der Marshall-Plan und Europa' in Raymond Poidevin (ed.), *Origins of European Integration* (European Community Liaison Committee, publication no. 1), Brussels, 1986, pp. 47–70; Michael J. Hogan, *The Marshall Plan: America, Britain, and the Reconstruction of Western Europe 1947–1952*, Cambridge, 1987, pp. 36f.

3. See the basic paper by George F. Kennan, 'Policy with Respect to American Aid to Western Europe', May 23, 1947, in A. K. Nelson (ed.), *The State Department Policy Planning Staff Papers 1947–1949*, 3 vols., New York, 1983, vol. 1, pp. 3–11. President Truman endorsed the same line of thinking two years later: 'Memorandum of Conversation. Participants the President, the Secretary of State, the Secretary of Defense, Atlantic Pact Foreign Ministers', April 4, 1949, published by Cees Wiebes and Bert Zeeman, 'Eine Lehrstunde in Realpolitik', in *Vierteljahrshefte für Zeitgeschichte*, vol. 40, 1992, pp. 417f., 421f.

4. Policy Planning Staff, 'Certain Aspects of the European Recovery Problem from the United States Standpoint', in Anna K. Nelson (ed.), *Policy Planning Staff Papers*, vol. 1, pp. 55–9; Policy Planning Staff, 'Resumé of World Situation', November 6, 1947, ibid., p.130, 133f.

5. Pierre Melandri, *Les États Unis face à l'unification de l'Europe 1945–1954*, Paris, 1980, pp. 779ff.

6. Hogan, *The Marshall Plan*, pp. 42 and passim.

7. John Gimbel, *The Origins of the Marshall Plan*, Stanford, 1976, pp. 250ff.

8. George F. Kennan, 'Certain Aspects of the European Recovery

Problem from the United States Standpoint', in Nelson (ed.), *The State Department Policy Planning Staff Papers*, vol. 1, pp. 48ff.

9. See for example Marshall to US embassy in Belgium, January 10, 1948, in *Foreign Relations of the United States 1948* (henceforth quoted as *FRUS*), vol. 3, Washington 1974, pp. 358f.

10. Melandri, *Les États Unis face à l'unification*, pp. 144f., 203, 248f.

11. Hogan, *The Marshall Plan*, pp. 56ff., 119; Schwabe, 'Der Marshall Plan und Europa', pp. 52f.

12. Marshall and Caffery, August 27, 1948, *FRUS 1948*, vol. 3, pp. 222f.

13. ERP Committee of the State Department, Memorandum, March 3, 1948, record group 353, box 31, National Archives, Washington.

14. *FRUS 1949*, vol. 3, p. 239.

15. Acheson in 'Memorandum of Conversation', April 4, 1949, in *Vierteljahrshefte für Zeitgeschichte*, vol. 40, 1992, p. 422; Summary of Discussion on Problems of Relief, Rehabilitation, and Reconstruction of Europe, May 27, 1947, in *FRUS 1947*, vol. 3, p. 235.

16. Truman in 'Memorandum of Conversation', *Vierteljahrshefte für Zeitgeschichte* 40, pp. 417, 421f.; Robert Murphy to Dean Acheson, March 23, 1949, *FRUS 1949*, vol. 3, pp. 120f., Annex: Paper prepared in the Department of State, undated [spring 1949], p. 133: 'Without the creation of the institutions necessary to ensure that separate national interests are subordinated to the best interests of the community, an adequate means for incorporating Germany will not exist and the objectives with respect to Germany...cannot be attained. It is also doubtful whether our other objectives in Western Europe...can be obtained in the absence of the creation of adequate community institutions.' The term 'contain' applied to the case of Germany appears in contemporary sources; see e. g. Policy Planning Staff, Meeting, May 25, 1949, record group 59, Policy Planning Staff Papers, box 27, National Archives, Washington. See also Hogan, *The Marshall Plan*, p. 292.

17. Hogan, *The Marshall Plan*, pp. 275ff.; Anne Deighton, *The Impossible Peace: Britain, the Division of Germany and the Origins of the Cold War*, Oxford, 1990, pp. 193, 197.

18. Hogan, *The Marshall Plan*, p. 280.

19. The initiator was the Foreign Office: Jebb and Kennan, 7 April 1949, Public Record Office (henceforth quoted as PRO) FO 371 76383. Jebb wanted to discuss with Kennan four topics: 1) the possibility of a Western European political union within the next five years; 2) the extent of a British 'association' with it, 3) Germany's role in a European union, 4) the position of a United Western Europe as a 'third force' between the superpowers. See also Millar to Jebb, 29 April 1949, PRO FO 371 76383.

20. Policy Planning Staff Meeting, May 20, 25, 27, June 7, 13, 14, 1949,

record group 59, Policy Planning Staff Papers, box 27, 32, National Archives, Washington.

21. Policy Planning Staff, 'Outline of US Stance towards Question of European Union', 7 July 1949, in Nelson (ed.), *The State Department Policy Planning Staff Papers 1947–1949*, vol. 3, pp. 82–100; paraphrase and comment in George F. Kennan, *Memoirs 1925–1950*, New York, 1967, pp. 452–6.

22. 'Outline', p. 95: 'No concept which does not envisage a possible place for an eventually-liberated Eastern Europe should be regarded as anything more than provisional unless we are really decided to accept as permanent the division of Europe along German and Austrian frontiers.' This was the only underlined paragraph of the whole paper.

23. Ibid., p. 96: The combination US-Britain would 'keep Britain out of continental groupings and thus remove existing ceiling on development of union among continental countries...'

24. Foreign Office, Memorandum, European Integration, 26 July 1949, PRO FO 371 76383. According to this account Kennan actually advised against the British joining a European union 'beyond the point of no return'. On the other hand, he was misunderstood by his British interlocutors in so far as they ascribed to him the view that Germany would ultimately dominate a European union, and that Franco-German relations had to be improved in order 'to induce the French to accept this ...' See also the following footnote!

25. 'Outline', pp. 85: 'We see no answer to German problem within sovereign national framework. Continuation of historical process within this framework will almost inevitably lead to repetition of post-Versailles sequence of developments... Only answer is some form of European union which would give young Germans wider horizon and remove introverted, explosive, neurotic quality of German political thought...' See also pp. 94, 97, 100. The paper was not entirely consistent, as it concluded by warning that 'nothing should be done during this period which would carry UK *or Western Germany* [my italics] into arrangements envisaging actual merging of sovereignty with other western nations...' Did the paper argue simply on the basis that West Germany did not have sovereignty as yet and, therefore, could not merge with other Western European nations? Or did he fear West Germany's armament – to which he was opposed – as a result of such merger? (For this see the Foreign Office Memorandum of 26 July 1949 cited above.) But how would a tighter European organisation become effective and serve the purpose that Kennan assigned it, if it did not encompass West Germany ? At any event, keeping Germany from dominating Europe again was the thrust of Kennan's argument, and opposed to what Hogan (*The Marshall Plan*, p. 269) states, there is no evidence that Kennan was resigned to a future military or political supremacy of a sovereign German state on the conti-

nent of Europe. For the contrary see Policy Planning Staff, Meeting, May 20 and 27, June 14, 1949, record group 59, Policy Planning Staff Papers, box 27, 32, National Archives Washington; Kennan to Bohlen, Oktober 12, 1949, ibid., box 27.

26. 'Outline', pp. 96, 99.
27. Foreign Office, Memorandum, 26 July 1949, PRO FO 371 76383.
28. 'Outline' , pp. 90
29. Wilson D. Miscamble, *George F. Kennan and the Making of American Foreign Policy 1917–1950*, Princeton, 1992, p. 285.
30. Kennan, *Memoirs*, p. 456; Gérard Bossuat, *La France, l'aide américaine et la construction européenne 1944–1954*, 2 vols., Paris, 1992, pp. 702f., see also Kennan to Bohlen, November 11, 1949, The Papers of George Kennan, Mudd Library, Princeton, N. J.
31. Kennan, *Memoirs*, p. 457. For Kennan's view on the lack of British interest in Eastern Europe see Policy Planning Staff, Meeting, May 25, June 14, 1949, record group 59, Policy Planning Staff Papers, box 27, 32, National Archives, Washington.
32. Roger Making, Minute, 21 July 1949, PRO FO 371 76383 .
33. Kennan, *Memoirs*, pp. 427, 462.
34. Bohlen to Kennan, October 6, 1949, record group 59, Papers of the Policy Planning Staff, box 27, National Archives, Washington.
35. Kennan to Bohlen, November 7, 1949, Papers of George Kennan, Mudd Library, Princeton, N. J.
36. Acheson to Embassy, London, October 24, 1949, in *FRUS 1949*, vol. 4, Washington 1975, p. 345; similar language used by Kennan according to Bossuat, *La France*, vol. 2, p. 711. On the basis of this evidence I do not agree with David Mayers, *George Kennan and the Dilemmas of US Foreign Policy*, Oxford, 1988, p. 151, who discounts Kennan's influence on the formulation of the United States European policies at that time.
37. Acheson to Embassy Paris, 19 October 1949, in *FRUS 1949*, vol. 4, p. 470.
38. Acheson to Schuman, October 30, 1949, in *FRUS 1949*, vol. 3, p. 623. At a meeting in September 1949 Acheson had addressed Schuman apparently in a similar vein, see Bossuat, *La France*, vol. 2, p. 742; Raymond Poidevin, *Robert Schuman – homme d'État 1886–1963*, Paris, 1986, p. 272.
39. Klaus Schwabe, ' "Ein Akt konstruktiver Staatskunst" – die USA und die Anfänge des Schuman-Plans' in K. Schwabe (ed.), *Die Anfänge des Schuman-Plans 1950/51*, Veröffentlichungen der Historiker-Verbindungsgruppe bei der Kommission der Europäischen Gemeinschaften, vol. 2, Baden-Baden, 1988, pp. 211–40; John Gillingham, *Coal, steel, and the rebirth of Europe, 1945–1955. The Germans and French from Ruhr conflict to economic community*, Cambridge, 1991, pp. 228ff.
40. Acheson to Bruce, October 17, 1950, *FRUS 1950*, vol. 3, p. 385; Dean Acheson, *Present at the Creation*, New York, 1969, p. 459.

41. Acheson/Lovett to Truman, July 30, 1951, *FRUS 1951*, vol. 3, pp. 849f.; Acheson and Bruce, June 28, 1951, ibid., p. 806; K. Schwabe, 'Fürsprecher Frankreichs? John McCloy und die Integration der Bundesrepublik', in Ludolf Herbst, Werner Bührer, Hanno Sowade (eds), *Vom Marshallplan zur EWG. Die Eingliederung der Bundesrepublik Deutschland in die westliche Welt*, München, 1990, pp. 523ff.

42. Georges-Henri Soutou, 'France and the German Rearmament Problem 1945–55', in R. Ahmann, A. M. Birke and M. Howard (eds), *The Quest for Stability: Problems of West European Security 1918–1957*, Oxford, 1993, pp. 501ff.

43. Brian R. Duchin, 'The "Agonizing Reappraisal": Eisenhower, Dulles, and the EDC', in *Diplomatic History*, vol. 16, 1992, pp. 202, 205ff., 212ff.

44. For example Dulles to Bruce, May 18, 1954, *FRUS 1952–1954*, vol. 5, p. 925.

45. Hans-Peter Schwarz, *Adenauer*, 2 vols., Stuttgart, 1986–91, vol. 2, *Adenauer. Der Staatsmann 1952–1967*, pp. 296, 301ff.

46. Alan S. Milward, *The European Rescue of the Nation-State*, London, 1992, pp. 214ff.; Hanns Jürgen Küsters, *Fondements de la communauté économique européenne*, Bruxelles, 1990, pp. 212f.

47. Schwarz, *Adenauer*, vol. 2, p. 291; Ennio di Nolfo, 'Gli Stati Uniti e le origini della Comunità Economica Europea', in Enrico Serra (ed.), *The Relaunching of Europe and the Treaties of Rome*, European Community Liaison Committee of Historians, publications vol.3, Bruxelles, 1989, pp. 339– 50.

GUSTAV SCHMIDT

'Tying' (West) Germany into the West – But to What? NATO? WEU? The European Community?[1]

The Focus

> All were agreed that the policy was to integrate Germany into
> the Western system. To assure this there must be first of all
> some definite Western system into which to integrate
> Germany.[2]

The basic concern of the Western Allies after 1945 was to prevent
the control of West Germany and Western Europe from falling
into the hands of the Soviet Union, whose interests and postures
appeared hostile to the 'West'. The situation in Europe and elsewhere in the world dictated the implementation of American,
British and French policies.[3] The US was called into Western
Europe to contain the Soviet Union and to provide security
against, as well as for, Germany. Washington tried to link
America's economic and military commitments in Europe to the
process of European integration by granting aid and security guarantees only on the condition that progress was made in creating a
united Europe.[4] Since the US was unwilling to meet its defence
needs without the support of allies,[5] the crucial problem was to
find partners in Europe willing and able to organise Western
Europe's coordination and integration. Conversely, the European
partners were resolved to 'have a policy of their own and try to per-

suade the US to make it their own.'[6] The coincidence of an American push to enhance European integration and the European pull to make America's posture as Europe's federator and 'pacifier' fit in with their own national ambitions is the main feature of the post-war decades. From the very beginning, the hallmark of the trans-Atlantic partnership is the linkage between commercial, economic and monetary interests on the one hand and military and security interests on the other, and the uneasy coexistence between European integration, a concept providing 'unity of purpose' in the US-led Atlantic Alliance, and the actual recovery and emancipation of Europe.[7]

The idea of linking Europe's integration to its defense, or even of using a common military strategy in Western Europe as a functional mechanism to promote integration, goes back to the start of the discussions for the alliance: 'Defense was, after all, the essential purpose of America's effort to bring stability to the region.'[8] As Alan Milward argues, the idea of combining the tasks of maximising rearmament and minimising its disruptive effects presented itself together with the possibility of doing so within a political structure embracing far more than the issue of armaments, tactics and strategy. Disillusioned with the OEEC (in autumn 1949), A. Harriman, in charge of the European Recovery Programme, looked forward to NATO as a new forum for political integration in Western Europe; others in Washington expected more rapid progress toward the political unification of Western Europe in a common framework of trade and payments.[9] However, as Milward and Schwabe emphasise, the inadequacy of US forces, the main reason for the strategies devised in late 1949, militated against the main aims of US foreign policy in Europe:

> ...the Schuman Plan...brought the solution to the central dilemma of American foreign policy...the issue of Germany's rearmament was so divisive that the United States had little choice but to pursue it through the proposed French device of an integrated European army under the control of a European Defense Community, no matter what delays this imposed. It followed that...OEEC must be maintained. The Federal Republic was a member there, but could not be in NATO... The idea that anything could be achieved along these lines in NATO had been given up completely.[10]

The preferences could, however, be reversed. Given the feeling (from the mid-1950s onwards) that the outbreak of a 'great war' in Europe was unlikely, there was a shift of emphasis to the struggle for economic influence.[11] Would the OEEC, led by Britain and encompassing the US and Canada, make the running, or would the continental Europeans, who had lost faith in the OEEC, accentuate the 'peace in parts' concept inherent in Western European integration? Would the US, because of the need to find a substitute for the West German 'magnet' theory concerning East Germany, back a Western European venture? Would a revival of the Schuman Plan idea centre on the use of atomic energy for civil purposes? Would France welcome American backing for EURATOM in order to prevent Germany from creating a bilateral link with the US in this crucial policy area? Or would Paris object to the American 'Atoms for Peace' programme because it restricted France's option to follow the US and Britain's example, i.e. to become a military as well as a civilian nuclear power?[12]

The focus of this article is on the consequences of the decisions resulting from compromises over the Schuman and Pleven plans. First, as K. Schwabe righly points out,

> Compared to the paramount issue of guaranteeing Europe's security, the problems of European integration lost, for the time being (until May/June 1949), much of their original importance and urgency... Once openly committed to maintaining the security of Western Europe, the US lost a powerful lever for a renewal of European efforts to integrate Europe – largely, or so it seemed, because of British obstructionism...[13]

Secondly, the North Atlantic Council (NAC) took in December 1950 a crucial step toward the reorganisation of NATO, approving the establishment of an integrated, collectively balanced military force under central command and control. This seemed to be the only way to implement the critical decision that alliance territory should be defended along a line as far east as practicable.[14] At the time of the Korean War, the US did not want to wait until France and Britain felt strong and confident enough to join together with a revitalised Germany.

> Instead, the US had to commit itself as a predominant factor in the European balance of power and in so doing reassure the French government that it would not face a Faustian choice between subservience to the Soviet Union and subservience to

Germany...NATO's new institutional structure was in part a means to accelerate Germany's return to semi-sovereign status.[15]

Washington's regard to both French and West German concerns was, however, contradicted by another development: the Nuclearisation of American, British and consequently NATO's strategy and defence posture. The nuclearisation was by no means a substitute for Germany's rearmament; on the contrary, SACEUR and the American military postulated that Germany's conventional forces were the prerequisite for the shift of emphasis in strategy and defence postures. The important aspect of this is that the US once again – as in 1949 – made a choice without much European involvement to place heavy reliance on nuclear weapons and a strike air force; the consequence of America's choice of a comprehensive nuclear strategy was to accentuate the differences between European countries. Once again, Washington's decision enhanced Britain's position and role in the Atlantic Alliance and encouraged the British resolve not to be a part of any integrated Europe. By copying the US defense posture, the Churchill–Eden government expected to revitalise the special relationship with the US; by developing into a second centre of residual power, as an independent civil and military nuclear power and as the hub of the sterling area, Britain aimed at maintaining an identity separate from Europe, but interacting with the US as a supplier of Europe's security:[16] 'Emphasizing a military role would give Britain more parity with the US, whereas economic integration would undermine the Commonwealth and Sterling area resources.'[17] Thanks to their nuclear power status, the US and Britain assumed that their territory had become a sanctuary; the other countries, especially Germany, were part of endangered zones. NATO became in effect an alliance of different zones of security and of power status.

The divisiveness of nuclear diplomacy since the autumn of 1953 gave another twist to the central question of tying West Germany to the West: which Western system could anchor Germany firmly and organically to the West? Who had to belong to the system which was to exercise *Zuverlässigkeitskontrolle* over the Bonn Republic and at the same time reassure West Germany that it could become an equal partner in such an integrated western system? France by herself could not do this, for the simple reason that it was suspicious of Washington's and London's interest in

German rearmament as a short-cut to reduce their own 'continental commitments'. For France, the willingness of the US and Britain to become 'European' powers was essential to attain a defense posture as far east as possible and to prevent Germany from exploiting the opportunities of an eventually integrated Europe.

If the Western powers – collectively and individually – needed Germany's help and wanted Germany to form part of the Western bloc, they had to make the FRG a full member of the club;[18] this, however, tended to mean German equality with Britain and France within a western European system as the West's second hub in the overall East-West conflict. The German question, then, has two aspects: first, how could Germany be anchored to the West in its global contest with the Soviet Union,[19] and second, how could Germany be placed as an equal partner in integrated Western – European and/or Atlantic – systems?

The US wanted the Western Europeans to develop European unity and real cohesion with respect to policies towards the USSR. In this respect, the FRG by the US was seen as an ever more important country in world affairs. In contrast to Britain, France or the Netherlands, the Bonn Republic was bound to be influenced by the US; the FRG could relieve America's burden and prop up America's global power. Germany was likely to become the powerhouse of an integrated European system, a favoured investment site for US corporations, and it would provide men for the armed forces necessary for a conventional part in the defense of Western Europe. However, in order to avoid the divisive effect of a German-American alliance within the trans-Atlantic community, the US had to make sure that Western Europe, too, benefitted from tying Germany firmly and organically to the West.

The Setting: Vital Interests of the 'Western allies'

1) The vital interest of the West in anchoring Germany firmly to itself was based on the assumption that the USSR had cut Europe in two and might be tempted to force Western Europe through blackmail, 'internal aggression', etc. into its zone of control; in reaction the western allies themselves resolved to cut Germany in two.[20] The contrast between the inherent weaknesses of France and Anglo-French tensions regarding

the shape and scope of any organisation reflecting Europe's
need for unity of purpose on the one hand, and the USSR's
advantage, namely that Moscow held the trump cards (occupation of the GDR and Russian control of the Oder-Neiße border) whenever it should come to bargaining for supremacy on
the other hand, made the US conscious of the need 'to exercise the greatest attraction to enable the Germans to overcome Soviet blandishments stemming from these Soviet
trump cards.'[21] Consequently, the US tied itself to a role as
'European power' and as an advocate of 'integration with
equality' towards the FRG. The West was frightened by the
prospect of having to face the choice between a deal or a duel
between the Soviet Union and Germany. In this situation, the
US became the arbiter, since Washington had the option to
come to terms with the Kremlin and/or to enhance Western
European integration. The German situation was specific, too:
whenever the balance of power between the US and the USSR
in Europe was to be changed – e.g. through negotiations
about zones of arms reduction, perhaps in connection with
German unification – the 'German question' was bound to
occupy the front stage.

The integration of Germany into the West was an act of
preventive diplomacy: should East-West tensions decrease
and should the US and the Soviet Union disengage or pull
back their forces from outposts in Europe, the FRG had to be
a committed member of the Western bloc; Dulles, in
September 1953, defined 'the cementing of Germany firmly
to Europe and the West' and European integration as the
most important prerequisites for a policy of 'easing in tensions' (détente). Britain and France, on the other hand,
feared that they might then be confronted with a united
Europe, but under German hegemony. For London and
Paris, 'Western integration' was instrumental to the control of
Germany's rise to power; the western systems had to impose
ceilings on the rearmament of Germany. For the US, however, Germany was needed to close the gap between the West's
security requirements and actual available resources.
Integrating West Germany into western system(s) was regarded a matter of survival in the global contest between the West
and the Soviet bloc, but it was also an attempt to keep a check
on the course which German policy might take in the future.

From the NATO summit at Lisbon (February 1952) to Germany's entry into NATO (May 1955), it was plain that the Western powers intended to let nothing deter them from the primary objective of bringing Germany into their system of alliances (EDC and NATO/WEU).[22]

2) The West had always to worry about the German and the Russian problems simultaneously. After the First World War, it was the USSR that was temporarily a marginal or peripheral factor; in the era of the first and second Cold War (1946–1953), Germany was the object of Western and Soviet conflicting strategies. Western, and particularly American, policy planning on and about Germany was, however, related to security arrangements which took into account the need to satisfy legitimate Soviet security concerns. It was, of course, also related to what was estimated the minimum requirements for maintaining the American presence in Western Europe.

3) Welcome as the US was as an European power, it was important for France and also for Britain to prevent the US from concentrating on an easy alliance with the FRG. In return for American support on the Berlin question, on unification and (after 1955) on non-recognition of the GDR, the FRG was inclined to follow the American lead more easily than were Britain or France. France's weakness, Britain's decline and the rivalries between American imperialism and European colonialism designated the FRG as America's foremost ally. American-German bilateralism, which was more attractive to some German industrialists and ministries than European integration,[23] tended to restrain the US from pursuing a more flexible *Ostpolitik* and from treating Germany as a supportive member of the US hegemony by promoting the FRG to first-class status within western systems. In order to counteract far-reaching American proposals in this direction, London and Paris could and did call for four-power negotiations to make sure that the power-status difference between Britain or France and non-nuclear Germany was reaffirmed.

4) Once the option of a self-reliant, free Europe was beyond reach (after 1948), the alternatives were European dependance on the US through NATO or an integrated Western Europe but within a divided Europe.[24] The latter, however,

implied that the subject of deploying nuclear weapons in Europe had to be placed at the top of a European agenda. These issues became prominent with the demise of EDC, which was due to French ambitions to attain at least equal status with Britain in the Alliance, and tripartite leadership instead of US-led alliances which were designated to encircle the Soviet Empire.

5) Britain and France realised that only the US was capable and willing to reintegrate Germany and Japan into the western orbit. However, British and French views on the Far East differed from those of America; America's atomic sabre-rattling in the Far East (against China in 1950, 1954 and 1957–8) irritated the European allies. Although the US assured Britain and France that 'massive retaliation' was not the answer to Europe's security dilemma, the suspicion grew that American unilateralism implied unreliability and unpredictability (*Unzuverlässigkeit und Unberechenbarkeit*). For Britain and France, and after 1956 also for Germany, it became apparent that there was a need for other options than dependance on the US. However, as British, French and German thinking on self-assertiveness did not coincide, and as Germany had no real alternative but to restore the American connection, the conflicting priorities did not lead to a serious split. NATO, however, as the linchpin of American influence on European and especially German affairs, was in chronic crisis. Hence, American politicians – for example Dulles in 1955 – and diplomats wondered whether NATO was a strong enough anchor with which to tie Germany to the West.[25]

6) The British were instrumental in persuading the US to become and remain a European power. To them, any mutual reinforcement between American isolation and German neutralism represented the worst-case scenario. On the one hand, Britain had to commit itself to the defense of Western Europe; on the other hand, Britain would do so only on condition that the US entered into similar or at least equivalent obligations: 'Britain would not join in European military arrangements to include a rearmed West Germany without the close involvement of the US.'[26] Britain was unable to consider 'making friends' in Europe by stepping forward to fill the gap if the US threatened to reduce its forces in Europe.

However, tying the US as well as Britain to the defense of Western Europe was designed to safeguard the UK's ability to sustain its global power status, based on the sterling area and the Commonwealth links. In consequence of NATO decisions to move towards unity of command, Britain resolved to put forward its non-European tasks as a contribution to the defense of the West, a defense strategy which was, however, based on the American nuclear deterrent.[27] Britain welcomed 'unity of control', but at the same time sought to be exempted from integration into NATO-Europe.[28] Britain also aimed at reducing its commitments to Europe, whilst at the same time accelerating the build-up of its own nuclear deterrent. The UK as well as the US because of their global commitments:

> ...should not be subjected to the same provisions as the European NATO countries, but in return they would be required to accept special responsibilities (i.e. the nuclearisation of the guarantee in NAT Art. 5)... Moreover, such specialisation would justify a reduction of British troops in Germany, thus alleviating the financial strain of maintaining the BAOR when the West Germans began their own rearmament.[29]

At a later stage – in March 1957 – Macmillan justified this turnaround by reminding France that it seemed no longer interested in Britain's European role. The foundation of the EEC was regarded a clear sign of the new balance of power in Western Europe, with France emphasising communality of interests with Germany and Italy and Britain opting for the revival of the Anglo-American special relationship (see below).

7) Britain and France were concerned not only about European security, but also about Europe's role in Africa and Asia. Macmillan criticised Foreign Secretary Eden for his support of the EDC project with the argument that if France concentrated on Europe, it would neglect the position of the West in Africa and Indochina; this in turn would endanger Britain's position overseas.[30] It is noticeable that Adenauer, in spite of his many differences with Britain over European integration, shared the view that Britain and France should sustain 'Europe's mission' in Africa and Asia.

Compatible interests and conflicting objectives[31]

Lack of progress on Western integration and the resulting disillusionment in West Germany raised the thorny question (*Gretchenfrage*) of whether Germany belonged to the West, and of what was the appropriate western system into which Germany should be integrated. Only one thing was certain: no integrated Western system which was not seen to be European would be viable.[32] In order to balance Germany's potential strength, such a union would need to include Britain. London regarded reconciliation between France and West Germany to be in its own vital interest. The problem was that Britain neither wished to be submerged in a 'European federated political body' nor to join European structures designed by France and backed by the US. The Kennan model, which ultimately prevailed, placed the burden of supranational integration on the continental nations of Europe;[33] Britain was left to do what London wanted to do anyway, namely develop ties with the US and Canada and support Western Europe from outside. But the temptation for American leaders to push Britain into Europe remained. As a minimum, Washington expected Britain – in 1950 as well as in 1955–57 – not to torpedo European initiatives.[34] In 1950, the French initiative superseded American efforts to create a suitable NATO framework for the integration of West Germany.[35] The US and Britain accommodated this move, since French territory and goodwill were central to NATO and Europe's defense. However, the US and Britain did attach the condition to the French project that any European defense force should be part of and under NATO's umbrella: 'Aus einem Instrument, das den Willen der E(V)G in der Atlantischen Allianz zur Geltung brachte, wurde ein Mittel, das umgekehrt dem Willen des Atlantischen Bündnisses in der EVG Einfluß verschaffen sollte.'[36]

France, until 1956, was highly interested in sustaining and enlarging the scope and capacity of NATO because cooperation in NATO might first, ensure French influence on and in Washington, second, assuage the fear that the US would pull its forces back from Europe once a European army was constituted,[37] and third, so that France could count on US cooperation in a European association within a NATO framework, thus putting an end to both the threat of German domination[38] and to the prospect of a Soviet invasion. As to promoting the EDC project in

May 1952, the US and Britain confirmed their earlier guarantees to support France in case of Germany's possible secession from the EDC, and they assured all members of EDC that the US and the UK would consider any threat to the integrity of the EDC as a threat to their own security.[39]

Britain hoped for a remodelled NATO, i.e. some form of Atlantic confederate force.[40] Such a solution provided for a NATO with more integrated structures; it had the advantage that neither the US nor France could press Britain to become more entangled within a supranational European organisation, and that Germany would be more safely and tightly bound to the West in NATO than in integrated European structures.[41] Within NATO, Britain – trusting in the special relationship with the US which linked the two powers with global responsibilities – reckoned that it might be able to lead Europe from London, a claim which was denied to Britain in 1950 and again in 1955–57. Nevertheless, the Attlee, Churchill, Eden and especially Macmillan governments expected to achieve a more equal partnership with the US both in the tasks of attaining a German contribution to the conventional defense of the West and in regulating East-West relations.

Britain and France – at least until 1958–9 – asserted that any peripheric strategy would mean ruin for Europe;[42] both objected – in the transition period from the demise of the EDC to the reconstitution of the WEU – to American proposals which envisioned a more independent German national army.[43] Both favoured in principle a strong European group within NATO, including Britain. But Brzezinski's view 'that Europe should be allowed to reconstitute itself because that is what it wants' had no appeal to Britain. This was partly due to the concern 'that too much of [British] military power [had been] tied down in Europe where it can easily be by-passed.'[44]

The most important coincidence of the major strategic-political objectives of the four Western powers occurred in the context of the search for a replacement for the ill-fated EDC. In some ways, the demise of the EDC was a blessing in disguise. Whereas the US, Britain and France were 'going nuclear' but did not want to see the FRG moving in the same direction, Adenauer deliberately ruled out – for the time being – such a move for Germany. The three Western allies were given time to consider their options for adopting the security guarantee under NATO Article 5 to the conditions of the nuclear age, i.e. the introduction of thermonuclear weapons as well as 'theatre weapons' into the armed forces on both sides of the East-West divide. Could Europe, by pooling its resources and establishing an integrated nuclear power based on the nuclear weapons of Britain and France, induce the Kremlin to consider serious negotiations about relaxation of control over Eastern Europe and German unification?[45] There were French deliberations in this direction,[46] but there was no chance for Britain and France to collaborate in the nuclear field; in 1954–55 as in 1947–50,[47] London held to the view that the military security of the UK did not require a commitment to a politically integrated Western Europe, which was the prerequisite for launching the WEU onto the nuclear power track.

In July–September 1954 the four Western powers modified their postures. Firstly, France regarded the reshaping of its defense posture to be predicated on close cooperation with the US, Britain and the FRG.[48] However, the precondition was French nuclear rearmament.[49] France drew its lesson from the debates within NATO's counsels and from the Bermuda Conference in December 1953 (see below). It is evident that France 'killed' its own brainchild, the EDC, with a view to preserving its nuclear option and thus maintaining equality of status with Britain in a US-led transatlantic security partnership.[50] The formula that nuclear material might be produced in safe (non-exposed strategic) zones permitted France, but not the FRG, to go nuclear; at the same time, the formula was a standing invitation to Germany (and Italy) to opt for an *entente nucléaire* with France.[51] The French could and did urge for cooperation between the three atomic powers in NATO and for shifting the burden of maintaining conventional forces to the non-nuclear members of NATO.[52] Any replacement of the EDC had to include Britain and British military commitment more or less permanently (for five decades). The WEU, therefore, should incorporate the EDC regulations allowing for 'control through integration', which was on Britain's agenda as well, but also grant more leeway to Britain and France so that they could pursue their non-European roles.

On the German side, the Amt Blank advised Adenauer (on 6–7 September 1954)[53] that in view of NATO's principle of balanced collective forces there was no need for military self-sufficiency and Germany could dispense with the nuclear option. As the defense of Germany's air-space (*Luftraum*) depended on the allies in any case, Bonn relied on its allies to provide a nuclear umbrella whilst at the same time contributing conventional forces of its own in order to relieve the burden on France and Britain.[54] This self-denial (*Verzichtserklärung*), however, was predicated on two German requests, first for equal and sufficient German representation in all of NATO's top organisations that had a say in questions relating to the defense of NATO-Europe territory, and second for integration of the operational command structures with due consideration for an effective and fair proportion of personnel from the participating member-states.[55] Fearing that France might discriminate against Germany even in NATO,[56] Bonn was open-minded toward British and American suggestions.[57]

The American position at that time was heavily influenced by developments in Southeast Asia and in the Far East, but: 'Our world position would be isolated and disastrous...if Europe were lost.'[58] Dulles' repeated threat that abandonment of the goal of European integration could have dire consequences for US policy toward Europe[59] was mellowed by consideration of the position of the US in the global contest with 'communist-nationalist forces':

> Most serious, however, is the fact that a resurgent Germany on the verge of disillusion could readily fall, initially, into an attitude of passive accommodation and subsequent collaboration with the Soviet bloc. France and...Britain...in apprehension of the implications of nuclear weapons and desire for trade, [are] tending towards arrangements with the Soviet Union which can only prove to be inimical to US interests.[60]

The rationale behind the creation of the Atlantic Alliance was reinforced: Washington sought to meet essential French and German requirements. On the one hand, it was thought that the Western nations now owed it to the Bonn Republic to do quickly 'all that lies in their power to restore sovereignty to Germany' (Dulles); there should be no second-class NATO membership for the West Germans and the solution should be straightforward, enabling the FRG to attain sovereignty. On the other hand, German membership in NATO must be acceptable to France and the other member-states of an integrated Europe; the contracting parties must accept the obligation not to use force or collaborate in military efforts to change boundaries. The German contribution was not to exceed the ceiling set by the NAC in September 1950, namely not more than 20 per cent of the land forces of NATO (Greece and Turkey were not included in this total).[61]

Britain agreed with Adenauer[62] and the US that a quick solution had to be found if only to make sure that domestic pressures on the Eisenhower Administration would not cut the ties that bound the US to Europe. If there was no replacement for EDC, and the US turned its back on Europe, then – according to Adenauer, but also to Britain – the Soviets would have won the cold war.[63] Although London was willing to help Mendès France out of his difficulties, and also to support German resistance against overly strong French discriminatory measures, any concept of 'unity of purpose' within the Western European system was limited.[64] Britain still wanted to distinguish European from Alliance policies, but with a view to maintaining its own balancing position and role: the US depended to some extent on Britain's ability to carry NATO-Europe along; NATO-Europe looked for some reassurance from Britain to assuage suspicions of US policies and to prevent continental Europe from falling victim either to a Franco-German condominium or to a struggle for leadership between them.

London was always frightened by the prospect that the US might prefer to deal with Western Europe over Britain's head. To regain its credentials as a European member of NATO (rather than building up a position as the first lieutenant of the US) Eden in August/September 1954 induced the British Cabinet to draw closer to Europe and accept new commitments in order to reaffirm Britain's identity in Europe. But once again the distance was also marked: Eden argued in Cabinet (on 27 August 1954)[65] that Britain would not agree to sharing with 'our European partners atomic and thermo-nuclear secrets'. The rationale behind this objection was that a plain European solution would not suffice to guarantee Europe's security against the Soviet Union; if, however, WEU proved efficient and sufficient for the defense of Western Europe, the US would sooner rather than later begin to pull back its land and possibly also its air forces; any self-reliant European system would serve the interests of the USSR and tempt the FRG to move toward a deal with Moscow.[66]

Developments and scenarios

At the Bermuda conference on 4–8 December 1953, the relationship between NATO, a European association and France's role in NATO was at the centre of the discussions. How urgent was

Germany's defense contribution and hence the need to establish a Western system into which a sovereign West Germany could be integrated? How far did the revolution in weapons technology affect NATO's defense postures and force requirements? Concerning the first question,[67] the debate was overshadowed by the projected four power conference in Berlin (February 1954); Dulles and Eden pressed the French on the question of EDC ratification.[68] However, the US gave in to two French requests in order to assuage their fear of German supremacy; first, a satisfactory solution to the Saar question must accompany, if not precede, the founding of the EDC, and second, the strength of American and British forces stationed in Europe 'should represent a definite proportion of the total forces and have a definite relationship to the German forces of the couverture.'[69] At Bermuda, Dulles also informed Bidault and Eden about the implications of the New Look strategy:

> We have entered an era where the quantity of atomic weapons and their military application necessitates a review of their impact on our strategy. We shall assume that such weapons will be used in military operations by US forces engaged whenever it is necessary to do so.[70]

The intention was to mesh atomic weapons with conventional forces, because the establishment of two separate land and air forces would be prohibitively expensive. Nuclear weapons were no substitute for conventional forces; rather, American forces in Western Europe and the full German contribution were both regarded as indispensable.

At about the same time President Eisenhower told NATO General Secretary, Lord Ismay, that the promulgation of the Atoms-for-peace programme required Western Europe to make progress on European unity, i.e. establish the EDC. In view of the 'nuclearisation' of NATO's strategy and forces posture, France and Italy began to enquire whether the introduction of nuclear weapons into American units assigned to NATO would mean that eventually NATO had to make first use of atomic weapons for defense purposes, as conventional forces would be too weak to respond. Who would then be in control? The US President? American generals as local commanders, to whom the president might have to delegate the authority? Or the North Atlantic Council?[71]

The mutual reinforcement, rather than the separation, of Atlantic and European integration[72] was as effective in 1955 as it had been in 1953. The growing criticism of Adenauer's decision to add the military dimension to the division of Germany and Europe, a criticism which was nourished by Moscow's position on the Austrian question, induced the US and Britain to do more to correct German tendencies towards neutralism.[73] The intensifying debate within NATO about the consequences of the December 1954 decision to supply SACEUR with atomic weapons was concerned with building up trust to prevent the eroding force of national egotism (the theory of 'national security first'), which had inspired the demise of the EDC, from spreading.[74] The idea that European integration was the only solid answer to the disruptive forces of nationalism induced Hallstein, Beyen, Spaak, Dulles and Monnet to call for European activities. A European safety net had to be put in place before the siren voices from the Soviet Union[75] could catch the imagination of Western Europeans, or for that matter influence the domestic balance of power in West Germany.[76]

The observation that Khrushchev (at the Geneva summit of 1955) was more concerned with recognition of Soviet parity with the US than with looking for a deal with Germany (which might be an element in the June offer to Adenauer to visit Moscow) created a new situation concerning the tying of the FRG more firmly to the West; from now on, conflicts were more likely to occur between Bonn and Washington (and London, insofar as Britain copied the American role) than between Germany and its continental Western European partners. The US postulated that German unification depended on a 'global rapprochement with the Soviet Union on control of nuclear weapons, which in itself was the prerequisite for some sort of disengagement in Europe.'[77] But would the US, if such a process could be launched, bargain for German unification? Washington was aware of the limited effect which the policy of non-recognition of the GDR (which was a substitute for actively working towards reunification) could have on preventing the resurgence of German nationalism. There was a need to compensate for West Germany's disappointments.

This induced Eisenhower and Dulles to impress on Britain the need to associate or at least agree not to impede the pursuit of the Messina initiative. Dulles asked Macmillan to 'do something to capture the imagination of the Germans and European integration offers a means to this end.'[78] Dulles also attacked the French view that it might be preferable to adapt to two German states: 'If the Germans have nothing to occupy their minds in the inevitable period of waiting that lies ahead on reunification question... they might then look to Soviets.'[79] This was the more dangerous because the presence of atomic weapons in the hands of France might upset Germany's legitimate claim to equality, namely its request for its own national atomic energy policy, first on a civilian basis, but sooner rather than later a military policy as well.[80] But Adenauer was satisfied when Pinay – on 13 November 1955, after the Geneva Foreign Ministers' conference – assured him that in view of the negative attitude of the Kremlin, the West should concentrate on European integration.[81]

The problem then was what sort of multilateral agreements 'will yield the greatest benefits to the western partners: NATO? A grouping under OEEC? Or an approach through the Community of the Six?'[82] In view of the divisive nature of nuclear diplomacy, and in view of the fact that Germany was not likely to be united for some time to come, Eisenhower stressed the 'desirability of developing in Western Europe a third great power bloc'.[83] In that case, the West could display its advantage – in comparison to the Eastern block – as a 'peace and wealth creating community'. Furthermore, a united Europe based on EURATOM and/or the EEC might attract the Eastern European nations and in that way substitute for what earlier West German visions of the 'magnet theory' had implied: overcoming the East-West divide, but on Western terms.

These visions were strong enough to keep up the momentum, but the scope of the issues at stake in the EURATOM and common market projects inevitably draw attention towards the differences between the position of the Six and the rest of the OEEC, including Britain, Canada, and the US. Annoyance about the fact that Germany was devoting relatively little of its resources to the defence of NATO-Europe, while at the same time German exports were expanding,[84] also related the cooperation between the Six to the problems confronting the WEU/NATO in *1956*. Britain hoped that the US and the Commonwealth would support the British initiative to embed the EEC into a wider industrial free trade area. This would enable the British 'to maintain their Imperial preference system, while, at the same time, they would enjoy equal access with Germany, their strongest continental competitor, to the markets of the other states within the Free Trade Area.'[85] It was clear that Britain wanted to regain a leading role in European cooperation by modifying the OEEC and combining the best of two preferential trade zones (imperial preference and common market), at a time when Britain's shift of emphasis in strategy and force deployment was bound to disappoint the Six, who were Britain's partners in the WEU. At first, London took refuge in the escape clauses of the Paris Treaties and tried to justify the new defense policy in terms of the American Radford Plan. As France was facing a serious economic and financial crisis even before Suez and as there was serious doubt whether Italy and Germany would be willing to let Paris take the lead in European integration, the British decision to cut forces assigned to WEU/NATO came at the worst possible moment. That the Free Trade Area proposal was designed to let Britain have the best of two worlds did not increase the attractiveness of London's countermeasure from the point of view of the other OEEC countries.

The American blunder over the Radford Plan, however, convinced Adenauer of the need to revive and upgrade the WEU.[86] When the three Western partners made their presence as nuclear powers felt in Germany,[87] it was inevitable that Adenauer[88] would take two steps. First, he urged the establishment within NATO of a system of control in which the Bonn Republic, representing the territory most likely to be a nuclear target, was to participate (*nukleare Mitwirkung*); this was bound to affect East-West relations, but a German right of co-determination in NATO counsels was inescapable. Second, Adenauer proposed closer political and military cooperation, the pooling of European resources, and cooperation via WEU. The coincidence of a WEU meeting in mid-September with a meeting of the Three Wise Men, reporting on improved cooperation in NATO on non-military issues, for the first time set the stage for bringing German influence to bear on the whole question of troop reductions and NATO's strategy. In September 1956 Adenauer launched the idea of establishing a self-reliant (*eigenständig*) European political power, able to hold its own in the bipolar world.[89] Fearing that the US and the Soviet Union might work out an agreement which would leave the European members of NATO 'high and dry',[90] Adenauer made up his mind that in view of the serious danger of NATO disintegration, the Europeans had to come up with their own ideas.

In comparison with the desire of other NATO countries to have

US policy made in the North Atlantic Council, the German position was welcome to Dulles:

> ...one good feature...was evidence of closer German relations with the British and the French. The Germans readily accepted the principle of giving another year of financial support to the costs of British forces in Germany. The French and the Germans seemed to be working well on the Saar problem. The British are moving towards support of the Common Market...[91]

Realising that the balance of terror (*Gleichgewicht des Schreckens*) was bound to change the sentiment of American policy, Adenauer wanted Western Europe to start preparing for situations to come; no one could take for granted that by the mid-1960s American presidents would be able to persuade the American electorate to provide Western Europe's security. Hence the Europeans must begin working for self-reliance, i.e. to create a European nuclear force:

> ...it might be that support for NATO would gradually die away. This was a terrible prospect for the Europeans. But because it existed the Americans must get used to the idea that the Europeans might need to have their own atomic weapons.[92]

> France and Germany were known to be averse to relying entirely on the US for the provision of atomic weapons and warheads; there might well be advantage for Britain in cooperating with such European allies in the nuclear field.[93]

Adenauer knew that the incumbent US Administration was immensely alliance-conscious and would try hard to obtain multilateralisation of NATO decisions and the right of nuclear co-determination for the Federal Republic. Indeed, Dulles and Eisenhower acknowledged that

> from a political perspective the European doubt (about changes in US policy vis-à-vis the Soviet Union) was rational and that the crisis in the alliance was real... If the US did not provide a surer strategic concept, the consequence would probably be a move by the allies to try and develop their own nuclear stocks...or turn to neutralism and a withdrawal from NATO to cut separate deals for peace with the Soviet Union.[94]

For political reasons, the US should not deny its allies' legitimate aspirations to possess nuclear weapons.[95] The device hit upon to re-establish confidence in the military arrangements of the Alliance was the sharing of tactical atomic weapons by the US with all its NATO partners. Nuclear aspirations, properly channelled, could also become the crucial spur to European integration. This would solve the problem of Germany's special status; it was the best alternative to either independent nuclear arsenals or neutralism on the part of the allies, and it would place the American multipolarity scenario back on track.[96]

The European partners welcomed Adenauer's appeal to 'Europeanise' NATO- Europe's defense and to upgrade the WEU. At first (in the autumn of 1956) France was more interested in reintroducing the scheme of a European defense production community, which it had been unable to get accepted in the negotiations on the WEU and on implementing the agreements relating to it (November 1954–April 1955).[97] Under the impact of the Suez and Hungary crises and Adenauer's 'helpful fixer' role in settling the crisis in the EEC negotiations in early November 1956, the French acted on lines congruent with Adenauer's goals; France urged the US (in June 1957) to discuss within NATO councils the question of creating an integrated NATO stockpile of nuclear weapons.[98] France also appeared willing to contribute to an equilibrium between 'modern' and conventional weapons and support the principle of collective balanced forces, but the question of control over all nuclear weapons located on French territory had to be solved first.[99] Under the impact of the Sputnik shock, the US accelerated its deliberations and finally presented a scheme to the North Atlantic Council in December 1957. Further, France cooperated with Italy and the FRG on questions of research, design and development of rockets, missiles and atomic weapons; the US was not only informed about the trilateral impetus,[100] but offered morale and material support.

The problem was with Britain. At that time still the only Western European nuclear power, Britain wanted to become the trustee for all Western Europe in this matter. What could Britain give to Europe? Most importantly, how far could Britain afford to 'Europeanise' her nuclear power?[101] Was European cooperation more advantageous for expanding Britain's nuclear production than cooperation with the US on research and development? Some Cabinet Ministers, such as Selwyn Lloyd and Julian Amery, were convinced that Britain for political reasons could not afford to rebuff Western Europe[102] a third time, after leaving the round of Messina talks and cutting down the BAOR and the air strike component.[103] By pooling British resources with those of the European allies, Britain 'might be able both to reduce [her] own defense burden and to develop within NATO a group almost as powerful as the US'.[104] The idea behind the proposal for the WEU to become a nuclear force was that this might offer Britain valuable opportunities not only for cooperation with continental European countries in arms development and production, but also over the wider field of relations with the Six. It was a persuasive argument, well-tuned to the thinking of people like Adenauer, Spaak, Monnet, Pinay and Mollet.

The general agreement in Cabinet, however, was that a fresh initiative towards closer European cooperation should not be based on proposals for cooperation in the development of nuclear weapons. For one thing, Britain's position as first-class power after Suez seemed to depend upon American backing, especially with Britain's entering into the missile age of strategic deterrence and the continuing dollar support for British defense and the economy.[105] Conversely, British leverage in Washington was bound to increase after the US decision to base IRBMs (THOR) in the UK,[106] which dated back to July 1956. The US depended – at least for the interval period before ICBMs would become available (i.e. 1963) – on the UK in order to provide a strategic deterrent for NATO. Defense Minister Sandys had resisted American pressures[107] 'to leave the nuclear role chiefly to the US and to maintain their [the British] conventional forces with the financial savings that could thereby ensue'. Secondly, Britain would simply not be able over the next 7–10 years to supply the European allies with nuclear weapons; Britain herself depended on American supplies, and the US could supply European needs, if Washington so desired, within a year. Since the US policy was that Western Europe should remain dependent on the US for its supply of nuclear warheads, the US always had a headstart over the UK.[108] Thirdly, Macmillan and the Cabinet majority defined Britain's posture differently: '...the need for us is to trim our cloth on a world-wide basis before turning to European questions.'[109] Although Whitehall knew that 'Britain had to bear in mind the growing importance of Europe to our defence',[110] the view prevailed that 'it is doubtful if Europe is the right place to spend the money there, and in any event the money is not there to spend.'[111] Confronted with the choice between increasing dependance on the US and closer association with Europe, Britain attempted to become an independent third actor.

This was jockeying for position. The Macmillan cabinet wanted to explore the chances for rebuilding the Anglo-American Alliance to its former strength[112] and speculated that Britain might once again turn a European failure (EDC in 1954; possible failure of the EEC) to good account by a British initiative (Free Trade Area/'Plan G').[113] The fact was that from London's perspective the Europeans were more concerned about American weakness than about their own, and this did not seem a good basis from which the European countries could act together effectively and consistently as a political unit. Why, then, should not Britain try to become the third power centre? What Britain had to offer Europe – the capital markets of the City of London, access to the sterling area, nuclear deterrent – could be better used for revitalising Britain's role as the West's second centre of command: a highly effective sterling area could complement and temporarily substitute for the US in case a recession prevented the US from exercising constructive leadership in the world economy, and an independent nuclear deterrent could assure Europe and the Commonwealth that they were safe even though the US might temporarily fail to meet its responsibilities.

The British case could not convince France and Germany. To them, the new British defense priorities implied a rearrangement of tasks which would make the US and UK solely responsible for the nuclear deterrent.[114] The British insisted on reserving decisions on strategic systems for the Anglo-American Alliance within NATO; SACEUR should not be elevated into a position of authority over NATO as a fourth nuclear power.[115] The Macmillan government was worried about the intentions of France to go ahead with a programme for the production of nuclear weapons and that France might invite Germany to collaborate; if some measure of control over proliferation of nuclear weapons could be established, the British were in favour.[116]

Parallel to this claim for first-class status along with the US, Britain – for economic and financial, but also political-strategic reasons – consistently pursued with regard to her continental commitments the policy of 'fewer men and better arms'. Hence the WEU failed in its purpose as a platform for aiming at 'unity of purpose' in NATO-Europe: it discussed off-set agreements as a means of mitigating the immediate effect of British troop reductions, whereas the big issue of the right balance between conventional, tactical and strategic forces within NATO and NATO's positions in comparison to Soviet disposals were kept outside the scope of the WEU. The FRG had hoped that after the settlement of the Saar question (in October 1956) the WEU could be developed into an instrument for coordinating the foreign and defense policies of the Seven; as there was no other European organisation in place to meet the demand for political consultations, the WEU should be designated for these tasks.[117]

The German interest in elevating the scope and level of the WEU, however, went beyond political consultations. In a series of interviews in the aftermath of the Bundestag debate on 2 April 1957, Defense Minister F.J. Strauß made the continued self-denial of Germany in the nuclear field conditional on German participation in a WEU framework. The Treaty, Strauß postulated, neither prohibited German research nor ruled out German participation in producing parts of the weapons system, provided the WEU partners agreed to this. Weapon systems thus developed and produced would then come under WEU control. Strauß obviously assumed that his French opposite number, Bourgès-Maunory, had the French Government's approval when discussing atomic cooperation with the Germans since January 1957. In a press conference on 5 April 1957, Adenauer mentioned the possibility of German participation in the joint production of atomic weapons with her European partners. The FRG obviously attempted to turn the WEU into an 'nuclearised EDC'.[118]

The Americans welcomed closer cooperation on research, development and production of armaments in the WEU,[119] but they were against the political development of WEU.[120] For Britain and France the WEU was primarily a controlling agency, or perhaps a means for getting arms production agreements, but on their own economic terms; the German concept implied that the control functions should be reduced or eliminated in order to establish the basis for consultations among equals. France wanted to follow the British model, if the US allowed this, or 'go nuclear on its own'; both ruled out the possibility that the FRG – via WEU and/or NATO – should become a nuclear power. If the WEU were to become the means for importing the consequences of the Anglo-Saxon nuclear strategy for NATO into continental Western Europe, it would have to reconsider whether the restrictive attitude towards German rearmament should be revised, or alterna-

tively whether the British and the French might have to accept
some WEU controls in order to attain non-discrimination and
equality of status for the FRG. If France and Britain were appre-
hensive about Germany getting free access to nuclear weapons in
the WEU framework, and if the European nuclear powers developed national independent deterrent forces, then Germany could
and did turn to the US in order to gain the right of nuclear co-
determination within NATO.[121]

Since discussion of the critical issues became taboo within the
WEU, the organisation simply lived on with its natural defects.[122]
As long as the EEC did not venture into high politics or take decisions on security, defense and disarmament matters, there was no
need for Britain to play the WEU card; for London, the WEU was
a residual power. The Six were lacking in strength as WEU members, and were therefore unable to press too hard for the upgrad-
ing of the WEU. Germany was reminded of its defaults concerning
the contribution expected from the Bundeswehr. The French
were criticised for pulling forces out of NATO-Europe to meet
their Algerian burden, whilst at the same time shifting funds into
the nuclear field. Why, then, did Paris and Bonn insist that Britain
remain faithful to the 1954 obligations? On the other hand, the
British government was in a quandary as a result of its call on
SACEUR to assess Britain's force reductions in the context of the
Minimum Forces Requirements planning exercise (MC 70,
1957–63). London feared the effect SACEUR's presentation might
have on the difficult negotiations for the association of the Free
Trade Area with the EEC, comprising Britain's six partners in
WEU.

The unexpected success of the EEC and the likelihood that
France would and could prevent the British FTA project from sub-
merging the EEC into a modified OEEC pattern caught Britain on
the wrong foot: 'If the Common Market were created without the
Free Trade Area, that would cause a division in Europe.'[123] This
split had ramifications not only for the economic, but also on the
political-strategic, landscape in Europe.

> France was now envisaging creating a community with
> Germany, whereas then she had been seeking British participa-
> tion to balance the German contribution... The conditions
> which underlay the UK guarantees a few years back to maintain
> specified forces on the Continent were out of date, since it had
> become obvious that France no longer feared Germany, but on

the contrary was proceeding with ever closer cooperation and integration with Germany in such fields as atomic energy, common market...[124]

Germany was prepared to pay an economic price for French political help, since a Franco-German alliance could prevent the 'Anglo-Saxons' from doing a deal with the Soviet Union at Germany's expense over disengagement, zones of arms limitation, recognition of the Oder-Neiße border, and permissiveness towards the GDR's acting as agent of the Soviet Union with regard to access routes to Berlin. This was the basic new determining factor in the balance of power within the Alliance. British expectations that for economic reasons the FRG would have to support Britain's interests – first by supporting the FTA idea, then by helping Britain into the EEC – and would therefore be forced to restrain France, were wishful thinking.

Britain, however, had three options. The first option was to attempt to come to terms with France directly. However, until late 1959, the view prevailed that Britain should do nothing to advance French weapons programmes, due to the agreements at the March 1957 Bermuda Conference.[125] The second option was that Britain could calculate that neither the EEC Six nor the WEU would survive if NATO collapsed; if Britain could contribute to holding NATO together and at the same time maintain the privileged position of principal influence on US policy,[126] it could expect Western Europe to take a helpful attitude over British interests in Europe. Third, London could postulate that closer political cooperation (e.g. via the WEU) had to depend on the willingness of the Six to accommodate to Britain's vital interest in the Free Trade Area project:[127] As Macmillan said to Adenauer in October 1958:

> No British Government could continue to take part in the military defence of a continent which had declared economic war on her.[128]

Conclusion

Confronted with Stalin's deliberate manoeuvres to incorporate Eastern Europe into the communist orbit but at the same time claim a voice in the affairs of Western Europe, the Western powers decided in reaction to cut Germany in two and merge West

Germany into the West. This move seemed inescapable because the USSR possessed important advantages when bargaining for supremacy over Germany. There was first Moscow's determination to make the Western powers accept the Oder-Neiße line as the western border of Poland, which enabled the Kremlin to remain the arbiter in any comprehensive settlement of European Security and Germany; there was second its hold on the GDR and Berlin, which allowed the Kremlin to test West Germany's willingness to cooperate with the Western allies as well as the Western powers' resolve to compete with Moscow in supporting the vital interests of their own German state.

The problem for the Western powers was that their individual and collective interest in tying West Germany firmly to the West did not easily translate into an agreement about the particular system into which West Germany should be integrated. Such a system had not merely to suit the political, military-strategic and economic interests of the USA, Britain and France, which regarded themselves as global actors, but also had to grant West Germany, the potential hegemonic power in the region, 'integration with equality'. Germany's claim to parity with France and Britain – inherent in any scheme of European integration – was conceivable in Western economic systems (OEEC/OECD, IMF/World Bank) and practised in the ECSC and EEC, but Britain and France were resolved to mark the difference between themselves and the Bonn Republic in the domain of defence (*Sicherheitspolitik*).

In order to attain parity with the US and Britain in the Nuclear Age France risked the demise of the EDC, which had been invented by the French to solve Western Europe's security dilemma. At first, the demise of the EDC was a blessing in disguise: Bonn, with a view to the principle of balanced collective forces in NATO, surrendered its claim to nuclear rearmament, whilst France at this stage (the late summer of 1954) still conceived of the *force de dissuasion* in the context of a security community with the US and Britain within NATO. Nevertheless, the nuclearisation of NATO's strategy and force structure enhanced the divisiveness of nuclear diplomacy: the differences in status and in capacity to influence the White House as the bringer of security to NATO-Europe were replicated in differences between zones of security (for example, British and French territory was regarded as a sanctuary). These differences were further enhanced by the nuclear powers' interest in negotiating with the USSR about zones of force reduction; the

USSR's full-fledged military power (ICBMs, MRBMs, sea power, theatre weapons and conventional armed forces) allowed the Kremlin to threaten simultaneously both the US and Western Europe.

Realising that NATO was in chronic crisis, Washington, Paris and Bonn considered European solutions to ensure that West Germany would be anchored firmly in the West. Although Britain shared this goal, London was not willing yet to give up its ambitions as a global power and to accept merely a European role. Rather, the Eden and Macmillan governments' 'three No's' to Europe – no to reducing the land and air force contributions to WEU/NATO, no to non-participation in founding the EEC, and no to building up an independent nuclear force rather than cooperating with Western Europe – reflected their resolve to re-activate Britain's position as an independent, though US-connected, second centre of command of the West. Without Britain, no Western European organisation could even think of tackling the problems of community-building, including defense and foreign relations with the US and the East. Britain still thought of leading Western Europe from outside – via the Anglo-American duopoly within NATO and as the hub of the Sterling area – but also envisaged an era of negotiations with the USSR in which the problems of European security and Germany might be settled. For Britain, there were other means than 'entanglement' in European integration to solve the problems deriving from the division of Europe and of Germany.

Notes

1. Footnotes are restricted to direct references to sources and the most relevant literature. Whenever documents have been published elsewhere, the footnote refers to the more accessible printed work.
2. Record of Third Tripartite Official Meeting, 27 April 1950, in *Documents on British Policy Overseas (DBPO)*, R. Bullen and M.E. Pelly (eds), London, 1987, 2nd ser., vol. II, No. 40, p. 149.
3. K. Schwabe, 'The Origins of the United States' Engagement in Europe, 1946–1952', in F. Heller and J. Gillingham (eds), *NATO: The Founding of the Atlantic Alliance and the Integration of Europe*, London, 1992, pp. 185f.
4. Schwabe, 'Origins', p. 175; cf. T. Ireland, *Creating the Entangling Alliance: The Origins of the North Atlantic Treaty Organisation*, London,

1981; L.S. Kaplan, *The United States and NATO: The Formative Years*, Lexington, 1984; M. Knapp (ed.), *Transatlantische Beziehungen. Die USA und Europa zwischen gemeinsamen Interessen und Konflikt*, Stuttgart, 1990; W.C. Cromwell, *The United States and the European Pillar: The Strained Alliance*, London, 1992.

5. National Security Council (NSC) 162/2, in *Foreign Relations of the United States (FRUS)*, vol.V, p. 714.

6. The phrase was coined by Orme Sargent with a view to the 1945 Potsdam Conference, in *DBPO*, 1st ser., vol. I, No. 102.

7. In view of the ambiguity between common vital interests and conflicting objectives of the western powers, it is not surprising that the American, British, French and German options for closer cooperation either within an expanded or reformed NATO or EDC-WEU framework or within OEEC or EDC/EEC shifted according to their recent experience, such as how far NATO served British or French purposes to attain an 'equal' role with the US in the planning of Western defense (tripartism or Anglo-American duopoly?) and to what extent the US were able and willing to support British and French ambitions as global actors. The option also depended on the view of NATO/WEU or European integration as the principal organisation for solving the question of German 'equality'.

8. A.S. Milward, 'NATO, OEEC, and the Integration of Europe', in Heller/Gillingham (eds), *NATO*, p. 242.

9. Ibid., pp. 241ff.

10. Ibid., p. 247.

11. United States Mission to the NATO and European Regional Organisations (USRO) to Livingston Merchant, Assistant Secretary of State for European Affairs, 23 September 1955.

12. President Eisenhower announced his programme on 8 December 1953; at about the same time, he warned Lord Ismay, Secretary-General of NATO, that non-ratification of the EDC would not only provoke an agonising reappraisal of the US's commitments, but also hinder the cooperation in the use of atomic energy for civilian purposes. Jacques Martin, French chargé d'affaires at the French Embassy in Washington, regarded the Eisenhower proposal – atoms for peace – as a threat to France's independent freedom of choice; G.-H. Soutou, 'La politique nucléaire de Pierre Mendès France', *Relations internationales*, no. 59, 1989, p.319.

13. Schwabe, 'Origins', p. 176f.

14. St. Weber, 'Shaping the postwar balance of power: multilateralism in NATO', *International Organisation*, vol.46/3, 1992, pp. 650 f.

15. Ibid., pp. 651/2.

16. H. Macmillan, 'European Integration', Memorandum, 16 January 1952, *DBPO*, 2nd. ser., vol. I, pp. 812ff.; see B. Ebersold, *Machtverfall und Machtbewußtsein. Britische Friedens- und Konfliktlösungsstrategien*

1918–1956, München, 1992, pp. 350ff., on European objections to Britain's claim for leading Europe from London.

17. C.S. Maier, 'Alliance and Autonomy: European Identity and US Foreign Policy Objectives in the Truman Years', in M.J. Lacey (ed.), *The Truman Presidency*, Cambridge, 1989, p. 289.

18. W.I. Mallet, Assistant Undersecretary of State superintending Western Organisations department, *DBPO*, 2nd ser., vol. III, No. 105.

19. The US, due to its role as the central provider of security, might benefit, if NATO was transformed into a comprehensive military, economic, fiscal and political organisation; on the other hand, however, expanding NATO in such manner would require the US to become a member on full terms of an integrated system; this was not to be expected of the Western superpower. Furthermore, from the very beginning of NATO the US was aware that British (Bevin's) and French (Bidault's) proposals of a Western European Union 'had only one specific aim, to enlist American support in the military defense of Europe'. This was Marshall's reaction to Bevin's plan for a Western European Union; see Schwabe, 'Origins', pp. 169ff. Washington suspected that the invitation to the US to bolster European morale and guarantee Western Europe's security was based on the assumption that Britain, France and the other Western European colonial powers would thereby feel relieved on the European 'front' and concentrate their resources instead on maintaining their overseas assets. The view from Washington was that the Allies' willingness to follow the lead of the US and have NATO turned into an economic organisation reflected the hope of extracting some more money and aid out of the US: J.F.Dulles and Eisenhower, NAC meeting, 5 May 1956, in *FRUS*, 1955–1957, vol. IV, p. 75.

20. P. Windsor, *German Reunification*, London, 1969, p. 23.

21. Robinson, Special Assistant to the American Ambassador in France, to Bowie, Policy Planning Staff, 27 December 1955, in *FRUS*, 1955–1957, vol. IV, pp. 378ff.

22. H.-J. Rupieper, 'Die Berliner Außenministerkonferenz von 1954', *Vierteljahrshefte für Zeitgeschichte*, vol. 34, no. 3, 1986, p. 433.

23. In response to President Eisenhower's atoms-for-peace campaign, Strauß and Erhard supported German industrialists in their claim for a bilateral agreement. See W. Bührer, 'Der BDI und die Außenpolitik der Bundesrepublik in den 50er Jahren', *Vierteljahrshefte für Zeitgeschichte*, vol. 40, no. 2, 1992, p. 258; also *FRUS*, 1955–57, vol. IV, pp. 335ff.

24. G.F. Treverton, 'America's stakes and choices in Europe', *Survival*, vol. 34, no. 3, 1992, p. 22; Gustav Schmidt, 'Großbritannien, die Gründung der Europäischen Wirtschaftsgemeinschaft und die

'Sicherheit des Westens': "The American Connection"', in M.
Salewski (ed.), *Nationale Identität und Europäische Integration*,
Göttingen, 1991, pp. 169–231.

25. Bedell Smith, according to Watson's report to Frank Roberts, 16
August 1954, FO 800–810, in reaction to Churchill's message to J.F.
Dulles; G. Schmidt 'Großbritannien' (note 24).

26. S. Dockrill, *Britain's Policy for West German Rearmament 1950–1955*,
Cambridge, 1991, p. 111.

27. G. Schmidt, 'Die politischen und sicherheitspolitischen
Dimensionen der britischen Europapolitik 1955/6 – 1963/4', in
Schmidt (ed.), *Großbritannien und Europa – Großbritannien in Europa*,
Bochum, 1989, pp. 169–252.

28. The 'classic statement' of Britain's posture is by Prime Minister
Attlee, 30 August 1951, CP (51) 239, CAB. 129–47: '...it is our aim to
foster the idea of an Atlantic rather than a purely European community, although we believe that closer continental integration on a
supranational basis is not necessarily inconsistent with our conception of the larger entity...the independent position of the U.K.
enables us in cooperation with America to play a very special and
important role in the free world... closer dependance on the
Continent would impair that position...it is thus in the interests of
the US and the other Western countries that we should maintain
our independent position.'

29. S. Dockrill, *Britain's*, p.110 (concerning Britain's stocktaking in
1952); G. Schmidt, 'Die sicherheitspolitischen und wirtschaftlichen
Dimensionen der britisch-amerikanischen Beziehungen
1955–1967', *Militärgeschichtliche Mitteilungen*, vol. 50, 1991, No. 2, pp.
107–42.

30. Macmillan, 'The EDC and European Unity,' 19 March 1953, CAB
129–57.

31. The competing models within the national political systems for
organising Western Europe are analysed in a masterpiece by W.
Loth, 'Französische Deutschlandbilder nach dem zweiten
Weltkrieg', in M. Grunewald and J. Schlobach (eds),
*Médiations/Vermittlungen. Aspects des relations franco-allemandes du
XVIIe siècle à nos jours*, Bern, 1992, pp. 343–52. I am aware that pass-
ing over this aspect in my article might be misleading.

32. B. Thoß, 'Sicherheits- und deutschlandpolitische Komponenten
der europäischen Integration zwischen EVG und EWG 1954–1957',
in L. Herbst et al. (eds), *Vom Marshallplan zur EWG*, München 1990,
pp. 476f.

33. Schwabe, 'Origins', pp. 176ff.

34. In this sense, the US was willing to win over the French on the main
issues at stake and comply to French requests; see *DBPO*, 2nd ser.,
vol. II, No. 62, on French objections to Germany's rearmament.

The Americans supported French demands for economic and political controls on Germany.

35. Schwabe, 'Origins', pp. 180ff.

36. G. Wettig, *Entmilitarisierung und Wiederbewaffnung in Deutschland, 1943– 1955*, München, 1967, pp. 571ff.

37. K. Maier, 'Die Auseinandersetzungen um die EVG als europäisches Unterbündnis der NATO 1950–1954', in B. Thoß and H.-E. Volkmann (eds), *Zwischen Kaltem Krieg und Entspannung. Sicherheits- und Deutschlandpolitik im Mächtesystem der Jahre 1953–1956*, Boppard am Rhein, 1988, p. 450. President Eisenhower was the leading representative of the view that the US commitment of armed forces was temporary, until Europe recovered; a united Europe would have the resources to sustain a reliable defense force against the USSR, if EDC (and later on WEU) and the US – via NATO – were connected.

38. Acheson to Schuman, December 1950, cf. Schwabe, 'Origins', pp. 181–3.

39. Ibid., p. 184.

40. Dockrill, *Britain's*, pp. 110ff.

41. C (52) 434, 'EDC and Alternative Plans', 10 December 1952, CAB. 129 – 57.

42. W. Churchill, August 1954, in K. Maier, 'Auseinandersetzungen', p. 462. The British Chiefs of Staff, in a memorandum of 15 September 1954, agreed that the Government had to accept the risks involved in the commitment to station its present forces indefinitely on the Continent, if that would prevent the US from adopting a strategy of periphery defense, but the commitment had to be subject to financial and overseas escape clauses; Ambassador Steel (from Bonn), on 10 September 1954, had recommended a similar position. Prime Minister Churchill, however, opposed these 'forward ideas' for that meant to honour France for her contemptuous attitudes: Churchill to Eden, 9 September 1954, Ge/54/28, FO 800–795.

43. Maier, 'Auseinandersetzungen', p. 463; H.-H. Jansen, *Großbritannien, das Scheitern der EVG und der NATO-Beitritt der Bundesrepublik Deutschland*, Bochum, 1992, pp. 167ff.

44. Hancock (Foreign Office) in conversation with Robertson, Canadian High Commissioner, 27 November 1956, Canadian High Commission to Department of External Affairs, Ottawa, Tel. 1674, 'NATO Military Reappraisal', Public Archives Canada (PAC), Record Group (RG) 25, file 50030–AG–I–40.

45. On Britain's views see below.

46. On the connection between the planning exercises of the General Staff of the French Army in June and September 1954 and the briefing of Mendès France for his meeting with Molotov on 21 July 1954, see K. Maier, 'Auseinandersetzungen', pp. 456ff., 459f.; Maier refers to R. Girault's contribution in F. Bédarida and P. Rioux (eds), *Pierre*

Mendès France et le Mendésisme, Paris, 1984. The Quai d'Orsay recommended the finding of an alternative solution to EDC for the FRG and consulting Britain about this; *Documents Diplomatiques Francais*, vol. 27.7.–31.12.1954, No. 1, pp. 1ff. The Soviet Union sent a note on 24 July calling for a European Security Conference; the proposal to include Red China raised doubts about the sincerity of the proposition. On 4 July Churchill, too, initiated a conference project.

47. Milward, 'NATO', p. 250.
48. Maier, 'Auseinandersetzungen', pp. 459ff. summarises the available information.
49. Therefore the government pushed for amending the stipulation in the EDC Treaty – which was to be transmitted into any replacement – so that France did safeguard an option for developing into a military nuclear power. France insisted on altering the regulation that any annual production of more than 500g nuclear fuel had to be registered as nuclear war material and must be approved by the Commissariat.
50. J. Bariéty, 'Das Scheitern der EVG und das Pariser Abkommen vom Oktober 1954 aus französischer Sicht', Vortrag auf dem Internationalen Kongreß zur Zeitgeschichte der Akademie Tutzing, 13.–17.Mai 1991, published in R. Steininger et al., (eds), *Die doppelte Eindämmung. Europäische Sicherheit und deutsche Frage in den Fünfzigern*, Mainz/München, 1993, pp. 99–131; see also the contributions by A. Coutrot, 'La politique atomique sous le gouvernment de Mendès France', and R. Girault, 'La France dans les rapports Est-Ouest au temps de la présidence de Pierre Mèndes France', in Bédarida and Rioux (eds), *Pierre Mendès France*; G.-H. Soutou, 'Die Nuklearpolitik der Vierten Republik', *Vierteljahrshefte für Zeitgeschichte*, vol. 37, 1989, pp. 605–10; K. Maier, 'Auseinandersetzungen', p. 459ff.
51. Soutou, 'Politique nucléaire', pp. 322ff.; E. Conze, 'La coopération franco-germano-italienne dans le domaine nucléaire dans les années 1957/8: un point de vue allemand', *Revue d'Histoire diplomatique*, vol. 102, 1990, pp.115–32.
52. Maier, 'Auseinandersetzungen', p.460.
53. Jansen, *Großbritannien*, pp. 181ff., 238 ff.
54. The 'high' principle did not pay any political dividends, because the delays in the build-up of the *Bundeswehr* undermined Germany's claims for parity.
55. Amt Blank, Memo, 'Forderungen der BR im Falle einer anderen Lösung als der EVG für deutschen Verteidigungsbeitrag', 7 July 1954, quoted by Maier, 'Auseinandersetzungen', pp. 463ff.
56. France, indeed, demanded safeguards, i.e. control and denial of producing certain weapons systems in strategically exposed areas;

Britain wanted to put a number of ceilings on certain weapons systems, but was less rigid; Germany could comply with Britain's demands. Jansen, *Großbritannien*, pp. 232ff., 238ff.

57. Adenauer extended his declaration on ABC weapons to comprise rockets, missiles of wider range, strategic bomber aircraft. Mendés France was not satisfied with Adenauer's statement. Jansen, *Großbritannien*, pp. 180f., 240ff.

58. 'US Policy toward Europe – post EDC', Memo by Fuller, 10 September 1954, *FRUS*, vol. V, pp. 1170–7.

59. Report on Secretary of State's Conversations with Chancellor Adenauer and Foreign Secretary Eden, September 16–17, 1954, in *FRUS*, vol. V, pp. 1209–23, p. 1217.

60. Joint Chiefs of Staff Memo to Dulles, 22 September 1954.

61. Maier, 'Auseinandersetzungen', pp. 463ff.; Jansen, *Großbritannien*, pp. 224ff.

62. Eden–Adenauer meeting in Bonn, 12 Sept. 1954. Adenauer moved towards Eden's ideas; he no longer pursued association models or assigning German forces directly to SACEUR, as he had suggested on 3 Sept.1954 to Hoyer Millar, much to the dismay of Blankenhorn and Hallstein. Hallstein seemed to prefer to get on with Britain, without caring for the US; the German minutes tell about Britain's 'Mittler-Stellung'; Hoyer Millar did not wish to consider passing over the US.

63. Memo of conversation between Adenauer and Prime Minister Scelba, 26 March 1954, Archiv des Auswärtigen Amtes, Politische Abteilung, III, 232–00. Adenauer explained that if the Russians could not succeed in separating the US and NATO-Europe, they would realise that they had to accommodate to the presence of the US as a European power and therefore could not induce one country after another to court the Kremlin.

64. Jansen, *Großbritannien*, p. 67. However, some crucial decisions had already been taken: in November 1953, London decided to participate in integrated headquarters for the air defence of the EDC; in March 1954 the assignment of one armoured division to an European Army, if SACEUR asked for this, was envisioned. S. Dockrill, 'The Evolution of Britain's Policy towards a European Army 1950–54', *Journal of Strategic Studies*, vol. 12, 1989, pp. 38–58, pp. 54ff.

65. C (54) 276, 'Alternatives to the EDC', 27 August 1954, PREM 11–618.

66. FO Memo, August 1954, listed the arguments pro and contra a European solution or a confederated NATO solution. Jansen, *Großbritannien*, pp. 67ff.

67. On the relationships between bloc consolidation, East-West negotiations and the division of Germany and Europe see G. Schmidt,

'Divided Europe – Divided Germany (1950–1963)', *Contemporary European History*, vol. III, no. 2, 1994, pp. 155–92

68. Dulles's comments and statements both at the Bermuda meetings and at the NAC meeting on 14 December 1953 were tuned to the 'agonizing reappraisal' theme.

69. Maier, 'Auseinandersetzungen', p. 451.

70. *FRUS*, 1952–54, vol. V, pt. 2; cf. Dulles Memo to Joint Chiefs of Staff, 16 Oct. 1953; R.J. Watson, *History of the Joint Chiefs of Staff*, vol. 5: *The Joint Chiefs of Staff and National Policy 1953–1954*, Washington, D.C. 1986, p. 27.

71. K.A. Maier,'Amerikanische Nuklearstrategie unter Truman und Eisenhower', in Maier and N. Wiggershaus, (eds), *Das Nordatlantische Bündnis 1949–1956*, München, 1993, pp. 225–240.

72. Thoß, 'Sicherheits- und deutschlandpolitische Komponenten' p. 476.

73. This aspect was related to deliberations on how to help Adenauer win the next election; on this see for instance: C.P.(57)6, 'The Grand Design', 5 January 1957, PREM 11–2136. The motivation was always present in British and US deliberations.

74. W. Hallstein, in the spring of 1955, quoted by Thoß, 'Sicherheits- und deutschlandpolitische Komponenten', p. 485.

75. The note of 15 January 1955 started the Soviet propaganda offensive.

76. H. Macmillan, *Riding the Storm: 1956–59*, London, 1971, p. 67.

77. Dulles, late January 1956, draft for meeting with Eden, in *FRUS*, vol. IV, pp. 399f.

78. Dulles-Macmillan conversation, 15 Dec. 1955, in *FRUS*, 1955–1957, vol. IV, p. 27.

79. Dulles, report to State Department on NAC meetings, 17 Dec. 1955, in *FRUS*, vol. IV, pp. 369–371.

80. Robinson to Bowie, 27 Dec. 1955, *FRUS*, vol. IV, pp. 378ff. It was irritating both to the US and to Adenauer that Britain's opposition to the projects of the Six might encourage a strange alignment with German industrialists, nationalists, but also 'free traders' (Erhard), who supported Strauß' endeavours to attain a national atomic energy policy and a bilateral treaty with the US. Conversation between Dulles, Monnet and Bowie, 17 December 1955, in *FRUS*, vol. IV, pp. 367ff.; Dulles to Macmillan, 10 December 1955, ibid., pp. 362ff.

81. Thoß, 'Sicherheits- und deutschlandpolitische Komponenten', p. 492.

82. Robinson to Bowie, 27 Dec. 1955, *FRUS*, vol. IV, pp. 378ff.

83. NSC, 267th meeting, 21 Nov. 1955, *FRUS*, IV, p. 349 and p. 351. Eisenhower added another reason: since the Soviet Union aimed at overtaking Western Europe's GNP – by 1975 or about – Western Europe had to accelerate the process of pooling resources and develop a strategy of common purpose; memo, prepared in the Office of European regional affairs, 6 December 1955, in *FRUS*, vol. IV, pp. 351ff.

84. Hancock's briefing for the 'old dominions' on British views on the 1956 NAC meeting, Canadian High Commission, London, to DEA, Tel. No. 1742, PAC, RG 25, file 50030-AG-1–40.
85. Parsons to Elbrick, 9 Oct. 1956, in *FRUS*, vol. IV, pp. 473 f.
86. Thoß, 'Sicherheits- und deutschlandpolitische Komponenten', p. 489.
87. The US and Britain resolved to deploy tactical atomic weapons with their land and air forces stationed in Germany; France, too, was about to restructure its forces. H.-P. Schwarz, *Geschichte der Bundesrepublik, vol. 2: Die Ära Adenauer*, Stuttgart, 1981, p. 359.
88. When Macmillan tried to 'sell' the philosophy of the Defense White Paper to Adenauer on his visit in Bonn in May 1957, Adenauer was confirmed in his view that the Bundeswehr had to get atomic weapons; see reports in *The Times* and *Frankfurter Allgemeine Zeitung* (FAZ), 8 May 1957. Replying to the *Große Anfrage der SPD* on 2nd April 1957, Adenauer explained his concerns about the centrifugal tendencies in NATO resulting from Britain's decision; this speech is known for Adenauer's made famous remark that atomic weapons were nothing else but an advanced type of artillery. President Eisenhower, formerly SACEUR, made similar remarks.
89. K. Adenauer, *Erinnerungen 1955–1959*, Stuttgart, 1971, pp. 219ff.; H.G. Pöttering, *Adenauers Sicherheitspolitik 1955–1963*, Düsseldorf, 1975, pp. 62ff. Adenauer explained his views to Gaitskell in mid-September 1956; H.-P. Schwarz, *Adenauer: Der Staatsmann 1952–1967*, Stuttgart, 1991, p. 296. Adenauer realised that the Soviet Union could make its influence felt in Europe as well as in North Africa, the Near and the Middle East, and in Southeast Asia; the US seemed uncertain as to how to react to the global presence of the USSR. This, then, surely was the moment where 'Europe' must begin to provide its own armed forces.
90. Report, Canadian Embassy to Department of External Affairs, 4 Oct.1956, on German Defense Contribution and US-German Relations; the report referred to a meeting between Adenauer and R. Murphy and Deputy Defense Minister Quarles, National Archives, Washington, Box 3560, File 762 A.5/10 – 456 OS/G.
91. Record of conference between President Eisenhower, J.F. Dulles, Goodpaster and Hoover, 15 Dec. 1956, *FRUS*, IV, pp. 164/5.
92. Record of meeting, Palais Schaumburg, 8 Oct. 1958, between Adenauer and Macmillan, PREM 11 – 2328; Adenauer recalled a conversation that he had with Dulles in December 1957 about possible trends in American policy.
93. GEN 564, 1st meeting, 18 Dec. 1956, 'Long Term Defence Programme', CAB 130 –122.
94. Dulles in a conversation with Adenauer, Dec. 1957; Weber, 'Shaping', p. 660.

95. Memorandum on conversation between Dulles and Macmillan, NAC, 15 Dec. 1957, *FRUS*, vol. IV, pp. 224 ff.

96. Weber, Shaping', pp. 641ff., 661ff.

97. Thoß, 'Sicherheits- und deutschlandpolitische Komponenten', p. 489.

98. Dulles to Radford, 27 June 1957, about General Ely's proposal for an agenda of the Franco-American talks in Paris (new weapons for the French Army, establishment of integrated parts for atomic weapons in Europe, equilibrium between modern and conventional weapons for western defense), NA 9B, RG 59, CDF 1955–59, Box 2507, file 611–51.

99. In December 1957, the NAC agreed to pursue the idea of an atomic stockpile; the French called for bilateral talks to resolve the control problem. When Dulles finally came to Paris in early July 1958, de Gaulle was in power.

100. General Heusinger, who accompanied Strauß to his talks with Bourgès-Maunory in January 1957, informed NATO staffs about the meetings.

101. Julian Amery to Macmillan, 12 June 1957, PREM 11–1333.

102. Selwyn Lloyd, 8 January 1957, C.M. (57) 3rd Conclusions, 'Political and military association', PREM 11–2136.

103. The Foreign Office warned that the Defense White Paper (March 1957) must create the impression that Britain was pulling out of Europe; Hoyer Millar to Secretary of State, 15 March 1957, FO 371–129 307.

104. Statement by Foreign Secretary, Selwyn Lloyd, in Cabinet, 8 January 1957. The FO paper – C.P. (57)6, 'The Grand Design', 5 January 1957; PREM 11–2136 – emphasised that Britain would bankrupt itself if it tried to possess the ingredients of great power status, i.e. conventional forces and the whole range of nuclear weapons. In a letter to Macmillan – 15 Febr. 1960, PM/ 60/12, PREM 11–2998 – Lloyd reviewed the development from 1956 to 1960; Macmillan to Lloyd, 22 Dec. 1959, PREM 11–2991.

105. Schmidt, 'Politische Dimensionen', pp. 180ff.

106. J.P.G. Freeman, *Britain's Nuclear Arms Control Policy in the Context of Anglo-American Relations, 1957–1968*, London, 1986, p. 89.

107. This refers to Sandys' visit to Washington in January 1957, DEFE 7-1756; Ambassador D. Wilgress, 15 Oct.1957, Tel. 4206, 'The present position of NATO', PAC, RG 25, file 50030-AG-1-40.

108. Cabinet Conclusions, 8 January 1957.

109. Briefing for Bermuda, GEN 572/2nd meeting, 6 March 1957, CAB 130–122.

110. Treasury memo, 'Basic International Economic Policy', 21 Febr. 1956, T 234–183, file 145/10/01.

111. Chancellor of the Exchequer, P. Thorneycroft, 'Economic Implications of the NATO meeting', 13 Dec. 1957, PREM 11–1828.

112. Macmillan to Selwyn Lloyd, 22 Dec. 1959, PREM 11–2991; Macmillan reviewed developments since he became Prime Minister (January 1957).

113. Zulueta-Note for Prime Minister, 29 May 1957, PREM 11–1844; Schmidt, *Großbritannien*, pp. 176ff.; London assumed that the 'Europeans' were waiting anyway for Britain to 'save'_critical situations for them.

114. Record of Meeting Macmillan/Lloyd-Mollet/Pineau/Faure, 9 March 1957, FO 371–129 327.

115. Briefing for Prime Minister's visit to Paris, 29–30 June 1958, No. III(d) 'NATO: IRBM sites in France', PREM 11–2326.

116. Meeting of Canadian and British Delegation at Bermuda, DL 369, 29 March 1957, PAC, RG 25, file 50030-AG-1–40.

117. Comment by Karl Carstens, 23 January 1957, on Hartlieb's analysis of the 'Three Wise Men'-report, Politisches Archiv des Auswärtigen Amtes, file 200 – 80.00/0.

118. Strauß, WDR interview, 13 April 1957; Edmund Taylor interview with Strauß, 18 April 1957, *The Reporter*; *Dokumente zur Deutschlandpolitik*, Reihe III, 1955–58, ed. Bundesministerium für Gesamtdeutsche Fragen Bonn/Berlin, vol. 3, pp. 598–603. *Frankfurter Allgemeine Zeitung*, 9 April 1957, reporting Strauß' press conference, 8 April 1957, on his return from US visit, reported that German soldiers would be trained in the use of *Mehrzweckflugkörper* and nuclear weapons but the latter would remain under US control. The Parliamentary Assembly of the WEU – in a meeting of early December 1959 – was in favour of aiming at an independent West European nuclear force, i.e. that the WEU should benefit from the revised McMahon Act, as Britain was doing.

119. Britain, partly in deference to American wishes, had dropped the idea of using the WEU framework for cooperation and had encouraged the use of NATO machinery, in the expectation that the US would join in and play a full part; Sandys-McElroy meeting, 23 Sept. 1958, DEFE 13–180. Sandys reminded the US Defense Secretary of this 'fact', and complained that the US supported 'European' missile production at the expense and exclusion of the UK.

120. UK Del. (Bermuda Conference) to FO, No. 93, ZP 28/60, 25 March 1957, FO 371–129331.

121. Heinrich Krone, Diary, 15 Febr. 1956, in H. Krone, *Aufzeichnungen zur Deutschland- und Ostpolitik 1954–1969*, in *Adenauer- Studien*, III, R. Morsey and K. Repgen (eds), Mainz, 1974, p. 140.

122. Thoß, 'Sicherheits- und deutschlandpolitische Komponenten', p. 479.

123. Record of meeting Macmillan-Mollet, 9 March 1957, ZG 243G, FO 371–129 327; PREM 11–1830A & 1831.

124. Macmillan-Mollet, 9 March 1957; Schmidt, 'Sicherheitspolitische Dimensionen', pp. 178f.

125. UK Del. (Bermuda) to FO, No. 93, ZP 28/60, FO 371–129 331; in two secret minutes, the parties agreed on prior consultation about new proposals regarding nuclear tests and military nuclear programmes of fourth countries, and 'that we should for the present treat the reported French plans for a military atomic programme cautiously and not assist it...', See Brief IVa &b, Prime Minister's visit to Paris, 29–30 June 1958, PREM 11–2326.
126. Selwyn Lloyd to Prime Minister, 13 Dec. 1959, PM/59/132, PREM 11–2987.
127. Cabinet Conclusions (57)1, 15 January 1957, minute 4.
128. Macmillan, meeting with Adenauer, Palais Schaumburg, 8 Oct.1958, PREM 11–2328.

CLEMENS WURM

Two Paths to Europe: Great Britain and France from a Comparative Perspective

The history of European integration is also a history of Anglo-French differences. This applies to the early stage, with its clashes over supranationality or intergovernmental cooperation, to the conflict over the British Free Trade Area proposal in the 1950s, to the 1960s when General de Gaulle twice blocked the United Kingdom's entry to the EEC, and finally to the quarrels in the seventies and eighties over the Community's budget and the Common Agricultural Policy. In all these disputes France was the main opponent of the UK. Great Britain is regularly portrayed in the literature as the 'insular outsider' of the EC,[1] whereas France is portrayed as the European power with long-term visions and 'very precise ideas on a European identity'.[2]

The present paper wants to draw out, using a comparative perspective, the pre-conditions, the fundamental principles, and the underlying continuities of the respective European integration policies pursued by Britain and France since the Second World War. I will attempt to show how the basic attitude of both countries towards integration has been remarkably stable since about 1950, and I will try to identify the motivations behind their policy choices. Both Britain and France have based their European policies on different concepts. They have been representatives of different forms of European integration and champions of conflicting ideas on Europe and its role in the world. The quarrels between Britain and France were not merely expressions of their struggle for the

leadership of Western Europe, though they are generally interpreted in this way. Behind these disputes were hidden conflicts
which were significant for European integration and which had a
marked impact on its history.

This analysis is founded on four issues. I will examine first the
basic principles and driving forces behind early post-war European
integration policies in both countries; secondly, the concepts and
forms of European integration; thirdly, French and British ideas
on the European institutions and how they sought to institution-
alise European cooperation and integration; and fourthly, the
issue of foreign relations, particularly with the US, and the views of
both countries on Europe's role in the world.

A preliminary note on methodology and the approach to the
subject: contrary to the federalist view, one which assumes an
awareness of a common community or European interest, the
national units will serve here as the basis for the analysis. Following
on from Stanley Hoffmann's approach,[3] this chapter will raise
questions about the domestic priorities and foreign policy objectives of the two countries, the impact of the external environment,
and finally, the institutional interplay between the actors.
European integration policy was much more closely linked to
domestic policy than was the case with foreign policy in general,
since it aimed at creating community structures which were to support, complement or, in the view of some, even to supersede
national systems. In one form or another, the factors and forces
shaping not only foreign policy but also the way national political
systems work left their mark on European integration policy.

I

During the early post-war years a strong impulse towards
Western European political and economic integration came
from France. The French government adopted plans initiated
by the European Movement at the Hague conference in May
1948. The European Coal and Steel Community (ECSC), the
Pleven Plan to build up a European Defence Community and, to
a great extent, the European Atomic Community resulted from
French initiatives. As is well known, the British government
rejected these initiatives and the European Movement's plans
were stripped of their far-reaching objectives for integration.

Britain, for the time being, remained aloof from the ECSC and the EEC.

Yet, Britain did not turn its back on Europe. Her European policy adapted itself to fit an international order changed by the cold war. The relationship between the USA, the Soviet Union and Great Britain – 'the crucial triangle'[4] – was the point of reference for London's policy, and British attitudes towards Western Europe were developed in this framework. Recent research has shown that the British government kept close watch on the situation on the continent and actively intervened to shape European developments. In early 1948 in particular, Foreign Secretary Bevin seems to have aimed at the creation of a British led-European third force that would give Europe economic independence from the United States and political security from the Soviet Union.[5] The British government played a leading role in implementing the Marshall Plan, initiated the Brussels Pact and was a driving force behind the founding of NATO.[6] The alternative solution adopted after the death of the EDC for West German rearmament – the transformation of the Brussels Pact into the WEU and the incorporation of the Federal Republic of Germany into NATO – was devised by Britain.[7] Political stability, economic recovery and military security were the goals Great Britain strove to attain in Western Europe. These goals were, in marked contrast to those of France, to be achieved without supranational integration. Loose forms of intergovernmental cooperation such as the OEEC or the Council of Europe were favoured and the contractual renunciation of national sovereignty rejected.

How can we explain the differences between British and French policies on integration? The question is a crucial one, and is the more important as both Britain and France had a great deal in common. Both countries were confronted in the post-war era with the same challenges. And both England and France were 'old', highly centralised nation-states. In both countries nation and nationalism formed strong emotive forces. France and Britain were colonial powers with authority over the largest empires of the period; both were confronted with the 'management of decline' and had to adjust to the rapidly changing conditions of the post-war world. The governments of both countries had to satisfy high expectations and a wide variety of demands. They had to provide not only welfare, redistribution of wealth, high consumption, democracy and participation, but also power, peace and security against the outside world. This made imperative new forms of cooperation **within** the states but also **between** the states. Only high economic growth would allow them to reconcile both domestic and foreign tasks, to provide butter and guns at the same time. The old dividing line between domestic and foreign policy, between economics and politics became obsolete; foreign policy became increasingly dependant on economic performance and vice versa.[8]

Yet the same challenges do not necessarily lead to the same political responses. In his comparative analysis of the political cultures of Great Britain and Germany, Karl Rohe has noted that each society has at its disposal different resources that enable it to cope in different ways with the same problems and to a different degree of success.[9] Peter Gourevitch has investigated from a comparative international perspective the responses of several countries to the world economic depressions of the last century, and has offered explanations why the political options in the various countries have differed so greatly and why they took one particular path rather than another.[10] Clearly one has to look at the distinctive features and structures of societies in order to understand their different policies on integration.

In spite of having a great deal in common, the initial positions of Britain and France in 1945 were very different. These differences were scarcely taken into account in most critical appraisals of British policy in the early post-war period. The criticisms were often strongly derived from the model of supranational integration without reference to the contemporary context, as in Walter Lipgens' accusation that the Labour government and Foreign Secretary Bevin made historically fateful errors when they rejected a federal Europe.[11] Four factors seem to be of particular relevance to our topic and will be analysed here: the respective role and importance of the colonial empires, structural elements of the economies of both countries, historical experiences and the impact of the war, and finally, the German problem.

A closer look first reveals great differences in the structure, function and significance of the colonial empires. In both cases the colonies provided additional sources of power, protected markets, supplies of raw materials and a source of dollar earnings. However, 'the French and British had entirely different colonial philosophies, the former's based on central control and "assimilation"... the latter's on ... evolution towards a much looser Commonwealth structure'.[12] The French Empire was much smaller and less significant to the metropolitan or world economy than that of Britain. The sterling area represented, besides the dollar area, the greatest trading and currency sub-system of the world. The Commonwealth enjoyed deeper loyalties than the Union Française; it lent identity and support to the political order in the United Kingdom. It was seen by many in London, not least the Labour Party, as a model for an alternative world system based on cooperation and consultation rather than integration. Even in the 1960s, there was among British elites 'a strong sense of attachment ... to the highly visible symbol of their historic grandeur, the Commonwealth.'[13] Close ties with the Commonwealth had priority over relations with Europe – unlike France which had always been a continental power: 'Dans ses profondeurs, la France n'était pas coloniale au XIXe et XXe siècle, quand elle a conquis et organisé un Empire dont le souvenir fascine encore les peuples étrangers.'[14]

Contrary to the British Empire, which was formed in a gradual process, the French colonies were created more recently and primarily for political reasons. According to French research the aim of colonialisation was to raise France's rank in Europe to compensate for the defeat of 1870-71 and the loss of Alsace-Lorraine and to regain lost 'grandeur'. The bitter struggle the French waged for the colonies in the 1950s was fought not least to improve France's position in Europe and especially with regard to Germany. The fate of the French position in Indochina was linked closely with that of the European Defence Community; it was widely assumed that only victory in Indochina would strengthen France sufficiently to enable it to take its place in an integrated European army alongside an economically, politically and militarily restored Federal Republic of Germany.[15]

The negotiations over the European Defence Community demonstrated, however, that military involvement overseas threatened conversely to lead to German dominance of the EDC. The objective of European unity gained measurable importance as France, under pressure from colonial nationalism and the superpowers, was forced to abandon its colonial illusions. The Suez fiasco, according to Pierre Guillen, was the major catalyst for the French Government's acceptance of the Rome Treaties.[16] Power through the Empire or through Europe was the French alternative.[17] In Great Britain too, the turn towards the EEC was closely linked to the dissolution of the Empire, but traditionally in Britain the force was the other way round. Here, European policy was only a function of wider British global policy; Europe did not have and did not get the status in London that it had in France.

Secondly, there were enormous differences in the economic structures of the two countries. Britain had relatively efficient and labour intensive agriculture and drew a large part of her food requirements cheaply from the Commonwealth. France, on the other hand, was strongly agrarian in character; agriculture employed about two-fifths of the workforce in 1945, and was much less productive than in Britain. France was eager to export its agricultural surplus to the British market and replace the Commonwealth as the main supplier. This difference partly explains the failure in 1948-9 to devise a common policy within the OEEC[18] and the later conflict over integration policy between the two countries, a conflict involving farming and the closely linked problems of the Common Agricultural Policy, its financing and the EC Budget.

Trade, finance and services were crucial to the British economy. The 'économie dominante' and the 'workshop of the world' in the nineteenth century, Great Britain was far more integrated into the world economy than was France. The ratio of goods exported was much higher in Britain (more than 20 per cent) than in France (around 8 per cent).[19] For Britain, expanding trade and promoting exports were used from 1947 to stimulate the economy, close the gaps in the balance of trade and finance the welfare state. France was only opened up to the world market within the framework of the EEC from the end of the 1950s onwards.

There were also major differences in the patterns of trade and foreign investment, although there were parallels in long-term trends. France's markets lay traditionally in Europe. From the middle of the nineteenth century onwards, the United Kingdom had gradually been gearing itself to trade with the overseas world away from the Euopean continent. In 1950 just over 10 per cent of Great Britain's exports went to the 'Little Europe' of the six Schuman Plan countries. Almost 50 per cent of exports and 40 per cent of imports were with the Commonwealth. Not until the mid-1950s was the direction of the flow of trade reversed, coinciding with Great Britain's gradual turn towards the EEC although the shift in trade began prior to entry into the Community. An even more pronounced concentration on the world outside of Europe can be seen in British investments. By the beginning of the twentieth century the City of London, which in 1830 or 1840 had shown considerable interest in Europe, was hardly any more interested in capital investment in European areas. Even in 1962 only around 10 per cent of foreign investment went to Europe (EEC and EFTA together).[20] The respective patterns of trade, finance and investment exercised an important influence on attitudes to Europe. As foreign trade and finance were aligned to the Commonwealth and the sterling area, for the Treasury and the Board of Trade involvement in a European customs union was out of the question – contrary to the Foreign Office which, until 1948, thought differently for political reasons.[21]

British policy – by concentrating on the Empire and the sterling area and rejecting European integration – has been criticised sharply in recent research. This criticism has been fuelled by the divergent economic development of most of the EEC states on the one hand and Britain on the other since around the mid-1950s, with impressive rates of growth in the first case, stagnation and symptoms of relative economic decline in the other. Certainly it can be said that British policy after 1945 was based on false assumptions. A world-wide shortage of raw materials was expected, as occurred in 1918-19. Trade with the Commonwealth and the sterling area would, it was assumed, secure for Great Britain leadership in world trade.[22] It transpired, however, that while trade between industrialised countries was growing quickly, especially in Western Europe, the Commonwealth and the sterling area formed a stagnating part of the world economy.

Great Britain found itself in the wrong trade block. Was this foreseeable? And from what time onwards? Alan Milward believes that already in 1948-50 it became clear that the 'Little Europe Bloc' (i.e. the later EEC) would offer a better framework for growth, productivity and national income than the Commonwealth as a direct result of the rapid expansion of intra-European trade.[23] One can maintain, however, that from the perspective of the year 1950, the European share of world exports had actually weakened during the previous fifty years, whilst the third world's share had increased. Not until 1952 did the prices of raw materials start to rise more slowly than those for industrial products. Therefore in 1950 those politicians in Britain who spoke out against Europe could justify their arguments on long term trends.[24]

Thirdly, we come to the consequences of the war and the wartime experience on public policy and national culture. These

are difficult to evaluate at the current state of research. Yet they
are of crucial importance to our topic. The impact of the war varied according to policy fields, and according to whether the war
was won or lost: 'Even if the war as a unit created numerous common experiences, the distinction between whether a nation
belonged to the winning or to the losing side remains a dividing
line which channels the ... workings of the national and individual
consciousness in different ways'.[25] Britain was a victor and one of
the 'Big Three', France a special case, first defeated, then a victor.
For Britain, one effect of the war was the linking of its security policy to that of the USA, and conversely a deeper mistrust of continental Europeans and misgivings about their political
dependability and stability. According to David Reynolds, the 'special relationship' is a product of the Second World War and the
fall of France in 1940.[26] Lack of faith in the political stability of the
French Fourth Republic was an important factor – lasting well into
the late 1950s – explaining why Britain feared close political ties
with Western Europe. The wartime experience reinforced long-
held beliefs; it promoted an inflated view of Britain's world role,
encouraged an over-extension of national financial and military
resources and helped prevent wider reforms.[27] France, on the contrary, with its history of defeat, occupation, and collaboration, was
doubly discredited. Yet, partly as a result of these experiences
there was a massive drive in France for renewal and modernisation[28] which will be discussed later.

   European integration grew partly out of the common experiences of the continental powers. Integration and the building of
common institutions were regarded as precautions against war and
guarantees of peace. But Britain's attitude was different; there was
no emotional commitment to Europe, and the war did not create
a sense of European identity. On the contrary, it reinforced a feeling of insularity, separateness and detachment from continental
Europe. As Kenneth O. Morgan has put it: 'Dunkirk, the Battle of
Britain, the image of "standing alone" and subsequently saving a
stricken continent from itself went deep into British folk memo-
ries. It was widely assumed that the wartime experience had
impelled Britain in a totally different direction from the defeated
continental nations between 1940 and 1945.'[29] Until the beginnings of the 1960s, Europe was not an issue in British politics.
Britain's role in the defeat of Germany was seen as an emphatic
confirmation of its own political culture, national identity and par-

liamentary system: 'The Second World War tested European countries' institutions and found them all, except Britain's, wanting.'[30] Defending the status quo abroad and – from 1948 onwards – at home, formed the broad outline of British policy. 'We intend to hold what we have gained here in this island', Hugh Dalton told the Labour Party Conference in 1950.[31]

The reforms of the Attlee governments strengthened the belief in the British nation-state and confirmed reservations about European integration. European integration and the nation-state were regarded as opposite entities. Why, most members of the British political elites were asking themselves, should Britain hand over sovereignty to supranational authorities or join in schemes of European integration at that moment, when her political and social system and readiness for reform seemed to have proved themselves? 'It is no accident', Denis Healey wrote in 1952, 'that in their approach to European unity since 1945 the socialist parties of Britain and Scandinavia have been most conservative – for they have most to conserve.'[32]

These differences in national experiences and structural conditions go a long way towards explaining why the integration policies of the two countries differed. The starting point for the early French initiatives, for the Schuman Plan and the Pleven Plan, however, lies elsewhere. Both countries differed fundamentally in their approach to Germany. For Paris, trying to solve the German problem was the most important impetus towards European integration. Britain, on the contrary, did not 'share French concern to the extent of accepting a loss of sovereignty in order to control Germany'.[33] In 1948-50 the two countries parted ways. Britain, at the zenith of its power in Western Europe, stuck to its model of a loose and pluralistic league of states without constitutional ties, based on consultation and cooperation. Britain became more Atlanticist in its orientation, and clear pre-eminence was given to relations with the Commonwealth and North America. By contrast a form of Western European integration, firmly backed by the United States and based on strong institutions and supranational structures including the Federal Republic of Germany, offered Paris a means of restoring France and containing both West Germany and the Soviet Union. It was also to be the basis of a new Europe.

'Germany is what French policy is fundamentally about. It was then and it is still today.'[34] 'Sécurité', political and economic security from Germany, was the dominant goal in French politics after both world wars. In the early period, 1944 to 1947, the French government, as after the First World War, aimed at the control of Germany through a system of alliances (including the Soviet Union), the dissolution of German state unity and separating the Rhineland, Ruhr and Saar from West Germany. The political and economic centre of gravity in the continent was to be shifted westwards, away from Germany towards France. And, just as after the First World War, French policy foundered on resistance from the USA and Great Britain. The Cold War, the Marshall Plan, the re-integration of Germany into the world economy promoted by the USA and Britain, the creation of a new West German state, the release of West Germany from production controls and restrictions and finally the desire for the re-arming of the Federal Republic: all these threw France onto the defensive and led Paris to a gradual adjustment of its policy to the new circumstances.

The final break with the old policy occurred in 1950 with the Schuman plan. France decided to move without Britain and to accommodate Germany in a cooperative structure, after all the previous French plans – in the OEEC or through a European customs Union – to create a regional West European bloc without West Germany and before Germany had recovered its strength had foundered, on British and American, but also on Belgian and Dutch resistance. European integration helped square the circle, to reconcile Germany's recovery with French political and economic security needs. Political motivations were inseparable from economic ones. By creating a common community of interests, initially of an economic nature, so Monnet intended, historical Franco-German differences were to be banished and a controlled partnership with the Federal Republic made possible. Binding Germany to European structures was to enable the development and the harnessing of the West German resources, without endangering France or the European states system. It would firmly anchor the Federal Republic to the West and prevent a new Rapallo, special arrangements with the Soviet Union or neutralist tendencies.[35]

As we know from recent studies, the shift to the new policy was highly disputed within the French administration. The shift was only partial, and was accompanied by setbacks. In one way the Schuman Plan masked the failure of previous French policy. Several lines of European policy coexisted uneasily in Paris, and the structure of the ECSC and the functioning of the High Authority had little in common with Monnet's original ideas.[36]

Nevertheless the Schuman Plan marked a turning point with far-reaching consequences.

Even industrial modernisation, strongly assisted by American capital, was now envisaged in the common European framework of the six Schuman Plan countries. 'The Schuman Plan was designed to save the Monnet Plan which in turn had meant to establish French industrial dominance in Europe.'[37] Only on the basis of economic strength, said the accepted wisdom since the war, would French security and international status be guaranteed. The Schuman Plan was to remove bottlenecks in coal supply and improve the competitiveness of the steel industry. The integration of atomic energy was meant to encourage economic growth flowing from what was then widely regarded as a new key sector of industry, and to keep the civil use of atomic energy by the Federal Republic of Germany under control.[38]

A third factor of French European integration policy, after the German problem and industrial modernisation, can be seen in the early stages of European integration. European unity was conceived as a stepping stone towards a stronger and more independent Europe, particularly in relation to the USA. France was heavily dependent on the US for its economic modernisation, for aid in fighting its colonial wars and for its security; this was a dependence that deeply affected French sovereignty and was much resented in France. Controlled limitation of national sovereignty in selected fields was accepted in order to achieve wider scope for action in a European framework. This will be discussed later.

Strong Anglo-French differences can be observed in all three areas. In France, industrial and agricultural growth was paramount. In London, it was the strength of sterling – the symbol of Britain's international standing – and monetary cooperation with the USA which counted most. The employment of the Marshall Plan's counterpart funds is instructive about the conflicting priorities of both countries. Whereas in France the fund was employed for industrial renewal (i.e. productive investment), in Britain it was employed to retire short- term public debt.[39] Both countries adapted to the post-war situation in different ways. In order to protect growth, rank and influence, Great Britain leant on the USA and the Commonwealth; France, to an increasing extent, on Western European unification. London welcomed the Franco-German rapprochement, but did not share the continental powers' belief in the potential of European integration to bring about power, stability and security. An integrated Europe, it was widely believed in London, would be politically as unstable and therefore militarily as weak as the French Fourth Republic. Close contacts with the governments of Western Europe were seen as a liability, not as an asset. In Britain's view, controlling and containing the Federal Republic was to be primarily the responsibility of NATO. Finally, London wanted to prevent the European institutions from becoming the starting point of Western Europe's independence from the USA. This point will also be discussed later.

II

Integration can be achieved in different ways. Roughly speaking these differences are those which result from the dynamics of market forces, technology, communication or social change, and those which follow the thrust of political decisions and channel the process of integration towards politically desirable goals. More narrowly speaking, market integration can be distinguished from political integration (*Politikintegration*).[40] Market integration seeks to remove trade barriers, to liberalise the factors of production, capital and labour and to create greater economic regions. By contrast, political integration involves placing individual policy fields under community institutions. In the first case those responsible for the integration process are the economic actors themselves; in the second case they are primarily national and supranational bureaucracies. The two methods are not contradictory; they must be seen as complementary forms as set out in the EEC treaty. The respective integration policies of the countries in question here – France and Britain – contain both aspects of integration, but, and this is the crucial point, they were given very different weight in the two countries.

Great Britain advocated, if anything, market integration; France rather championed political integration. Examples would be first the project for a large industrial free trade area (FTA) comprising the OEEC states proposed by the British government in 1956, and second, the European Free Trade Association (EFTA). The FTA proposition deserves more attention than it has received from historians so far, if only for the reason that it contained elements which shaped Britain's integration policy even in the following decades. And on the continent the concept of a free trade area was regarded with considerable interest by all those who saw the nascent customs union (i.e. the EEC) as protectionist, dirigiste and inward-looking. In the Federal Republic of Germany this applied especially to Ludwig Erhard and his followers.[41]

The FTA project was abruptly terminated by de Gaulle in November 1958, and became the basis of EFTA. EFTA was based on the conviction that political and economic integration could be kept separate from one another and that 'all one needed was a broad framework' of free trade between the member states. Integration (namely, specialisation and trade) could then be left to the market.[42] EFTA envisaged only minimal institutions. There were no common policies, no common tariff nor any independent authorities such as the Commission of the EEC. Agriculture was excluded. The British government eventually turned to the EEC, but was only partly willing to adopt the larger political objectives of the EC, namely political union. Integration was basically intended to promote a common economic market; politically it was meant to adopt the form of close cooperation between sovereign and independent states.

Not so with France. The Schuman Plan as well as the EAC were precisely the result of efforts to control Germany's economic potential and to direct it along politically determined channels. The liberal concept of integration as proposed by Britain was unacceptable, for it would leave France exposed to the free play of forces against a neighbour who might be potentially dangerous again and who, in the economic field, seemed to have many advantages. In the EC, in marked contrast to Britain, the drive behind Community policies often came from France.[43] Domestic objectives were formulated in European terms, and the European framework was to support and complement national policies. Examples abound and are well known: they include CAP, industrial policies, Europe as a social space and Europe as a technology community. The term *construction européenne* or *construction de l'Europe* – incidentally the term *intégration européenne* is rarely used in France – with its voluntaristic connotations suggests that the building of Europe is a political project that cannot be left to the market but needs the driving force or even the guiding hand of politics.

How can we explain the differences between France and Britain? These differences were the product of one or the other of the factors which shaped the attitudes of both countries on

European integration. They also resulted from opposing ideas about the role of the market and the state, from different state traditions and modernisation strategies which were transferred onto the European stage.

France has a long tradition of state intervention going back to Colbert and absolutism. The modernisation of the economy after 1945 was driven forward by 'planification'. It was part of a broader movement of renewal and was closely related to other structural reforms such as nationalisation, reform of industrial and company law and the construction of the welfare state. In all of the reforms the state played a central role in helping France catch up industrially, stimulating economic growth and overcoming Malthusian ways of thinking. Planning was made to serve not the construction of socialism but the furtherance of economic growth. Key sectors of industry like steel or electricity were promoted, and investment was channelled into them. Research gives varying assessments of the success of state measures: recently Serge Berstein and Pierre Milza have once again portrayed them in a positive light.[44]

Nationalisation, controls, welfare reforms and planning all also characterised British economic policy after 1945.[45] Yet, the nature (not the extent) of government intervention was different. The government was more committed to macroeconomic management, directing economic development by control over expenditure, fiscal and monetary policies.[46] The stability of sterling, full employment and social welfare were paramount.[47] In practice, 'planning' was much less ambitious than in France;[48] as one distinguished economist has put it: 'The balance of payments was the focus of the one really determined effort of planning in which the Labour government engaged.'[49] In its relations with the producer groups the British government, in accordance with English liberal traditions, relied on voluntary methods of consultation and partnership, not direction. Reforms or modernising programmes were not forced in the face of opposition from private industry.[50] The difference between France and Britain will become clearer when we examine the third topic of discussion, the institutions.

III

Institutions were important to European integration. They formed the framework for bargaining patterns, influenced attitudes and shaped modes of behaviour. They contributed to the growing development in Western Europe of a 'habit of coopera-tion'.[51] Alan Milward sees the institutionalisation of economic cooperation and interdependence as being fundamental to the success of political and economic reconstruction in Western Europe following the Second World War in contrast to the inter-war period.[52]

In the institutional sphere, French initiatives were highly con-tradictory. Marked as they were by shifts between federal, suprana-tional and strictly intergovernmental efforts. Sometimes France triumphed as the *nation animatrice* of European integration; at other times it acted as the brake on Western European union, such as with the rejection of the EDC, in the negotiations leading to the EEC and in the mid-1960s with de Gaulle's empty chair pol-icy. The French government at times profferred itself as the advo-cate of supranational solutions, while Great Britain came forward as the champion of national sovereignty. Since de Gaulle's time at the latest this conflict has lost a lot of its Franco-British enmity, and was probably only for a short while as important as was widely believed. Even in France the ideal of supra-nationality had always been hotly contested. Its importance for French politics has much to do with Jean Monnet, who lost a great deal of his influence in Paris after he took over the presidency of the High Authority of the ECSC and after Schuman had to leave the Quai d'Orsay in January 1953. The understanding between Pompidou and Heath over the EC as a body resting on the nation-states as the central units formed, alongside the wish to counter-balance the Federal Republic, the basis for Britain's entry to the EC.[53] Both countries were either sceptical or dismissive of an extension of the powers of the European Parliament or of strengthening the Commission and regarded the Council of Ministers or the European Council as the central decision-making body. In this area they acted – rarely enough – as allies.

There was, however, less agreement on the questions regarding the creation and the role of the institutions and the institutionali-sation of European cooperation and integration. From the very beginning, France had a strong influence on the integration process, its character and content. The process was to be influ-enced or shaped via new, strong institutions or treaties. According to the British, however, permanent and stable institutions could only develop gradually and after a long period of more intensive cooperation. Practical cooperation was to precede the institutional structure, and not vice versa (as the French wanted).

The British view was clearly revealed in Whitehall's reaction to the plans by the European Movement to set up a European assembly and to create a kind of federal European state with its own constitution. Foreign Secretary Bevin rejected the European schemes in 1948, claiming one could not put the roof on before the building had been built.[54] 'New constitutional forms', a Labour Party pamphlet said, 'can only follow, not precede, the growth of a genuine European community'.[55] 'To us', according to a British minister of state in 1983, 'institutions must be subservient to policies. Closer cooperation should not be forced, but must grow out of practical ways in which as a community we can work for our common good. Substance and reality must come before form'.[56]

Differences in the formation and working of national political systems, as well as diverse constitutional traditions, shaped different policies of integration. Great Britain has no written constitution, whereas France, often called a 'constitutional laboratory', has had an uninterrupted succession of constitutional documents ever since the 1789 revolution. As a consequence of these many changes, constitutions never had the significance of fundamental charters for the nation.[57] The British system of government has evolved gradually, and parliament constitutes an important part of the nation's identity. In contrast, France's modern history is marked by the instability of its political institutions and systems of government. This applies in particular to the Fourth Republic, whose weak governments were the object of controversy, dislike, derision and hostility. For this reason too it should be easier for France to define its national objectives within the framework of new European institutions.

IV

Did France and Great Britain share a belief in the autonomy of European interests in international policy as being the aim of European policy? Can we detect convergence between the two countries? What was their view of Europe's role in the world? In spite of their many common features, this question reveals strong differences between the two countries. Relations with the dominant western power, the USA, have been especially contentious.

British foreign policy after the war was guided by the concept of the three circles expounded by Winston Churchill in 1948, according to which Britain's overseas interests lay in three interlocking areas, Europe, the Empire/Commonwealth and North America. 'With Europe but not of it', Britain accorded the continent a much lower priority than the Commonwealth or the 'special relationship' with the United States.[58] The aim of British policy, as formulated in 1951, was 'to try to lead the integration movement away from exclusively European ideas towards an Atlantic community',[59] towards a Pax Atlantica.

Shifts in the international system, the disintegration of the Empire, sluggish economic growth and recurrent balance of payments crises, the growing strength of West Germany, the determination of the six Schuman Plan countries to pool their resources and to go ahead with the unification project irrespective of Britain: all of these caused Whitehall, from around 1956-7, gradually to adjust its political priorities. In London the EEC was increasingly seen, by Macmillan, as a new centre of power. The USA, which had strongly supported European integration from the beginning, regarded the EEC (not the EFTA or Britain) as its privileged partner. If Britain wanted to retain scope for its own European and Atlantic interests and for its self-perceived role as the bridge beween Europe and the United States, then it was important to secure a position within the EEC and influence its policies in the sense of British interests.[60]

Today, Britain is politically and economically tightly connected with the European continent. More than 50 per cent of its foreign trade is conducted with the EC. In practical matters the British government several times has emphasised the indivisibility of European interests, even vis-à-vis the USA. However, two continuities remained which mark strong differences with France: first, Britain advocated a wider, loosely structured Community, open in commercial dealings to the outside world, while France desired a Community more closed to the outside, grouped around a central core under French leadership. Second, British interest has always been to prevent the continental European states forming a regional European power bloc independent of the USA.

France thought differently. The French withdrawal from the military command structure of NATO in 1966 and the creation of a 'European Europe' stretching from the Atlantic to the Urals was meant to restore French independence, to overcome the division

of Germany and the continent (the legacy of Yalta), and to ensure
Europe's autonomy and manoeuvrability, especially in relation to
the USA. This conception is associated with the name of de
Gaulle.[61] In one form or another, however, it effectively shaped
French policy, insofar as France not only saw the organising of
Europe as a way of integrating Western Europe into the Atlantic
world (which was favoured in London) but also as a stepping stone
towards a more independent Europe (which was rejected in
London). Building up the EEC into a customs union instead of a
mere free trade area (as Britain wanted) was to establish the
Community as an independent economic power. The common
tariff would endow the Community with strong policy instruments
of its own and give substance to the Community's claim to secure
equal concessions from its trading partners.

Recent French literature stresses the continuities between the
Fourth and the Fifth Republics, particularly in the field of nuclear
and defence policies.[62] Yet, it is important to note that the goal of
the Fourth Republic was independence within interdependence.
France wanted to be regarded as equal in status with Britain and
strove for tripartite leadership of NATO. European integration
came to be seen as a means (by Guy Mollet for instance) to free
the French from excessive dependence on the US and to even out
the distribution of power within the Atlantic Alliance, not to leave
it.[63]

The contradictions in de Gaulle's view, notwithstanding its forward-looking and visionary elements, have been repeatedly
referred to in the literature. They stem from the insistence on
national independence and the claim to act as spokesman for
Western Europe, from a gulf between the objectives and the reality of French power, and from the rift between the national and
European elements in French policy. Whether de Gaulle was
aware of the full extent of this rift seems questionable. After all, his
ideas emanated from a belief in the identity of French, European
and universal interests which have characterised the French
nation ever since the 'levée en masse'. But they also reflected a
deeper dilemma within French integration policy. Integrating and
controlling the Federal Republic within European institutions
threatened to bind France to the same extent as the Federal
Republic, and in a community moreover in which France's partners had a much more 'Atlantic' security outlook than France.
The discussions over the Pleven Plan and the EDC showed this.

Paris attempted to escape this dilemma first by limiting the supranational elements of European integration and by trying, as in the 1960s, to transform the EC into a mere confederal Political Union; and second, by developing – outside the EEC – its own nuclear force (the crucial decisions to develop atomic weapons were taken under the Fourth Republic,[64] not in the Fifth Republic as is widely believed), by stressing military autonomy, by pursuing an active global policy and by emphasising the difference of international status vis-à-vis West Germany. A counter-balance was to be created against the growing economic and financial strength of the Federal Republic. A precarious balance was thus created in Western Europe, a balance which has been thrown into question by German reunification and the shift in emphasis from military to economic determinants of power.

Notes

1. Keith Robbins, *Insular Outsider? 'British History' and European Integration*, Reading, 1990; Stephen George, *An Awkward Partner: Britain in the European Community*, Oxford, 1990.
2. Rudolf von Thadden, 'Aufbau nationaler Identität. Deutschland und Frankreich im Vergleich', in Bernhard Giesen (ed.), *Nationale und kulturelle Identität. Studien zur Entwicklung des kollektiven Bewußtseins in der Neuzeit*, Frankfurt am Main, 1991, p. 507.
3. Stanley Hoffmann, 'Reflections on the Nation State in Western Europe Today', in Loukas Tsoukalis (ed.), *The European Community: Past, Present and Future*, Oxford, 1983, p. 30.
4. Avi Shlaim, *Britain and the Origins of European Unity 1940–1951*, Reading, 1978, pp. 104–14; Anne Deighton, *The Impossible Peace. Britain, the Division of Europe, and the Origins of the Cold War*, Oxford, 1990.
5. This point is argued forcefully by John W. Young and John Kent, 'The "Western Union" Concept and British Defence Policy, 1947–8', in Richard J. Aldrich (ed.), *British Intelligence, Strategy and the Cold War, 1945–51*, London, 1992, pp. 166–92; Young and Kent, 'British Policy Overseas: The "Third Force" and the Origins of NATO – In Search of a New Perspective', in Beatrice Heuser and Robert O'Neill (eds), *Securing Peace in Europe, 1945–62: Thoughts for the Post-Cold War Era*, Basingstoke, 1992, pp. 41–61; Sean Greenwood, *Britain and European Cooperation Since 1945*, Oxford, 1992, chs 2–3; John W. Young, *Britain and European Unity, 1945–1992*, Basingstoke, 1993, ch. 1. Yet, Bevin's ideas remained vague. It was unclear how the plan was to be realised. Moreover, the British government was not prepared at that time to give any firm military guarantees to continental Europe.

6. John Baylis, *The Diplomacy of Pragmatism: Britain and the Formation of NATO, 1942–49*, Basingstoke, 1993.

7. Saki Dockrill, *Britain's Policy for West German Rearmament 1950–1955*, Cambridge, 1991; Olaf Mager, *Die Stationierung der britischen Rheinarmee – Großbritanniens EVG-Alternative*, Baden-Baden, 1990; Hans-Heinrich Jansen, *Großbritannien, das Scheitern der EVG und der NATO-Beitritt der Bundesrepublik Deutschland*, Bochum, 1992.

8. Cf. René Girault, 'De la Puissance de la France d'Aujourd'hui', *Relations Internationales*, no. 58, 1989, pp. 162f.

9. Karl Rohe, 'Zur Typologie politischer Kulturen in westlichen Demokratien. Überlegungen am Beispiel Großbritanniens und Deutschlands', in Heinz Dollinger, Horst Gründer and Alwin Hanschmidt (eds), *Weltpolitik, Europagedanke, Regionalismus. Festschrift für Heinz Gollwitzer zum 65. Geburtstag*, Münster, 1982, pp. 581–96.

10. Peter A. Gourevitch, 'International Trade, Domestic Coalitions, and Liberty: Comparative Responses to the Crisis of 1873–1896', *The Journal of Interdisciplinary History*, vol. 8, no. 2, 1977, pp. 281–313; Gourevitch, 'Breaking with Orthodoxy: The Politics of Economic Policy Responses to the Depression of the 1930s', *International Organization*, vol. 38, no. 2, 1984, pp. 95–129; Gourevitch, *Politics in Hard Times: Comparative Responses to International Economic Crises*, Ithaca, 1986; see also the review article by Gabriel A. Almond, 'The International-National Connection', *British Journal of Political Science*, vol. 19, part 2, 1989, pp. 237–59.

11. Walter Lipgens, *Die Anfänge der europäischen Einigungspolitik 1945–1950*, vol. 1, *1945–1947*, Stuttgart, 1977; Lipgens, 'Labour und Europa 1945/46', in Ulrich Engelhardt, Volker Sellin and Horst Stuke (eds), *Soziale Bewegung und politische Verfassung. Beiträge zur Geschichte der modernen Welt*, Stuttgart, 1976, pp. 713–54.

12. John W. Young, *France, the Cold War and the Western Alliance 1944–1949: French Foreign Policy and Post-War Europe*, Leicester, 1990, p. 169; John Kent, *The Internationalization of Colonialism: Britain, France, and Black Africa, 1939–1956*, Oxford, 1992.

13. Two-thirds of the elite groups described this relationship as 'very valuable'. No one considered it harmful and only 3 per cent felt that it was of no real value. By contrast, membership of the European Common Market ranked in fifth place only – after the Commonwealth, NATO, the US special relationship and the United Nations. Mark Abrams, 'British Elite Attitudes and the European Common Market', *The Public Opinion Quarterly*, vol. 29, no. 2, 1965, p. 242. The survey was carried out in the spring of 1963. The results may have been influenced by de Gaulle's veto to British entry to the EEC in January 1963.

14. Charles-Robert Ageron, *France Coloniale ou Parti Colonial?*, Paris, 1978, p. 297. The same has been said by Max Beloff on Great Britain: 'The

British were not an imperially minded people; they lacked both a theory of empire and the will to engender and implement one.' Max Beloff, *Imperial Sunset*, 2 vols (1, *Britain's Liberal Empire 1897–1921*; 2, *Dream of Commonwealth 1921–42*), London 1969–1989, vol. 1, p. 19. However, for the strength of London's attempts to preserve Britain's financial and commercial authority in the Empire/Commonwealth even after 1945 see Peter J. Cain and A. G. Hopkins, *British Imperialism*, vol. 2, *Crisis and Deconstruction 1914–1990*, London, 1993.

15. Irwin W. Wall, *The United States and the Making of Postwar France, 1945–1954*, Cambridge, 1991, chs 7–9.

16. Pierre Guillen, 'L'Europe Remède à l'Impuissance Française? Le Gouvernement Guy Mollet et la Négociation des Traités de Rome (1955–1957)', *Revue d'Histoire Diplomatique*, vol. 102, 1988, pp. 319–35; Guillen, 'La France et la Négociation des Traités de Rome: L'Euratom', in Enrico Serra (ed.), *Il Rilancio dell'Europa e i Trattati di Roma*, Milano, 1989, pp. 513–24. Yet, there is no agreement on this question. According to Alan Milward and Frances M. B. Lynch, economic motivations were paramount. The French government, moreover, had made up its mind to sign the Rome Treaty before the dramatic international crises of October-November 1956. Alan S. Milward (with the Assistance of George Brennan and Federico Romero), *The European Rescue of the Nation-State*, London, 1992, pp. 214f.; Frances M. B. Lynch, 'Restoring France: the Road to Integration', in Alan S. Milward et al., *The Frontier of National Sovereignty: History and Theory 1945–1992*, London, 1993, pp. 59–87, 208–10.

17. Robert Frank, 'The French Alternative: Economic Power Through the Empire or Through Europe?', in Ennio di Nolfo (ed.), *Power in Europe?* vol. II, *Great Britain, France, Germany and Italy and the Origins of the EEC, 1952–1957*, Berlin, 1992, pp. 160–73. For the function of the Empire as a 'compensatory myth' after the defeat of 1940 see Charles-Robert Ageron, 'L'Opinion Publique Face aux Problèmes de l'Union Française (Étude de Sondages)', in Ageron (ed.), *Les Chemins de la Décolonisation de l'Empire Colonial Français*, Paris 1986, pp. 33–48; Ageron, 'De l'Empire à la Dislocation de l'Union Française (1939–1956)'; Ageron, 'La Décolonisation au Regard de la France', in Jacques Thobie et al., *Histoire de la France Coloniale*, 2 vols, Paris, 1990–1991, vol. 2, *1914–1990*, parts 4 and 5.

18. On the French long-term plan presented to OEEC and Britain at the beginning of 1949 see Gérard Bossuat, *La France, l'Aide Américaine et la Construction Européenne 1944–1954*, 2 vols, Paris, 1992, vol. 2, ch. XVI.

19. Alec Cairncross, 'The Postwar Years 1945–77' in Roderick Floud and Donald M. McCloskey (eds), *The Economic History of Britain Since 1700*, 2 vols, Cambridge, 1981, vol. 2, p. 389 (table 16.5); Jean-François Eck, *Histoire de l'Économie Française depuis 1945*, 3rd edn, Paris 1992, ch. 1.

20. J. H. Dunning and D. C. Rowan, 'British Direct Investment in Western Europe', *Banca Nazionale del Lavoro Quarterly Review*, vol. 18, no. 73, 1965, pp. 127–55, 129.

21. John W. Young, *Britain, France and the Unity of Europe 1945–1951*, Leicester, 1984; Geoffrey Warner, 'The Labour Governments and the Unity of Western Europe, 1945–51', in Ritchie Ovendale (ed.), *The Foreign Policy of the British Labour Governments, 1945–1951*, Leicester, 1984, pp. 61–82.

22. George C. Peden, 'Economic Aspects of British Perceptions of Power on the Eve of the Cold War', in Josef Becker and Franz Knipping (eds), *Power in Europe? Great Britain, France, Italy and Germany in a Postwar World, 1945–1950*, Berlin, 1986, pp. 237–61, 256–9.

23. Alan S. Milward, *The Reconstruction of Western Europe 1945–51*, London, 1984, ch. XI.

24. Harm G. Schröter, 'Sonderweg und (un)aufhaltsame Hinwendung zu Europa: Zur Entwicklung der britischen Außenwirtschafts-strukturen im 20. Jahrhundert', in Clemens A. Wurm (ed.), *Wege nach Europa. Wirtschaft und Außenpolitik Großbritanniens im 20. Jahrhundert*, Bochum, 1992, pp. 155–70.

25. Reinhart Koselleck, 'Der Einfluß der beiden Weltkriege auf das soziale Bewußtsein', in Wolfram Wette (ed.), *Der Krieg des kleinen Mannes. Eine Militärgeschichte von unten*, München, 1992, p. 332.

26. David Reynolds, '1940: Fulcrum of the Twentieth Century?', *International Affairs*, vol. 66, no. 2, 1990, pp. 325–50; Reynolds, 'Great Britain and the Security "Lessons" of the Second World War', in Rolf Ahmann, Adolf M. Birke and Michael Howard (eds), *The Quest for Stability: Problems of West European Security 1918–1957*, Oxford, 1993, pp. 299–325.

27. Kenneth O. Morgan, 'The Second World War and British Culture', in Brian Brivati and Harriet Jones (eds), *From Reconstruction to Integration: Britain and Europe Since 1945*, Leicester, 1993, p. 33–46. Morgan stresses that, at home, the war promoted positive values of social citizenship and national cohesion.

28. Jean-Pierre Rioux, *La France de la Quatrième République*, 2 vols., Paris, 1980–1983; see also the contributions by Harold Perkin and Marcel David on 'Welfare State and Economic Planning', in Douglas Johnson, François Crouzet and François Bédarida (eds), *Britain and France: Ten Centuries*, Folkestone, 1980, ch. 13.

29. Morgan, 'The Second World War', p. 43; see also Robbins, *Insular Outsider*, pp. 6, 12.

30. Vernon Bogdanor, speaking at BBC Radio 4 on 1 December 1991, cited by Jill Stevenson, 'Britain and Europe in the Later Twentieth Century: Identity, Sovereignty, Peculiarity', in Mary Fulbrook (ed.), *National Histories and European History*, London, 1993, pp. 230–54, 243. According to Stevenson this is to overstate the case: Britain's

institutions had not been put to the same test as those of continental Europe.

31. The Labour Party, *Report of the 49th Annual Conference*, Margate, October 2 to October 6, 1950, p. 166.

32. Denis Healey, 'Power Politics and the Labour Party', in R. H. S. Crossman (ed.), *New Fabian Essays*, 3rd edn, London, 1970, p. 168.

33. Young, *France*, p. 228.

34. Eric Hobsbawm, 'Britain: a Comparative View', in Brian Brivati and Harriet Jones (eds), *What Difference Did the War Make?*, Leicester, 1993, p. 24.

35. Raymond Poidevin, *Robert Schuman. Homme d'État 1886–1963*, Paris, 1986; Jean Monnet, *Mémoires*, Paris, 1976; Douglas Brinkley and Clifford Hackett (eds), *Jean Monnet: The Path to European Unity*. Introduction by George W. Ball, Basingstoke, 1991.

36. Klaus Schwabe (ed.), *Die Anfänge des Schuman-Plans 1950/51*, Baden-Baden, 1988; John Gillingham, *Coal, Steel, and the Rebirth of Europe, 1945–1955: The Germans and French from Ruhr Conflict to Economic Community*, Cambridge, 1991 (ch. 6, 'The success of a failure'); Jean-Marie Palayret, 'Jean Monnet, la Haute Autorité de la CECA Face au Problème de la Reconcentration de la Sidérurgie Dans la Ruhr (1950–1958)', *Revue d'Histoire Diplomatique*, vol. 105, 1991, pp. 307–48.

37. Irwin M. Wall, *The United States and the Making of Postwar France, 1945–1954*, Cambridge, 1991, p. 199. For earlier expositions of this view see Frances M. B. Lynch, 'Resolving the Paradox of the Monnet Plan: National and International Planning in French Reconstruction', *The Economic History Review*, 2nd ser., vol. 37, no. 2, 1984, pp. 229–43; Milward, *Reconstruction*; Gillingham, *Coal, Steel, and the Rebirth of Europe*.

38. Wilfried Loth, *Der Weg nach Europa. Geschichte der europäischen Integration 1939–1957*, Göttingen, 1990, p. 114 (for Monnet's views).

39. Bossuat, *L'Europe Occidentale*, ch. 7. In 1948–51 the percentage of the counterpart funds in the credits of the 'Fonds de Modernisation et d'Équipment' amounted to 40 per cent.

40. For the distinction see Michael Kreile, 'Politische Dimensionen des Binnenmarktes', *Aus Politik und Zeitgeschichte. Beilage zur Wochenzeitung Das Parlament*, B 24–25/89, 9 June 1989, p. 26. William Wallace distinguishes between 'formal' and 'informal integration'; William Wallace, *The Transformation of Western Europe*, London, 1990, 53–6; Wallace, 'Introduction: The Dynamics of European Integration', in Wallace (ed.), *The Dynamics of European Integration*, London, 1990, pp. 8–12. 'Politikintegration' is not identical with 'political integration' as understood by Wallace, *The Transformation*, pp. 54–5.

41. Daniel Koerfer, *Kampf ums Kanzleramt: Erhard und Adenauer*, 2nd edn, Stuttgart, 1988, pp. 128–46, 199–205; 206–20; Hans-Peter Schwarz,

Adenauer, vol. 2, *Der Staatsmann: 1952–1967*, Stuttgart, 1991, esp. pp. 439–67. According to Frances Lynch, Britain's proposal for a free trade area in July 1956 was crucial for the French government's acceptance of the customs union proposal. The fear was that Britain's proposal might be more attractive to Germany and undermine France's foreign and economic policy, which aimed at close links with the Federal Republic; Lynch, 'Restoring France', in Milward et al., *The Frontier*, pp. 83f.

42. Victoria Curzon Price, 'Three Models of European Integration', in Ralf Dahrendorf et al., *Whose Europe? Competing Visions for 1992*, London, 1989, pp. 24–6.

43. Françoise de la Serre and Helen Wallace, 'The European Dimension: Conflict and Congruence', in Françoise de La Serre, Jacques Leruez and Helen Wallace (eds), *French and British Foreign Policies in Transition. The Challenge of Adjustment*, New York, 1990, pp. 96–129.

44. Serge Berstein and Pierre Milza, *Histoire de la France au XXe siècle*, vol. 3, *1945–1958*, Bruxelles, 1991. For details see Richard Kuisel, *Capitalism and the State in Modern France. Renovation and Economic Management in the Twentieth Century*, Cambridge, 1981, ch. 8; Philippe Mioche, *Le Plan Monnet. Genèse et Élaboration 1941–1947*, Paris, 1987; Irwin W. Wall, 'Jean Monnet, the United States and the French Economic Plan', in Brinkley and Hackett (eds), *Jean Monnet*, pp. 86–113, 101–4 (for assessments of the achievements of the Monnet Plan); William J. Adams, *Restructuring the French Economy: Government and the Rise of Market Competition since World War II*, Washington, D. C., 1989, especially ch. 3.

45. On the expansion of the British state in the twentieth century and the debates on the state in Britain see James E. Cronin, *The Politics of State Expansion: War, State and Society in Twentieth Century Britain*, London, 1991.

46. Alec Cairncross, *Years of Recovery: British Economic Policy 1945–51*, London, 1985; Kevin Jefferys, *The Attlee Governments 1945–1951*, London, 1992, especially pp. 44f.

47. The British after 1945 went further than other European countries in the construction of the welfare state. David W. Ellwood, *Rebuilding Europe: Western Europe, America and Postwar Reconstruction*, London, 1992, ch. 8. In 1949 real wages stood on average 20 per cent higher than in 1938; ibid., p. 138.

48. See Mikkal E. Herberg, 'Politics, Planning, and Capitalism: National Economic Planning in France and Britain', *Political Studies*, vol. 29, no. 4, 1981, pp. 497–516; the contributions by Harold Perkin and Marcel David on 'Welfare State and Economic Planning', in Johnson et al. (eds), *Britain and France*, ch. 13. For the shortcomings of British planning see the introduction by Bernard W. E. Alford, Rodney Lowe and Neil Rollings, *Economic Planning 1943–1951: A Guide to Documents*

in the Public Record Office, London, 1992, ch. 1.

49. Cairncross, *Years of Recovery*, p. 503.
50. Helen Mercer, 'The Labour Governments of 1945–51 and Private Industry', in Nick Tiratsoo (ed.), *The Attlee Years*, London, 1991, pp. 71–89, especially 84; Helen Mercer, Neil Rollings and Jim D. Tomlinson (eds), *Labour Governments and Private Industry: The Experience of 1945–1951*, Edinburgh, 1992.
51. Ralf Dahrendorf, 'The Future of Europe?', in Dahrendorf et al., *Whose Europe?*, p. 9.
52. Milward, *Reconstruction*, passim.
53. Uwe Kitzinger, *Diplomacy and Persuasion: How Britain Joined the Common Market*, London, 1973; Christopher Lord, *British Entry to the European Community under the Heath Government of 1970–4*, Aldershot, 1993; Wolfram F. Hanrieder, *Germany, America, Europe: Forty Years of German Foreign Policy*, New Haven, 1989, part III.
54. House of Commons, *Debates*, 5th series, vol. 456, 15.9.1948, col. 106.
55. The Labour Party, *European Unity: A Statement by the National Executive Committee of the Labour Party*, London, 1950, p. 11.
56. Cited by David Judge, 'The British Government, European Union and EC Institutional Reform', *The Political Quarterly*, vol. 57, no. 3, 1986, p. 324.
57. Henry W. Ehrmann, *Politics in France*, Boston, 1968, p. 15.
58. David Reynolds, 'A "Special Relationship"?: America, Britain and the International Order since the Second World War', *International Affairs*, vol. 62, no. 1, 1985/86, pp. 1–20; Wm. Roger Louis and Hedley Bull (eds), *The 'Special Relationship': Anglo-American Relations since 1945*, Oxford, 1986; Geoffrey Warner, 'The Anglo-American Special Relationship', *Diplomatic History*, vol. 13, no. 4, 1989, pp. 479–99; Christopher J. Bartlett, *'The Special Relationship': A Political History of Anglo-American Relations since 1945*, Harlow, 1992.
59. 'Memorandum for the Permanent Under Secretary's Committee', 9 June 1951; *Documents on British Policy Overseas (DBPO)*, ser. II, vol. 1, London 1986, p. 594.
60. Miriam Camps, *Britain and the European Community 1955–1963*, Princeton, 1964; Gustav Schmidt, 'Großbritannien, die Gründung der Europäischen Wirtschaftsgemeinschaft und die 'Sicherheit des Westens': "The American Connection"', in Michael Salewski (ed.), *Nationale Identität und Europäische Einigung*, Göttingen, 1991, pp. 169–231.
61. For de Gaulle's integration and European policies see Edmond Jouve, *Le Général de Gaulle et la Construction de l'Europe 1940–1966*, 2 vols., Paris, 1967; Wilfried Loth, 'De Gaulle und Europa. Eine Revision', *Historische Zeitschrift*, vol. 253, 1991, pp. 629–60; Hans-Dieter Lucas, *Europa vom Atlantik bis zum Ural? Europapolitik und Europadenken im Frankreich der Ära de Gaulle (1958–1969)*, Bonn, 1992;

Institut Charles de Gaulle, *De Gaulle et Son Siècle*, vol. 5: *L'Europe*, Paris, 1992.

62. Maurice Vaïsse, 'Aux Origines du Mémorandum de Septembre 1958', *Relations Internationales*, no. 58, 1989, pp. 253–68; Vaïsse, 'Le Choix Atomique de la France (1945–1958)', *Vingtième Siècle*, no. 36, 1992, pp. 21–30; Georges-Henri Soutou, 'La politique nucléaire de Pierre Mendès France', *Relations Internationales*, no. 59, 1989, pp. 317–30. According to Frédéric Bozo, *La France et l'OTAN. De la Guerre Froide au Nouvel Ordre Européen*, Paris, 1991, in 1958 at the end of the Fourth Republic all the main elements were present that induced de Gaulle after his return to power to define in a radically new way France's attitude towards NATO (p. 24).

63. Gérard Bossuat, 'France and the Leadership of the West in the 1950s: A Story of Disenchantment', in Heuser and O'Neill (eds), *Securing Peace*, pp. 105–24.

64. Jean Delmas, 'Naissance et Developpement d'une Politique Nucléaire Militaire en France (1945–1956)', in Klaus A. Maier and Norbert Wiggershaus unter Mitwirkung von Günther Hebert (eds), *Das Nordatlantische Bündnis 1949–1956*, München, 1993, pp. 263–72. France killed the EDC with a view to preserve its own nuclear option; see Jacques Bariéty, 'Frankreich und das Scheitern der EVG', in Rolf Steininger et al. (eds), *Die doppelte Eindämmung. Europäische Sicherheit und deutsche Frage in den Fünfzigern*, München, 1993, pp. 99–131.

WILFRIED LOTH

The Process of European Integration: Some General Reflections

The process of subordinating the nation-state order existing in Europe by establishing European Community structures – one of the major topics in the history of the twentieth century – is essentially attributable to two different underlying factors. On the one hand, this process is due to the inter-state anarchy representing the fundamental structural deficit of the nation-state system, the explosive effect of which was continuously intensified along with the increasingly destructive nature of modern warfare; on the other hand, this process is due to the development of productive resources in the industrialised era, which led to a situation where national markets became too narrow for rational production, where an international commodity culture came into existence, and where the transnational communication process was selectively accelerated. The resulting functional deficits of nation-states did not, of course, assume uniform proportions; people did not everywhere become aware of the problems on the same scale, and the solutions envisaged were likewise not always identical. Hence, European integration turned out to be a complex process, provoking reciprocal obstacles as well as benefitting from cumulative changes. Given this situation, a delayed perception of events was often unavoidable and mobilising action could only be taken on a short-term basis.

I will try to outline the different driving forces of European Community formation in their chronological order and development. Although my chapter is limited in scope, I hereby intend to illustrate clearly the foundations of today's European Community and the nature of its potential development.[1]

I

Plans for a unification of Europe have existed ever since the outset of modern state formation in Europe. The yearning for the lost unity of the Christian world, a universal struggle for harmony and, in numerous cases, imperial ambitions, gave rise repeatedly to the development of new schemes designed to overcome the inter-state anarchy in Europe. For a long time, however, such plans only became politically relevant in connection with hegemonial aspirations, such as Napoleon's plans to create a continental power block or the plans for Central Europe drawn up in the era of German imperialism during World War I. It was only subsequent to the disturbance of the equilibrium in Europe's nation-states in the course of World War I that European integration, as an alternative to the power ambitions of nation-states, became the aim of political movements and political operations.

The hitherto unparalleled extent of military force involved in this war, as well as the ensuing tremendous grief, gave rise a new urgency in seeking ways to guarantee a lasting peace. At the same time it became more and more obvious that new techniques of industrial production were rendering the national borders of European states irrelevant, and that the pressure exerted by dynamic, forward-looking American competitors could be felt in Europe's national economies. Moreover, a lot of representatives of the European landed and bourgeois classes were alarmed by the revolutionary claims of the Russian October Revolution and its supporters, who challenged their social and state order and predicted its rapid downfall. 'Europe must federate or perish', the slogan formulated by Clement Attlee in 1939,[2] became a slogan which entered into rivalry with the dominating nation-state principle and gave rise to plenty of Europe-oriented initiatives such as Coudenhove-Kalergi's Paneurope Campaign and Briand's Europe Plan, to name the most spectacular ones.

The longing for peace and the striving for restoration of the integrated economic system of the nineteenth century consequently called the whole principle of the nation-state into question. The initiatives towards unification which emerged from this period, however, failed due to the combination of nationalist regression and the nation-states' strategies to meet the world-wide economic depression. In view of the increasingly aggressive nature of German revisionism and the general concentration on protectionist measures to find a way out of the economic crisis, it was – for the time being – not possible to establish the foundations required for the development of an integration policy which would have been something different, going beyond the hiding of a nation's hegemonial ambitions.

As soon as the failure of the Versailles peace order became evident, the initiatives towards unification were, however, again given a strong impetus. The successful revisionist policy and the rapid triumphal march of National-Socialist Germany in 1939–40 opened the European peoples' eyes to the painful fact that the European nation-states were no longer in a position to guarantee the safety of their citizens, and that even the conventional type of alliances and intergovernmental allignments no longer provided sufficient protection against armed aggression. This intensified the demand for the creation of collective security structures, which made it possible to eliminate the inter-state anarchy at least on European territory; at the same time all those nations which felt threatened by German National-Socialist expansion moved closer together. In Great Britain this development (which, for a long period, was hardly recognised) appeared in outline as early as the time of the Munich Agreement, which was widely perceived as a disgraceful event. Authors like Lord Lothian and Clarence Streit, who came out in favour of a federation of democratic states, attracted enormous attention. Churchill's union offer to France in June 1940 must also be seen against this background.[3]

Afterwards, however, when in France the advocates of an armistice asserted themselves and when Great Britain alone resisted for more than a year the German offensive, the British people's willingness to establish long-term ties with the Continent declined markedly. Lasting peace was now expected to emerge from a close collaboration with the United States, and the British themselves believed they had taken on the role of one of three world powers watching over the peace. On the other hand, those who actively resisted German occupation not only witnessed the failure of the League of Nations, but also experienced national humiliation and breakdown. Owing to this, the rejection of the nation-state principle was expressed with even greater radicalism and, as soon as the prospect of overcoming the National-Socialist empire in Europe became more plausible, the receptivity to federal ideas gained ground. Léon Blum, for instance, expressed his opinion in the spring of 1941 during his imprisonment under the Vichy government as follows: 'One may tell it to the whole world with the deepest and most uncompromising conviction: this war must finally give rise to fundamentally strong international institutions and must lead to an international power taking far-reaching effect, as otherwise other wars will certainly follow.'[4] And, like Blum, dozens of other resistance authors, as well as the overwhelming majority of resistance groups, expressed in writing what would be required for such a degree of effectiveness: the restriction of national sovereignties in favour of a so-called 'super-state' with its own institutions and its own leadership.[5]

The reasoning of the resistance élites was not only shaped by the war and national breakdown, but also – the longer the war-related strains persisted – by the experience of an increasing loss of power in relation to the new world powers. While European resources suffered an extensive loss in value due to war, the United States of America – as the beneficiary of this situation due to her function as main supplier of materials to the anti-Hitler coalition and due to the absence of the European countries from the world market – extended her volume of production to more than double the previous output. The United States achieved standards of economic production which definitely surpassed the limits imposed by the European nation-states, thus calling the competitiveness and consequently the independence of the European countries into question. Simultaneously the outcome of the war enabled the United States, from a strategic point of view, to rise to become the world's leading military power, whereas the Soviet Union advanced to being the strongest military power on the European continent. This resulted in a situation where the old states of the continent not only suffered a considerable loss of their previous influence in international politics, but also themselves became more and more vulnerable to the power and influence exerted by the two main victorious powers which emerged from the war.

Both the accelerated development of productive resources and the obvious loss of political power and importance by the European nation-states produced the impression that a consolidation of European resources as a means of self-stabilisation against the previous 'wing-states' of Europe was now a matter of top priority. The European exile politicians, who were most concerned about this aim, primarily envisaged regional unification. In view of the relative homogeneity of the countries involved and given the intensity of economic interchange already achieved, such regional unions appeared to be within reach and were thus intended to serve as the initial starting point for more comprehensive political unions. In any case those politicians who were now engaged in the development of regional union initiatives normally considered a 'bigger' Europe as the most desirable objective; however, they first concentrated on those things that seemed to be realisable in a post-war situation marked by general upheaval. This is true for both Western and Eastern European exile governments during the Second World War, whereby – in view of the current situation – it is a particularly remarkable fact that the most concrete plans were developed by representatives of the Eastern European governments in exile and resistance.[6]

The readiness to find supra-national solutions was even intensified by the fact that numerous resistance fighters perceived the totalitarian suppression exercised by the fascists to be the final consequence of the absolute nature of the nation-state principle of sovereignty. They rediscovered the mutuality of traditional European values when fighting against the extreme, fascist, form of etatism and nationalism. What urged them to resist was not so much their fight against foreign rule as their rebellion against the suppression of human rights. They were thus induced to move closer together by overcoming ideological, social and national barriers, as well as to take precautionary measures in order to prevent a repeated abuse of nation-state power. In the summer of 1941 Ernesto Rossi and Altiero Spinelli wrote the following statement as a result of long discussions with co-prisoners on the Italian prison island of Ventotene: 'The absolute sovereignty of national states has given each the desire to dominate.' According to them, the nation-states' efforts to maintain a dominant position would necessarily lead to totalitarian regimes; therefore the European peoples would have to oppose the beneficiaries of the old order by eliminating the partition of Europe into sovereign nation-states: 'A free and unified Europe is the necessary prerequisite for a development of modern civilization, which came to a standstill in the era of totalitarianism.'[7]

The longer the war persisted and revealed the atrocities of the National-Socialist regime, the more it became obvious that federative structures had to be established in order to solve the German problem. 'Hatred cannot be wiped out by hatred and violence cannot be removed by violence', Léon Blum wrote in 1941. 'There is ... only one way to dissolve the contradiction in order to render Germany harmless on the basis of a peaceful and secured statute: namely the integration of the German nation into an international community.'[8] Along with the disclosure of realities in the totalitarian power state, it became more and more obvious that the social roots of German imperialism could only be eliminated by a controlled restructuring of German society by the victorious powers. As Claude Bourdet in the French resistance paper *Combat* put it in March 1944: 'This guardianship will, however, only be endurable and tolerated, if Europe's nations partially renounce their national sovereign rights in favour of a European federation.'[9] Without the prospect of development within a federal community of Europeans, the enforcement action taken by the victorious powers would only threaten to produce a new spirit of revengefulness amongst the Germans.

It stands to reason that this line of argumentation was likewise well received among those Germans who reflected on their nation's future following the defeat of the Third Reich. Democratic resistance to Hitler could only really imagine a future for Germany which would be acceptable for all European nations within the framework of a federative international order. When the chances of revolting against National-Socialism dwindled, they intensified their efforts to direct the Allied powers' attention to the effective connection which would exist between the process of democratisation and federalisation. And the conservative resistance around men like Ludwig Beck, Ulrich von Hassell and Carl Goerdeler, which was first marked by certain affinities to the traditional hegemonial conceptions of 'Mitteleuropa', found itself more and more compelled to show greater modesty. Some of them, such as Goerdeler, were convinced of the necessity for economic integration and controlled disarmament, and finally declared themselves in favour of a federative Europe, 'where neither Germany nor any other power would claim predominance'.[10]

The experiences of World War II up to 1943 led to a broad unification movement in Europe. This movement was somewhat uncertain about the geographical boundaries of a unified Europe and Europe's role in a global peace organisation. There were different conceptions about attitudes towards the Soviet Union and about Germany's role within a unified Europe; there were, furthermore, different social objectives and political strategies, different levels of rejection of traditional power politics. There was also no united view on the political implementation of the ideals represented in the European Movement, and there were different attitudes towards the need for certain regional unions. However, the unification movement was marked by a consensus of opinion and similarity of motives which went beyond national and ideological borders, particularly in pointing out the inadequacy of and the threat to peace posed by the traditional nation-state system, as well as the need for federative regulations. This consensus was typical of the majority of politicians in exile and the overwhelming majority of resistance élites in the occupied countries from France to Poland, except for a minority of conservatives and the communist resistance. This consensus could not be found in Great Britain where, following an initial turn towards federative solutions, there was an increasing confidence in the country's own power; the same applied to the Nordic states, which traditionally oriented themselves towards Great Britain. For continental Europe in a narrower sense, however, this consensus of opinion constituted a basis for developing an alternative solution to the restoration of the collapsed nation-state system.

II

The numerous unification plans which had been developed during the resistance period all over Europe did not immediately take the shape of a concrete unification policy at the end of war. Stalin blocked any kind of union in Eastern Europe; at the same time each step towards unification in Western Europe threatened to deepen the division of the continent between East and West, a divisive process which was already under way. It was thus doubtful whether the unification initiatives did justice to the ultimate aim of safeguarding the peace, and numerous supporters of the unification idea shrank back from overly ambitious initiatives. Given this hesitant attitude of the forces demanding integration, it was – particularly in France – still possible to cling to conservative positions aiming at a combination of integration measures with the enforcement of the nation's own leadership. The concept of unification advocated in France by de Gaulle was, however, not acceptable to the neighbouring states. Hence, a great number of unification initiatives were unable to get beyond their tentative beginnings.[11]

It was the increasing gravity of the East-West conflict, escalating into the Cold War, which was decisive for the political break-through of the unification movement. On the one hand, this aggravated conflict produced a clear decision regarding the question of the continent's division, which could no longer be avoided by the Europeans; on the other hand, the need for unification by the nations of Western Europe appeared to be even more urgent than before. The economic weakness of the European countries was now felt to be more worrying, as was their powerlessness in the face of global confrontation, the presence of the United States in Europe and the necessity to intervene in the global conflict in order to save the peace. At the same time there was an increasing fear of Soviet aggression, especially since the communist assumption of power in Czechoslovakia in February 1948. With the inclusion of West Germany into the containment programme, the problem of creating a framework for integration in order to control the German recovery had to be approached in a new manner.

Henceforth a safe position with respect to Germany could neither be guaranteed by a joint control exercised through the four victorious powers, nor by unilateral discrimination against the West German state. The Germans were now able to request a reward for their new role as an indispensable partner of the Western alliance; even though it could not be excluded that Germany, having shaken off the chains put on it by the occupying powers, might decide to link up with the Soviet Union, which disposed of the key to the reunification of Germany. It was especially this perspective (reviving the 'Rapallo trauma') which led to a situation where the creation of supra-national structures in Western Europe became a matter of top priority. In early September 1948, for instance, Jacques Tarbé de Saint-Hardouin, political adviser to General Koenig, put it in the following way: 'We have still the opportunity to integrate Germany into Europe, but this opportunity must rapidly be seized; in one year's time it will already be too late.'[12]

On the whole, these impulses were now effective enough to manage a first attempt towards a European integration within the area of the Marshall Plan. It is true that the United States' decision to support the Western European union made it much easier to realise the integration plan, which appeared in outline in 1948–49 behind the initiatives to establish the Brussels Pact, the OEEC

(Organisation for European Economic Cooperation) and the Council of Europe, and which was now especially hastened by the French government. However, the real driving force behind the integration process was a forthright independent European movement which went beyond the European associations which had meanwhile been formally established, and sometimes even ignored them. It was influential within some national governments, and – at least in the countries forming part of the later established 'Community of Six' – met with wide-spread public approval. A precise analysis of public opinion and voting behaviour shows that, in 1948–49, these countries disposed of clear majorities in favour of a real integration with supra-national elements, and that the Council of Europe was understood as the embryo of a future federative Europe.[13]

It was, however, only possible to fill the public with enthusiasm for a European project if Great Britain participated in such a project. Only if this condition was fulfilled would a unified Europe have sufficient weight to be active in the field of world politics. Britain's presence was also necessary for the maintenance of a reliable counterweight, compensating for the possibly dominant position of Germany within Europe. Third, Great Britain's participation was considered by left-wing factions within the European movement as a guarantor for a Europe which, certainly as far as domestic policy was concerned, would develop into a 'third force' between American capitalism and Soviet communism. This threefold necessity of British participation serves as explanation for the persistent attempts – made especially by France and the continental leftists in the years 1948 and 1949 – to convert the British people to the unification project. The fact that, at the first attempt, these parties were content with the constitution of a Council of Europe with mere advisory functions had nothing to do with a lack of determination or readiness for real integration. The Council of Europe was rather called into existence in order to convince the obviously hesitating British of the necessity to create a European union under British leadership.

Integration policy soon reached a deadlock due to the effort made to gain Great Britain's support. Although the British Foreign Minister, Ernest Bevin, repeatedly made arrangements for a contribution from his country to the integration process, both the British President of the Board of Trade and the Chancellor of the Exchequer continually put obstacles in his way. Therefore the

British attitude remained reserved and self-contradictory; the continental advocates of British participation in the unification project again and again gathered fresh hope, but in each case the negotiations came to a standstill. In early November 1949, the British government blocked all recommendations pronounced during the first session of the consultative assembly of the Council of Europe which aimed at an extension of the authority of the Council, thereby destroying the hope of creating a European constituent assembly through the evolution of the Council itself.

However, conclusions were not rapidly drawn from this restriction on the scope of the Council of Europe. The hopes pinned on British leadership ability remained too high, the fear of West Germany's weight in a Europe without Great Britain remained too strong, and the domestic resistance of left-wing parties to a Europe characterised by capitalism and Cold War remained too great. It was only when nothing else functioned – namely when the preparations for German rearmament threatened to bring about the removal of production restrictions imposed on West German heavy industry, thus causing a relaxation of the occupation statute – that the French Foreign Minister Robert Schuman made up his mind, after long inner conflict, to take the plunge into a state of supra-nationality without Great Britain. The basic idea of the Schuman Plan of May 9, 1950 – which consisted in entrusting a supra-national European body with the competence to issue guidelines and to coordinate the planning of Europe's basic industries – had been discussed ever since World War II, and since 1948 several initiatives had already begun in order to translate this plan into reality. What was new was Schuman's readiness to realise the project even in the absence of British participation. By proclaiming from the very beginning that the French government would insist upon the supra-national authority of the Coal and Steel Agency, he confronted the British in an unmistakable manner with a crucial decision: did they want to participate in the first steps of the unification process or did they not?[14]

III

It was due to this resoluteness that the plans which had been made in times of war finally began to take shape after a delay of five years. The so-called 'Europe of Six', which started with the establishment of the European Coal and Steel Community (ECSC), was of course merely a modest version of the European proposals developed since the war. The European Coal and Steel Community was far less popular than the European idea as propagated in the late 1940s; and an enlargement of the Community of Six going beyond the coal and steel area was not, either in 1950 or at a later date, advocated by a clear and determined majority, whether among the public or in the decision-making centres of the six member states. Politicians on the left in particular showed a slackening in interest in a Europe which was evidently closely attached to American power, and which showed a liberal-conservative tendency, with the apparent commitment to solve the problem of the Cold War.

Support for the integration project lost further ground when, in the course of the years 1951–52, it became evident that, even through European Community structures, the Germans could not be placed under the guardianship of their European neighbours on a lasting basis. Despite their insight regarding the necessity of European unification, the victims of German aggression – understandably enough – found it hard to accept West Germany as an equally privileged partner. For this reason a majority of unification supporters had first taken refuge under the concept that Germany would put up with a so-called 'minor status' within the future Community. Most of the planning for integration during the first few post-war years merely provided for a very restricted German participation in political responsibility. Even in the first version of the project aiming at a European Defence Community, namely the French Pleven Plan of October 1950, the element of discrimination was still much in evidence: according to the original French conceptions, Germany – and only Germany – should renounce its own general staff and military infrastructure, as well as air forces and troops outside the common command.

However, it was in defence matters in particular that such discriminatory treatment could not be enforced: The population of the Federal Republic of Germany could only be persuaded to make a defence contribution if, in return for such a contribution, it was granted the same degree of security as all other Community members. In the negotiations concerning the European Defence Community, Adenauer, though having to struggle hard, was able to gain almost full equality of rights for the Federal Republic of Germany in the field of security policy. Thereafter unilateral discrimination was out of the question in other political fields as well. However, as this became evident, reservations about the European Defence Community likewise gained ground. Objections were increasingly raised against a widening of the integration process, and these could not be overcome in the short term. The learning process, which was particularly required in France, did not everywhere attain the speed necessary in order to save the European Defence Community. Consequently, after more than two years of agonising discussions, the plan to create a Defence Community failed, being rejected by the French Parliament in August 1954.[15]

Added to this, the integration project became less urgent in the course of the early 1950s for several reasons. Due to the Soviet détente initiatives, especially after Stalin's death in March 1953, integration intended to ward off the Soviet danger was no longer a matter of top priority; and as soon as economic reconstruction was successful, the first symptom of a historically new and impressive 'economic miracle', both the economic and the political weaknesses of the old nation-states seemed less urgent than in the immediate post-war period. Moreover, the functions which had originally been assigned to a unified Europe were now partially performed by the Atlantic Alliance. This was true not only of the safeguarding of Western Europe's position against the Soviet Union, which could hardly be guaranteed by European efforts alone, particularly in view of the fact that the nuclear deterrent was now gaining increasing importance; it likewise applied to security against the Germans, which was guaranteed – admittedly to an insufficient, but nevertheless reassuring degree – by the permanent presence of American troops on West German territory. This became so obvious that the French, following the emotional discussion about the European Defence Community, were now able to accept the direct integration of the Federal Republic of Germany into NATO.

Thereafter, European Community structures were basically only necessary to prevent West Germany's economic domination, to stabilise the general economic upsurge, to strengthen the European role in international politics, and to ensure a long-term survival of solidarity among Europeans. These were all highly respectable grounds for continuing the integration process, despite the failure of the European Defence Community. But the aforementioned motives still did not arouse a sufficient driving force in order to eliminate at the first attempt the nation-state oriented structures and interests that were opposed to the integration project.

Given this situation, the treaties for the foundation of the European Economic Community (EEC) and of the European Atomic Energy Community (EURATOM) of March 1957 represented an attempt to save the European idea, insofar as it was not already irretrievably lost.[16] This attempt was first of all politically motivated and, just like previous integration projects, aimed at the creation of a politically-united Europe. However, the underlying idea was for the first time a consolidation of such economic interests which, independent of political considerations regarding their utility, came out in favour of a closer cooperation among the six member states. Efforts were made to reduce three different types of interests to one common denominator: firstly, the interest of the French modernisation planners in the intensified use of nuclear energy, which was by no means vital but was politically attractive in France and was therefore brought up for discussion by Jean Monnet; secondly, the interest of the Dutch and of an increasing number of French farmers in a European agricultural market with modernisation projects and sales guarantees, aiming in principle at the integration of other nations outside the circle of the six member states, but in the last resort also accepting a restriction to this limited circle; and finally, the interest of the Dutch and of an increasing part of German and Belgian industry in the removal of trade barriers, especially among the countries of the European Coal and Steel Community (ECSC).

The mere consolidation of these interests was, of course, not sufficient for the revival and advance of the integration process. On the one hand, it was possible to consolidate the atomic energy community, the common agrarian market and the removal of trade barriers in terms of a 'quid pro quo' for those involved; on the other hand, these interests encountered the resistance of those having to expect disadvantages from such a consolidation. The countries importing agrarian products resisted the expected high consumer prices, and the farmers' lobby in those countries with a less competitive agricultural output put up a fierce resistance to the abandonment of national protectionism. In France, major sectors of industry and commerce, but also most of the workers' representatives, recoiled from open competition within a European market. In the Federal Republic of Germany the industrial complex, even encouraged by the liberal philosophy of

Ludwig Erhard, resisted common external tariffs, anti-cartel regulations and the harmonisation of social burdens, which – it was feared – would threaten the expansion of the German economy. What was required to overcome such opposition was not only the counter-attraction of economic compensation arrangements, but also the intention to continue the integration project for what could be described as superior political reasons.

That this political intention was able to prevail was first of all attributable to a situation where those political forces which had originally advocated a European union, but had meanwhile been disappointed by the possibilities of its realisation, did not simply return to a traditional nation-state policy. The great majority of these forces wavered between their belief in the necessity of the European union on the one hand, and a feeling of regret at not being able to carry out this unification under the desired conditions on the other hand. They held back when it came to concrete unification projects, but did not completely abandon their hopes for a future realization of their ideals. In France, where the prevailing political attitude was once again of decisive importance, the pressures exerted by the Americans in the question of a European Defence Community had actually given rise to additional resistance to the integration project, which even persisted after the failure of the European Defence Community. At the same time, however, the strong rejection by West Germany of all Soviet reunification offers meant a gradual lessening of reservations towards a de facto partnership with the Federal Republic of Germany.

Given the state of public opinion and the attitude of organised interest groups, an attitude which was basically characterised by indecision and conflicting impulses, politicians acting with determination and tactical cleverness had a good chance to establish new structures. The actual existence of such leaders, who were keenly interested in carrying on the integration project for political reasons, was a further and indeed independent prerequisite for the accomplishment of the Treaties of Rome. In particular, three politicians should be named in this context, who – not because of their ideas, but due to their ability to take resolute action directed towards specific objectives – can rightfully be designated as the 'founding fathers' of the EEC and EURATOM: Paul-Henri Spaak, who managed to turn the loose group of experts appointed by the Messina conference into a political instrument with a binding commitment; Guy Mollet, who managed by masterly tactics to carry the project through in France despite public resistance; and Konrad Adenauer, who once more summoned up the required flexibility and readiness to make concessions to his French partners.

IV

However, the extraordinary difficulties arising in connection with the implementation of the Treaties of Rome are also indicative of the fact that the state of European integration had reached the highest level possible in the 1950s, and that the Community's further development was by no means programmed in advance by the signing of these treaties. The reservations regarding the transition to the second and third level of the Common Market, which were included in the EEC Treaty on the insistence of France, represented real reservations; and the acknowledgment of the Community's political finality was no more than an introductory declaration of intent without any binding commitment. Whether the suggested and, if only from an economic point of view, urgently required further development of the European Community would in fact be realised was essentially dependent upon whether it would at a later date be possible to reach an understanding regarding the Community's political finality. This question was for tactical reasons left out when concluding the Treaties of Rome.

However, this was precisely what did not happen. The negotiations on political union, pushed forward by De Gaulle in 1961–62 within the scope of the 'Fouchet Plans', developed rather into a *dialogue des sourds*. The political partners of France were afraid of a French hegemony, and most rejected the idea of the Community's own identity in terms of security policy; whereupon de Gaulle was piqued and returned to a national policy.[17] British applications for membership were abruptly rejected twice (in 1963 and in 1967); with its *force de frappe*, France began to establish an autonomous defence structure, and in July 1965, de Gaulle reacted to attempts to strengthen the European Community organs by pursuing the 'policy of the empty chair', which gave rise to a crisis in Community development. This threatened to turn into reality the worries of Jean Monnet and Konrad Adenauer in the early stages of negotiations: namely that the creation of economic control authorities without the corresponding formation of a political union would, in the long run, discredit the integration plan.

The fact that the European Community outlived the crisis triggered by de Gaulle is primarily due to the increasing power of attraction of the Common Market. Its early machinery already proved to be an instrument for raising productivity in a socially acceptable manner within the circle of the six member states. Later the Common Market was courted by new applicants for membership and thus continuously gained more importance and weight. In 1979, the hope of overcoming dependency upon currency speculators following the abandonment of the Bretton Woods system gave rise to the introduction of the European Monetary System. In 1985–86, the fear of Japanese competition led the decision to complete the internal market before 1993.

On the other hand, the project of a politically united Europe always remained a precarious problem. The objective difficulties facing its realisation were too great. These included the bipolar system of deterrence, the uncertainties regarding the definitive orientation of West Germany, and the persistent French insistence on a special nuclear role (which was actually intensified by the entire situation). The Community's ultimate political objectives were not even discussed when new member states joined the Community at a later date; political cooperation exhausted itself in occasional manifestations of goodwill, accompanied by an endless series of national single combats and mutual frustrations.[18]

Of course, the termination of the post-war order in 1990 and the reunification of Germany have necessarily resulted in increasing the political importance of the European Community. The decay of the Soviet empire and the ensuing reduction of the American presence in Europe have strengthened the role of the European Community in world politics as well as its function as a force for order on the European continent; and the reunification of Germany has rendered the Community's function as a control instrument, serving to restrain the Germans, even more important.[19]

The Maastricht Treaties are an attempt to take account of these modifications in the situation. However, they still leave open the question of the democratic legitimation of a supra-national Europe. As long as this problem is not solved, the danger of a repeated breakthrough of nationalist trends cannot be excluded. While such a breakthrough will not lead to a restoration of the pre-war order, as is sometimes predicted in speculative accounts or nostalgic versions of history, it may well result in a general incapacity to practise governmental control, which might lead to even more disastrous consequences. There is no way back to the nation-state order, but this does not yet guarantee that the benefits of civilisation achieved by the nation-states will develop positively within a European Community.

Notes

1. Parts I-III are based on my *Der Weg nach Europa. Geschichte der europäischen Integration 1939–1957*, Göttingen, 1990.
2. C.R. Attlee, *Labour's Peace Aims*, London, 1940, p. 12.
3. See J. Pinder, 'Federal Union 1939–41'. in W. Lipgens (ed.), *Documents on the History of European Integration, vol. II: Plans for European Union in Great Britain and in Exile 1939–1945*, Berlin/New York, 1986, pp. 26–155; A. Bosco, *Federal Union and the Origins of the Churchill Proposal: The Federalist Debate in the United Kingdom from Munich to the Fall of France, 1938–1940*, London, 1992.
4. L. Blum, *A l'échelle humaine*, Paris, 1945.
5. See W. Lipgens (ed.), *Documents on the History of European Integration, vol. I: Continental Plans for European Integration 1939–1945*, Berlin/New York, 1985.
6. W. Lipgens, 'East European Plans for the Future of Europe: the Example of Poland', ibid., pp. 609–58; F. Gross/M.K. Dziewanowski, 'Plans by Exiles from East European Countries', in *Documents, vol. II*, pp. 353–413.
7. *Documents, vol. I*, pp. 474 and 479.
8. Blum, *A l'échelle humaine*.
9. C. Bourdet, 'Future Allemagne?, *Combat* Nr. 55, march 1944.
10. '"Peace plan, late summer-autumn 1943"', printed in *Documents, vol. I*, pp. 430–2
11. See Loth, *Der Weg*, pp. 22–47.
12. Letter to Robert Schuman 7.9.1948, quoted in R. Poidevin, 'Le facteur Europe dans la politique allemande de Robert Schuman (été 1948–printemps 1949)', in R. Poidevin (ed.), *Histoire des débuts de la construction européenne (Mars 1948–printemps 1949)*, Bruxelles, 1986, pp. 311–26. For the context see W. Lipgens and W. Loth (eds), *Documents on the History of European Integration, vol. III: The Struggle for European Union by Political Parties and Pressure Groups in Western European Countries, 1945–1950*, Berlin/New York, 1988.
13. Ibid. and W. Lipgens and W. Loth (eds), *Documents on the History of European Integration, vol. IV: Transnational Organisations of Political*

Parties and Pressure Groups in the Struggle for European Union, 1945–1950, Berlin/New York, 1991.

14. See my 'Der Abschied vom Europarat. Europapolitische Entscheidungen im Kontext des Schuman-Plans', in K. Schwabe (ed.), *Die Anfänge des Schuman-Plans 1950/51,* Baden-Baden, 1988, pp. 183–95.

15. For the details, see Militärgeschichtliches Forschungsamt (ed.), *Anfänge westdeutscher Sicherheitspolitik 1945–1956, Bd. 2: Die EVG-Phase,* München, 1990.

16. Much new evidence on the origins of EEC and EURATOM can be found in E. Serra (ed.), *Il rilancio dell'Europa e i Trattati di Roma,* Milano, 1989. For a general assessment of the decision-making process see Loth, *Der Weg,* pp. 113–33.

17. For the scope of de Gaulle's project, see my 'De Gaulle und Europa. Eine Revision', in *Historische Zeitschrift,* vol. 253, 1991, pp. 629–60.

18. Recent overviews are D.W. Urwin, *The Community of Europe: A History of European Integration since 1945,* London/New York, 1991; and J. Pinder, *European Community: The Building of a Union,* Oxford/New York, 1991.

19. For an assessment of the implications of the end of the Cold War, see my 'Das Ende der Nachkriegsordnung', in *Aus Politik und Zeitgeschichte,* B18/91, 1991, pp. 3–10.

HARTMUT KAELBLE

The Social History of European Integration

Introductory Remarks

This paper[1] intends to show what contribution to the historical analysis of European integration can be made by social historians. I do not claim to be presenting a fundamentally new interpretation of general history by a social historian. My idea of a social history of European integration is much more modest and much more pragmatic. It is a plea for a broader and more comprehensive historical analysis of European integration.

I shall start with some brief remarks on what could be regarded as a social history of European integration. I shall then present a concept which consists of what I would see as the four essential aspects of social history of European integration: first, the interconnections and exchanges between European societies; second, the social differences between European societies and the convergence of European (mainly Western European) societies since the Second World War; third, the social commonalities and at the same time the social peculiarities of nineteenth and twentieth century Europe compared to non-European industrial societies; and finally, awareness among Europeans of a common European society and civilisation.

Let me first make some initial remarks on what could be understood as the social history of European integration. In theory, the social history of European integration could be written in three different ways, one of which I shall select for this paper.

219

The first way of writing the social history of European integration is that which is expected normally by political historians and
political scientists. Social factors and social preconditions for the
emergence and further development of supra-national or intergovernmental European institutions are investigated as well as
policies and political ideas. Historians and political scientists hope
to learn from social history about neglected but powerful factors
affecting European integration. They seek social factors underlying the foundation of the European Coal and Steel Community of
1950, or the social background to the foundation of the European
Economic Community in 1957, or even try to find social reasons
for the failure of the European Defence Community in 1954 or the
reinforcement of European integration in the late 1980s. This sort
of social history of European integration has not so far been written, mainly because it is extremely difficult to demonstrate that
social factors played a role in the motivation of European decision-
makers; they certainly cannot be detected in the European
archives.

A second type of social history of European integration investi-
gates the direct or indirect social results and consequences of the
policies of European institutions. It describes the direct results of
European policy in various fields, e.g. the mobility of labour, the
mobility of students, occupational chances for women, social
funds for the workers in the declining coal and steel regions, social
funds for European farmers, and the social history of the
European bureaucracy. If the European social chapter comes into
effect, this history will also include European regulations for working hours and perhaps eventually European regulations for industrial relations or a European social policy, which at the moment is
in only an embrionic stage.[2] This type of social history of European
integration could also include more indirect social consequences
of European integration which are usually linked to specific policies only in a loose way, e.g. the rise of a European consumption
pattern, the improvement of the European standard of living,
changes in regional disparities, changes in national consciousness
and new mental horizons among national administrative and political elites. This type of social history of European integration
would be written in the activist spirit of the motto of Jean Monnet:
'We do not only ally governments, we also unite peoples.' In this
sense, this social history describes not only the cooperation
between European governments, but also the wider effects of

European integration on the coexistence of European societies and on the way Europeans live together in everyday life. However, the direct social results of European policies are usually not very impressive, and the more impressive indirect results are difficult to trace and to prove. So far, I am not aware of any historical book which follows this way of the social history of European integration.

There is, however, a third type of social history which does not begin with the policies of European institutions. Rather, it stands back from the history of European integration and tries to find out whether European societies or in particular Western European societies, became more integrated in the sense that they became less dissimilar and less separate from each other during the second half of the twentieth century. This approach to the social history of European integration does not presume any direct link between the foundation of supra-national European institutions and a more intensive integration of European societies: integration of European societies might start earlier or come later than political integration. It might include only a few societies of the European Community, but it could also include societies outside the European Community. The integration of European societies might be most intensive in fields which are not covered by European policy, and might be least intensive in fields in which European institutions have intervened. Integration in European societies might be totally unintended or even unnoticed by European politicians. This social history of European integration starts from a broad concept of European integration which includes not only the foundation of European institutions but also the emergence of a European civilisation, of common European characteristics under the precondition that cultural, economic, social and political integration might even develop independently from each other. The central interest of this type of approach to social history of European integration is actual societal differences.

A further general remark: historians who work on European social integration can not build upon theoretical concepts and extensive theoretical debates for two reasons. Theories of supra-national integration usually concentrate upon political integration in the narrow sense. They normally leave out any social aspects, factors or preconditions. In addition, concepts of supra-national integration which regard European integration as a special case of

nation-building or as a special case of multinational empire building do not really fit into European reality. The stimulating theoretical concepts of European integration which were developed,
especially in the 1950s, started with the assumption that Europe
would become a sort of a nation-state. It is difficult to share this
basic assumption after forty years of European political integration. Nor can the historical analysis of multicultural empires be
applied to the European Community, since it is a unique supranational institution; it did not come into existence by military conquest, by immigration or by marriage as all other multinational
empires have done, it is based not on the hegemonial leadership
of one ethnic group such as the Russians in the Soviet Union, the
Austrian Germans in the Habsburg Empire or the Serbs in
Yugoslavia but upon a partnership which includes an important
input from the small member-states, and finally, the European
Community is integrating rather than suppressing nation-states
and national identities. European integration is so unique that neither theories nor precise terms exist for it. Hence, historical analysis of European integration has to be pragmatic rather than led by
the theoretical concepts which are normally helpful for the historian.

Because of lack of space I shall only briefly deal with the four
main aspects of the concept mentioned above, and will give only
an overview rather than a detailed analysis. For the same reason I
shall concentrate mainly upon the period after the Second World
War, though one might also wish to treat these events in a much
longer perspective to show more clearly whether integrative tendencies since the Second World War in fact replaced disintegrative
tendencies during the nineteenth and early twentieth centuries.
This paper also cannot deal with individual European countries.
This may be seen as a disadvantage, since individual European
countries by no means always follow the main European trends.
Presenting such a general concept has its dangers; many of the
special aspects which I touch upon are almost totally neglected by
research and I would need the whole space of this article to present individual integrative tendencies in a convincing way. I am
therefore fully aware that in many ways this paper will lead to questions and reflections rather than to firm arguments based on
detailed empirical proofs.[3]

Interconnections between European Societies

Social interconnections between European societies are an important aspect of European integration. In his theory of European integration, Karl Deutsch saw communication between societies as the major social factor of political integration.[4] Some studies of bilateral relationships between European countries put social interconnections at the centre of their analysis. Nevertheless, the interconnections between European societies as the result of education in other countries, migration, travel, international communication, or the international transfer of goods, ideas, lifestyles and social values have rarely been investigated. They have been explored if at all in terms of bilateral relationships rather than on a European or even on a Western European level. European investigations do face serious difficulties because of the lack of general European sources, lack of standardisation of national European statistics, and also lack of methods by which Europe or groups of European countries can be isolated from international worldwide interconnections. Hence, the history of the weakening and the intensification of inner European social connections and exchanges has in many ways to start from scratch.

Moreover, the development of interconnections within Europe was not simply in the direction of intensification. On the contrary, disconnections also exist. I want to refer to four major weakenings of social connections between European societies during the twentieth century. First, the kinship relations between European power-holders, which had existed between most of the European monarchies and national aristocracies, were seriously weakened with the decline of monarchies in many European countries and lost their political importance. Second, the migration of workers within Europe also lost its former importance. In the earlier period, in which Europe was clearly divided into an economically developed inner Europe and an economic periphery, the migration of wage-earners created a strong connection between European societies, although it often produced ethnic and national discrimination and even ghettos. However, after Europe became fully industrialised during the 1960s and 1970s, labour migration between European societies ceased to grow. The number of Italian workers migrating to France, the number of German employees migrating to England and the number of Dutch workers migrating to Germany did not increase, and even declined. The third weakening of international communication lay in the field of international scholarship. The international scholar, whose best known exemplar was Erasmus of Rotterdam, and who still existed in the nineteenth and early twentieth centuries, became more and more marginal because of the national separation of scientific cultures since the First World War, and also in a different way because of the rapid expansion of research personnel since the 1960s. It is not clear that the internationalisation of research since the 1970s actually compensated for this decline in the internationalism of scholars. Finally, for about forty years, international communication and exchanges were also strongly reduced by the political division of Europe between Eastern Europe and Western Europe. It will undoubtedly still take years until the interconnections across the former Iron Curtain will get back to a normal level of intensity.

Despite these weakenings, it seems in general that the interconnection between European societies has intensified since the Second World War in a double sense: on the one hand, the quantity of exchanges between European societies has distinctly increased, especially during the 1970s and 1980s,[5] and on the other hand, the experience of geographic space by Europeans expanded beyond regional and national borders and at the same time concentrated more upon Europe.

The development of quantitative social exchanges between European societies has still to be investigated on the European level. Statistics vary strongly between countries, standardised statistics do not exist even for the European Community. Hence, I have to illustrate the quantitative development by taking the example of Germany, which does not look to me to be an exceptional case. Social exchanges increased between European countries in all major fields, in education as well as in professional migration, in travelling as well as in marriages, in the consumption of foreign goods as well as in the knowledge of foreign languages.

Education of Europeans in foreign European countries has clearly expanded. In Germany, the number of German students at foreign European universities increased from some 100 university students around 1910 to 7000 students during the 1960s and to more than 25,000 students in 1989. At the same time the number of foreign European students in Germany increased from about 6000 in 1910 to about 11,000 during the 1960s and to about 18,000 in the 1980s, though German universities (and the German language) lost much of their international attraction during the twentieth century for political and scientific reasons. These numbers may seem small, but many of these students were later to assume important and influential positions.

Short-term and long-term migration between European countries also increased, especially in the 1970s and 1980s. Once again let us take the German example: around 1980 more British and French than ever before lived in Germany. The number of Europeans in Germany coming from member states of the European Community was larger than one might expect; it is as large as the largest group of immigrants from outside the European Community, the Turks. It is highly probable that these migrants between European countries were not just blue-collar workers but came from all sorts of occupations including those demanding highly qualified employees; in Southern European countries they were also migrants after retirement. Since the decline of the inner-European migration of mostly unskilled workers from peripheral to industrial countries, a new trend towards short-term and long-term socially diversified migration between industrialised European societies seems to have emerged.

Travel between European societies also seems to have grown rapidly. Hotel bookings by European foreigners in Germany rose from about 800,000 in 1950 to almost 15 million in 1989. In other Western European countries as a whole, hotel bookings by European foreigners increased even more rapidly. European statistics show that this increase in travel not only brought Northern Europeans to the South, but more recently also Southern Europeans to the North. Among the young Europeans, in 1990, only a small minority had not visited other – mostly European – countries.

Family connections between European countries also increased, though at a lower level than one might expect. Again to use the German case, the number of male Germans who married European foreign women increased from somewhat more than one-half of 1 per cent in 1955 to almost 2 per cent of all marriages in Germany in 1980. The percentage of female Germans who married a foreign European man increased from around 1 per cent to more than $2\frac{1}{2}$ per cent over the same period. A final important interconnection between European societies lies in the increasing exchange of consumer goods, which has created not only an economic momentum but has also led in many ways to changes of lifestyle. The separation of national consumer cultures became less distinct and gave way to the beginnings of a European consumer culture consisting of goods from all European countries.

One major precondition for exchanges between European societies, knowledge of foreign languages, has also changed dramatically. Once again, because of the lack of general European case studies we shall use the German example: among those who went to school before the Second World War only a small minority, about 15 per cent spoke English. Among West Germans who went to school after the Second World War, about half spoke English; by the end of the 1980s the overwhelming majority, 90 per cent, of young West Germans spoke English. West Germany is no exceptional case; among the young Europeans in the European Community in 1990, about 90 per cent had learned a foreign language, about two-thirds could make a conversation in a foreign language.

All these interconnections (except of the knowledge of English language) opened up links mainly to other European societies. Once again using the German example, about 80 per cent of the West German students who were at a foreign university in the 1980s studied at European universities. Three-quarters of the foreigners who booked hotels in West Germany in 1990 were Europeans. Around 80 per cent of West Germans who made their holidays in foreign countries went to other European countries. Marriages between Germans and foreigners were predominantly (males) or increasingly (females) with other Europeans. Foreign consumer goods in Germany were overwhelmingly European consumer goods; three-quarters, in terms of value, came from European OECD countries. Increasing international connections seem to have remained either predominantly European or to have become even more European.

Among the reasons for the growth in international connections between European societies, I would distinguish between two categories. On the one hand, there are general explanations which apply to European as well as to non-European industrial societies: the unique rise of the standard of living especially since the 1950s and 1960s, the unique development of educational qualifications and the rapid expansion of university graduates and secondary schooling, and finally the traffic revolution and the information revolution have led to a more intensive social exchange between all industrial societies. On top of these explanations, there are special European reasons for more intensive European interconnections: the long period of inter-European peace which is needed to tear down the economic, political and mental barriers between European societies, the negative experience of two wars felt by most Europeans which gradually opened European minds to other European countries, and finally also the European Community which has in indirect ways also made social exchanges easier.

Interconnections between European societies became more intensive not only due to more quantitative exchanges, but also due to a new geographical experience. Before approximately the middle of the twentieth century, most Europeans knew only their own country, often only their own region or locality, from direct personal experience. They usually knew other European countries only indirectly from journals, books, radio broadcasting, or hearsay. Only for a very small group of businessmen, higher civil servants (mostly diplomats), internationally active academics, artists and intellectuals, and for special occupations such as railway employees or seamen, was direct experience of other European countries part of normal life.

Mass experience of other countries was to be had in two different and clearly exceptional ways. On the one hand, direct personal experience of foreign countries was had by many Europeans in countries outside Europe, either by emigration, mainly to the Americas where they usually stayed, but where quite a number of Europeans also came back after shorter or longer stays; or by immigration, temporary work or travelling in the European colonies. This experience of foreign countries did not render other parts of Europe more familiar. On the other hand, direct personal experience of foreign European countries was made by many Europeans under extreme, often traumatic conditions. Probably the most frequent situation was the war, which led to experience of other European countries as soldier, prisoner of war, displaced person, deportee, refugee, or prisoner in a concentration camp. These experiences were not only traumatic in the sense that they created a total separation from normal life, but they also took place in a fundamentally hostile situation.

Another still frequent experience was the migration of usually unskilled workers and servants into other European countries, often leading to ghettos and deprivation and often also experienced as a major upheaval in life. More limited to the European middle class was the experience of other European countries through work in foreign firms owned by relatives or friends as sons of business families, or through work as a governess or as an au pair girl in foreign middle class households. This experience again was exceptional in the sense that it was usually part of middle class adolescence and thus limited to a specific phase of male or female middle class life. On the whole and with the exception of a few occupations, Europeans had either no direct personal experience of other European countries, or only in exceptional, peculiar and often traumatic situations.

From roughly the middle of the twentieth century the direct personal experience of other European countries changed fundamentally in two directions. On the one hand, direct experience of foreign countries became more Europeanised. With the decline of the colonial empires of Britain, France, Belgium, the Netherlands, Spain, Portugal and Italy fewer Europeans from these countries lived in the European colonies outside Europe and knew them. In fact, many Europeans lived through a dramatic 'Europeanisation' of their lives in being forced to leave the colonies and to go back to a Europe which they sometimes did not know at all. In addition, with the decline of emigration to the Americas after the end of the short-term post-war revival of emigration, fewer Europeans than before emigrated from this part of the world. This was not compensated by expanding tourism and business travelling in non-European countries; these were much more superficial experiences, not real continuity. On the other hand, from roughly the middle of the twentieth century on, a mass of Europeans started to cross the borders into other European countries under normal conditions of peace through business travel, through tourism, or for the purpose of education or work. They also experienced European countries by marrying, contact with foreign visitors, business relations, or buying consumer goods from abroad. These growing interconnections not only became part of normal life, but were also repetitive rather than exceptional; they were usually linked neither to extreme situations such as wars, nor to a radical break with the society of origin, nor were they limited to a specific phase of life. Among young Europeans in 1990, three out of four had visited other countries, mostly European countries, at least once. One out of three Europeans in 1990 had stayed in foreign countries for longer than one month.[6]

It would be naïve to assume that these increasing exchanges

and increasingly normal personal experiences of other European countries led to a disappearance of confrontations between different European cultures and to a full abolition of prejudices, or to an automatic emergence of international minds or European identities. Some types of tourism in foreign European countries are undoubtedly caricatures of direct personal experience of foreign societies. The persistence of strong prejudices among citizens of the same national society with even more internal exchanges than between European countries is a definite warning. The precise consequences of these enlarging interconnections on the images formed by Europeans of other Europeans has in fact been little investigated. But one can expect, for good reasons, two major consequences. First, the image of other European societies would have a fundamentally different base and would be much more influenced by personal direct experience than before. Second, purchasing consumer goods from other European countries and travelling to other European countries has become so much part of normal life for the mass of Europeans that the abolition of these exchanges would be seen as directed against their material interests. The German or Spaniard of the 1930s who was prevented by the policy of autarchy of the Nazi regime or the Franco regime from travelling abroad and from consuming foreign products did not renounce many important things in his life. The German or Spaniard of the 1990s faced with a similar policy of autarchy would face a substantial reduction in his standard of life.

The convergence of European societies: less dissimilarities

A second major aspect of the social history of European integration is the mitigation, rather than full convergence, of the social differences between European societies. For lack of space it is impossible to go into details about the development of social differences between individual European countries. I can only touch upon the main trends.

Social differences between European countries have by no means disappeared. They were and are important. This is not only a matter of empirical evidence, but also a matter of wishes and hopes. Most Europeans appreciate intensive interconnections between European societies, but they do not necessarily wish to have less social differences between European countries. One of the major European peculiarities which makes Europe different from the United States of America is the way in which Europeans appreciate the peculiarities of national and regional societies. A rising number of European intellectuals also believe that the enormous internal social and cultural variety of Europe is its most outstanding characteristic, and a major protection against over-centralisation of power in Brussels and against economic over-standardisation in Europe.[7]

In addition, especially during the immediate post-war era, some differences between European societies were reinforced. First of all, the Second World War did not affect all European countries to the same degree. Some countries were much more affected by hunger, by scarcity of housing and fuel, by epidemic diseases, by the breakdown of the provision of basic needs, public administration and schooling. Contrasts in everyday life were very strong after the Second World War, especially between the small part of Europe which did not take part in the war, i.e. Sweden, Switzerland, Spain, Portugal and Ireland on the one hand, and the regions most affected by the war, i.e. Britain, France, the Netherlands, Belgium, Northern Italy, Germany, Poland, Yugoslavia, Finland and the Soviet Union, on the other hand. In addition, governments and societies drew varying lessons from the war. The continuity of elites, the political role of former resistance movements, and social reforms in a wide sense varied enormously from one country to another as a direct consequence of the war. In Britain for example, the war led to a fundamentally new concept of social policy, the Beveridge plan, which inspired the reforms of the British welfare state directly after the Second World War; in Germany the war and the Nazi regime strengthened the position of the opponents of any reform of public social insurance. In France, the war led to an awareness of the backwardness of the French economy and to a forceful modernisation policy by 'planification' after the Second World War; in Germany, the reaction to the highly centralised Nazi war economy was an important precondition for the strictly liberal economic policy adopted in the Western part of Germany. Finally there was a much more persistent reason for social differences within Europe; the division between Eastern and Western Europe. The fundamental social differences caused by the political division of Europe can be observed in contemporary

Germany, for example.

However, distinct convergences and reductions of the differences between European societies have also occurred, especially since the 1950s. Two major new momentums of convergences came into effect, an economic momentum and a political momentum. The economic momentum for the social convergence of European societies came from two directions. On the one hand, the period since the Second World War is a period of industrialisation in the whole of Europe, not only of inner Europe[8] but also of the former southern, northern and eastern peripheries. Whereas in inner Europe industrialisation was a long-term process which started in the late eighteenth and nineteenth centuries, for large parts of Eastern, Southern and Northern Europe industrialisation was a sudden economic upheaval during the 1950s and 1960s. Only from that time on can one say that Europe as a whole was industrialised, with the exception only of some isolated regions. On the other hand, the period since the Second World War was a period of a unique rise in the standard of living without any parallel in Europe's past. The timing and intensity of the rise in the standard of living was not the same in all European countries but the basic trend can be found everywhere, in the west as well as in the east, in the north as well as in the south. The industrialisation, as well as the rise in the standard of living, was reinforced though not fully explained by the new international economic order established in the West by the United States, by European economic integration since the 1960s and by different but highly purposeful national economic policies.

This economic momentum led to three major social convergences since the Second World War; not to full similarities, but to a reduction of dissimilarities. First, the strong dissimilarity in the active population decreased markedly. The sharp contrasts which still existed around 1950 between societies with marginal agrarian labour forces such as Britain or the Netherlands and societies with a predominant agrarian labour forces such as Portugal, Spain, Italy and various Eastern European countries were clearly reduced. The agrarian labour force became a minority everywhere in Europe, except in some isolated regions and in Albania. The huge differences in industrial labour forces which also could still be found in 1950, between countries with strong industrial labour forces such as Britain, Belgium, Germany, Austria, Switzerland and Czechoslovakia, and countries with a marginal industrial labour force such as Portugal, Italy and many Eastern European countries, also clearly diminished. The labour force in the service sector was always less dissimilar than in other sectors, but it became still more similar. During the 1970s and the 1980s some new divergences did emerge, especially between some Central European countries such as Czechoslovakia and the GDR which maintained strong industrial labour forces and Western Europe where the industrial labour force became steadily less important. In a rapid, brutal deindustrialisation process, the Central European societies have become more similar to the rest of Europe since 1989.[9]

Secondly, the strong dissimilarities in urbanisation were also mitigated. Directly after the Second World War, huge differences existed between the most urbanised European societies, Britain and the Netherlands, and predominantly rural European societies such as Portugal, Greece, Italy, Spain, Ireland, Norway, Finland and various Eastern European countries. After the urbanisation of the whole of Europe during the last decades, almost all European countries became predominantly urban. Most Europeans now live in urban environments and have taken over urban values.

The third and perhaps the most important convergence lay in the fact that, at least in Western Europe, the large differences in the standard of living have also been reduced. In the 1950s, impressive differences were to be found between the inner, industrialised Europe and southern Europe in particular. Private consumption expenditure in Portugal around 1960 was only one-fifth of the Western European average, and in Italy it was still just above two-thirds of the average. By 1990, private consumption expenditure in Portugal had reached two-thirds of the European average and in Italy it was equal to the European average. The huge differences which could also be found in the normal indicators of living standards (which in the mean time have become partly dubious) such as housing standards and possession of telephones, TVs, refrigerators and cars were also clearly reduced. Important differences in standards of living between European countries persisted in Western Europe, however, and demanded a more active regional policy on the part of the European Community; in addition, clear differences became more apparent between Western Europe as a whole and Eastern Europe. But the Western European standard of living in 1990 was clearly more homogenous than in 1960, and this in turn gives us some hope for a lessening of the difference between Western and Eastern Europe.[10]

These trends of reduced dissimilarities are not simply global trends to be found in all industrial societies. Though Europe did not divert from these global trends, it still kept distinct peculiarities. In the active population of Europe, industrial labour remained more important than elsewhere. The urbanisation in Europe remained special: huge metropolitan areas of several million inhabitants were less common among European cities than among American, Canadian, Australian or Japanese cities, and they did not grow as rapidly as in the Soviet Union. The process of de-urbanisation during the 1980s also was much less distinct in Western Europe than in the United States. Undoubtedly the indicators of the standard of living, i.e. the use of cars, of TVs and of telephones, for example, developed in a similar way everywhere. However, the clear reduction of international disparities in private consumption expenditure was a European peculiarity. Even among the OECD countries the same reduction cannot be demonstrated.[11]

Was the rise of interconnections and the weakening of social dissimilarities between European, especially Western European, countries not mainly a consequence of an Americanisation of the European societies? I think one ought to be careful when evaluating arguments on this topic. 'Americanisation' is not only a term which is loaded with ideologies and strong emotions, and, hence, difficult to define and to use as an efficient scientific term. We also do not know very much about the social impact of the USA on European societies. Few European historians have worked on this topic in social history, though it is usually understood that Americanisation has been strong since the Second World War.[12] Moreover in social history one ought to make a clear difference between two levels: the debate by contemporaries on Americanisation, and the actual social impact of the USA. In the debate by contemporaries since the Second World War, the term Americanisation was often used by conservative as well as left-wing commentators of social trends to stigmatise widely varying social changes. It would be highly problematic to use these debates as sources for the factual social impact of the USA. No doubt the factual impact of the USA has been distinct in specific social areas such as in scientific and social scientific research, business management, the cinema, and the commercialisation of consumption, such as in the introduction of supermarkets and fast food and also in the introduction of specific American products such as Coca Cola, computers, jeans or burger restaurants. However, one should also not overlook some fundamental limits of the American social impact.

One major limit which might look paradoxical at first glance is the long-term basic proximity of the societies of the USA and of inner Europe. Industrialisation and subsequent social change have advanced in close mutual connection on a similar level in the USA and Europe since the nineteenth century. Basic technologies and basic social innovations were developed on both sides of the Atlantic Ocean. Because of the destruction created by two European wars, a wide gap emerged in the interwar period between the United States and inner Europe in economic and social development and continued to exist for about two decades after the Second World War, especially in the field of management techniques, household techniques, the expansion of the automobile, housing standards and in the quality and standard of life in general. Because of this gap, many Europeans during that period believed that the model of the American way of life was alien to European societies.

But most of these techniques and principals of social life were also developed in Europe. The automobile, the motorway, skyscrapers, the refrigerator, canned food, fast food, the radio, the TV, even the supermarket were also European traditions. 'Americanisation' in many ways meant either reimporting or even merely encouraging social trends already present in inner Europe, rather than imposing a foreign way of life on Europe. In this way, 'Americanisation' in Europe – provided one still wishes to apply this term at all to the social history of inner Europe – means something fundamentally different from the social change brought about by the American model in Japan, South America, Southeast Asia and also in some peripheral European countries. No doubt for inner Europe, especially for West Germany, the American impact led to fundamental political upheavals, in particular for certain aspects of constitutional history, for international relations, and also for the change of the political and professional mentalities of the elites. But for social history, the notion carries with it the misleading image of an imposed alien hegemonial social culture.

Social peculiarities of Europe

A third crucial element of a social history of European integration is the existence of commonalities of European societies which at the same time distinguish Europe from non-European industrial societies. Such social peculiarities of Europe as a whole compared to non-European industrial societies did not only exist as common historical origins, as Judeo-Christian origins or as ancient origins and as medieval origins. Social peculiarities also did not only exist in the sense of an historical European civilisation compared to China or India or the Muslim world, as classical sociologists and historians such as Max Weber or Emil Durkheim or Arnold Toynbee have demonstrated. There are also social peculiarities of Europe during the nineteenth and twentieth centuries which were rarely discussed by social historians in a general sense. What we know comes from three sources: from the classical sociologists who analysed also the civilisations of their time; from research by social historians on some specific themes such as family history, the history of the welfare states or the history of specific social milieus; and finally from the historical research on the American 'exceptionalism', which usually compares the United States with Europe as a whole.

No doubt these social peculiarities do not include all European countries or even all Western European countries. They do, however, cover the situation of the majority of the Europeans. No doubt also these social peculiarities did not last during the whole of the nineteenth and twentieth centuries. Some of these social peculiarities emerged in the early modern period or became clear during the course of the nineteenth and early twentieth centuries. But all of them are still important for the period since 1945. It is also clear that the social peculiarities which will be treated on the following pages are not known outside the community of specialists; in general, Europeans are not aware of these social commonalities of European societies. The common European historical roots, the ancient, Judeo-Christian and medieval roots are much better known than the social commonalities of the present. Still, the social peculiarities and commonalities of post-war European social history are an crucial aspect of the reality of social integration of Europe.

Due to lack of space, I shall treat European social peculiarities only briefly.[13] I want to touch upon the five most important social peculiarities and at the same time the social commonalities of post-war Europe. For these five peculiarities evidence from social history research is available. Other social peculiarities of Europe could be added or should be more closely explored: the social history of religion, the social history of the city and of urban life, the social history of the intellectuals and their public, the social history of public bureaucracy and of attitudes towards law, the social history of business and management, the social history of industrial relations, the social history of migration and of minorities. However, the five major European social peculiarities and commonalities which I want to mention briefly are: the European family, European work, European social milieus, the European welfare state and the European consumption pattern.

First, British and Austrian social historians have demonstrated that a peculiar type of European family has developed since the early modern period. Its main momentum can be seen in an especially strong independence of European young couples from the household of their parents. Hence, marriage meant the establishment of an independent household. As a consequence, three-generation households were much more rare in Europe than elsewhere; the age of men at first marriage as well as that of women was distinctly higher because an independent household needed more professional independence and more savings. For the same reason, the rate of non-marriage was more substantial in Europe than elsewhere, and the late age of marriage also led to a lower birth rate than elsewhere. At the same time, specifically European family mentalities developed, such as an especially strong intimacy of the family and a especially strong separation of the nuclear family from the neighbourhood and from the other relatives, strong emotional links between husbands and wives and between parents and children, and a more distinct crisis of adolescence which prepared the separation from the household of the parents. This European family developed especially in Northwestern and Central Europe and spread over the whole of Europe only during the nineteenth and twentieth centuries. Though it became a global model during the twentieth century up to the present, the age of first marriage is still distinctly higher in Europe than in the United States or in Eastern Europe and the birth rate is still distinctly lower in Europe than in the rest of the world.[14]

A second social peculiarity of nineteenth and twentieth century European societies was and is the strong impact of industrial work.

The proportion of industrial labour in the active population was much higher in Europe than in all other industrial societies in America or in Asia. Only in European history can a distinct period be found in which industry was the largest employment sector. For some countries such as Britain, Germany or Switzerland, this period of industrial society lasted many decades and had already started during the nineteenth century. For Western Europe as a whole this period started in the 1920s and ended in the 1970s. As a consequence, European societies were much more strongly characterised by purely industrial cities such as Sheffield, Vervier, Gelsenkirchen, Katowice and St. Etienne. Industrial workers were clearly more numerous in European societies than in non-European industrial societies. Hence, working-class culture, working-class quarters and the trade unions had a much stronger impact in Europe than elsewhere. To be sure, tertiary labour became more important than industrial labour since the 1970s in Europe, and the Central European communist societies, in which high proportions of industrial labour had been preserved, followed this path in a brutal way after 1989. But industrial work is still more important in Europe than elsewhere.

All this is not true for all European societies, but is so at least for the majority of the Europeans. Perhaps because of these traditions of industrial labour, the separation between work and non-work outside the household became more distinct in Europe than elsewhere, especially since the Second World War: during the week, the working hours have been reduced further in Europe than elsewhere. During the year, holidays were longer in Europe than elsewhere and a peculiar European holiday culture emerged; during the worker's lifetime the period of work was shorter in Europe, the entrance into the labour market was later, the age of retirement was earlier and the proportion of women who never worked was larger than elsewhere in the world.[15]

A third social peculiarity consisted of a strong impact of unique social milieus on European societies in the nineteenth and twentieth centuries. The most important of these peculiarly European social milieus were the European middle class with its peculiar common family and economic values, with its strong internal connections by marriage, by education, by associations and culture, and with its strict social distinction from the aristocracy and from the lower classes; the European working class with its peculiar culture, its solidarity in individual crises and its more or less strong links to the labour movement; the European lower middle class with its strong sense of economic independence, strong family ties, high mobility into and out of the lower middle class and its peculiar lower middle class culture; the European milieu of peasants with its strong orientation towards the preservation of the family property, strong social isolation and strong family ties, weak formal school and professional training, and clear separation from urban culture and its peculiar lifestyles and values. European societies were not only characterised by these individual milieus, and also by very strict demarcation lines separating these social milieus, but also by many exchanges and mutual dependencies between these social milieus. Again, there is no room to present these milieus in a more detailed way. They weakened after the Second World War in most European societies but many of the institutions and mentalities of these social milieus still persist.[16]

A fourth social peculiarity of Europe emerged after the Second World War in the development of the modern welfare state. The modern welfare state was clearly more developed in Europe than in non-European rich industrial societies. Welfare expenditure in relation to GNP in most European countries was higher than in non-European Western industrial societies. The proportion of the active and non-active population which was protected by the modern welfare state was distinctly larger in Europe than in industrial societies outside Europe. In most Western European societies, almost the total of the population was protected in this way. Moreover, the European welfare state had a longer history than the welfare state in other non-European societies. In pioneering countries such as Britain, Sweden, Germany and Austria, it was already in the process of development in the late nineteenth century. The modern post-war European welfare state built upon this long welfare state experience. Moreover, during the whole period since the Second World War the most important pressure for the further development of the welfare state always came from Europe, especially from Britain and Sweden. Even in the deep crisis of the welfare state during the 1980s, distinct European peculiarities emerged. The alternative to the public welfare state was not only the family and the market, as in non-European societies, but also to a much stronger degree than outside Europe the idea of the non-profit making, non-bureaucratised small public association, an idea which built upon a long European tradition of 'friendly societies', 'secours mutuels' and 'Genossenschaften'.[17]

A final social peculiarity of Europe developed only after the Second World War. The European consumption pattern and way of life have unfortunately not been explored so far by social historians in the international comparative perspective. It seems, however, that strong national and regional divergencies in consumption became less distinct and were in part replaced by common European consumer goods which often are a mixture of goods from various European countries and regions: European food, European drinks, European clothes, European household machines, European cars, European furniture, European housing standards and housing designs. In the centre of European cities specifically European urban lifestyles have developed which have made shopping in Modena, Périgueux, Lausanne, Freiburg, Oxford, and Uppsala rather similar, and certainly more similar than immediately after the Second World War. A peculiar European holiday culture has emerged which is different from holidays in the Americas or in Asia. I repeat: though the impact of the American way of life after the Second World War became stronger than ever before, American consumer goods played only a marginal, though sometimes spectacular, role. Fundamental changes in consumption and the rise of European-wide consumption patterns were sometimes discussed as 'Americanisation'. However, these were mostly not an imposed alien culture, but basically an Atlantic culture which was merely sometimes more developed and more advanced in the US than in Europe.

The Awareness among Europeans of European Society

Contemporary Europeans were not always aware of the development of interconnections between European societies, of the rising or diminishing international differences, or of the evolution of European social commonalities. The debate among Europeans on social commonalities has another history than that which one might expect from what has been presented so far. The awareness of Europeans of the rising interconnections and diminishing differences between European societies was not clearly reinforced after the Second World War. It also did not always centre upon what social historians regard as European social commonalities. It was normally also clearly separate from politics, and few Europeans seem to have had the idea that the commonalities of

European civilisation might be the base for a political united Europe.

Once again, there is no room to present details about the development of the ideas of social commonalities of European countries. I want to present four final observations. First of all, the debate on social commonalities of Europe was far more vivid and far more intensive since the nineteenth century than one might expect in the period of nationalism and the nation-state. It seems that in this debate on the social characteristics of Europe, many more participants were involved than in the debate on the establishment of a politically united Europe. Famous names such as Simone de Beauvoir, James Bryce, Hugo von Hofmannsthal, Karl Kautsky, Wilhelm Liebknecht, André Siegfried, Werner Sombart, Alexis de Tocqueville, Arnold Toynbee, Max Weber, Carl Zuckmayer and hundreds of unknown writers, civil servants, professionals, professors and travellers participated in this debate. To be sure, the debate was restricted to public debate by educated Europeans. The horizon of the common European was too narrow, too regional and even too local. Nevertheless, the educated European often seems to have had an idea of a European society. This idea did not only cover the European past, the common ancient, Judeo-Christian and medieval roots of Europe; it also covered European society in the contemporary period. This idea of Europe was most clearly formulated in comparison with the United States, whereas comparisons with other civilisations such as the Muslim world, the Chinese world or the African world were normally made with Western civilisation as a whole including the United States, rather than with Europe alone.

Moreover, contemporary images of European society did not fully coincide with the results of the research by social historians. Contemporary Europeans were aware only of specific aspects of the European family such as the distinct division of role between husbands and wives, rather than the European family as a whole. They did not observe at all the specific importance of industrial employment; they often observed only fragments of the strict demarcation lines between social milieus in Europe and either defended or attacked this European peculiarity. Europeans only gradually became aware of more modern European social peculiarities such as the welfare state or the European consumption pattern. The same is true for other social peculiarities of Europe such as specific industrial relations, specific types of urbanisation, specific ways of business management and specific types of bureau-cracy. On the whole, contemporary Europeans had many impor-tant insights into the social peculiarities of Europe, but since they did not have the sources which we use today, they could not detect the whole range of social commonalities and particuliarities of Europe.

In addition, the social peculiarities of Europe were not simply a matter of scientific research. The debate on social peculiarities of Europe was part of a more comprehensive discussion of social modernisation of Europe during the nineteenth and twentieth centuries. The evaluation of the social peculiarities of Europe was often highly controversial. There was no consensus among Europeans about crucial aspects of modernisation: there was no agreement on whether Europe was the harbinger of modernisa-tion or whether it was falling back, especially behind the United States; whether social change in Europe was to be regarded as a positive result or as a danger; whether the possible model and future of social modernisation of Europe, i.e. the United States, was to be judged in a fully positive or totally negative way; or whether the predominant trends in Europe were acceptable for one's own country or one's own region, or whether a more favourable special way and a deviation from European norm was regarded as preferable. In the period of fundamental change such as the nineteenth and parts of the twentieth century, the discus-sion about the social peculiarities of Europe was also a discussion on the acceptance or the refusal of this social change. Therefore, a clear contradiction between a strong consensus about common European roots and highly controversial evaluations of the com-mon present European society was typical for that period.[18]

With the definite establishment of the European centre of power in Brussels, two developments are possible. On the one hand, the social peculiarities of Europe might become part of a European identity; but substantial symptoms for such a develop-ment do not yet exist. On the other hand, with the increasing eco-nomic integration and standardisation in Europe and with the rise of a strong power centre in Brussels, national or regional social and cultural identities might serve more and more as a protection against an economic over-standardisation and against too much power for the European institutions in Brussels. This trend has been expressed in recent years by various European intellectuals, who argue that the major particularity of Europe is her social and cultural variety and heterogenity. The recent debate is dominated by warnings of the weakening of cultural and social differences between European nations, rather by any enthusiasm for European social commonalities.[19]

Concluding Remarks

This concept of a social history of European integration is partly based on intensive empirical evidence, but partly also on preliminary indicators. The main arguments are that since the Second World War, three important social changes took place in the social history of Western Europe or Europe as a whole. First, despite contradictory developments, the exchanges and connections between European societies, especially between Western European societies, clearly intensified in the areas of work and education in other European countries, in tourism into other European countries, in the exchange of consumer goods between European countries and, though to much less clear degree, in family relations. All this was based upon a strong increase in the knowledge of other European languages.

Parallel to these social changes, the geographical experience of the mass of Europeans also changed. It Europeanised with the decline of European colonial empires and with the reduction of the emigration to non-European societies; the experience of other European countries at the same time became less exceptional and less dramatic. Geographical experience was no longer a matter of wars, enforced migration of the unskilled or ritual migration during adolescence, but became an experience of all Europeans in normal situations of everyday life and in almost all ages. Though we do not know very much about the effects of these wide and direct experiences on prejudices, people's images of other societies are now based much more on direct experience. In addition, travelling or living in other European countries and consuming goods from other European countries has become a normal part of the everyday life of Europeans and hence a part of the material interests of Europeans.

Secondly, despite new divergences – partly as a consequence of the Second World War and partly as a consequence of the division of Europe between East and West – in general social differences between West European societies have weakened, partly for economic reasons, i.e. because of the industrialisation of the whole of Europe including the periphery, partly because of the unique rise in the standard of living especially in the 1950s and the 1960s, and partly also for political reasons, especially because of the parallel intervention of European governments in social development. This mitigation of social differences between European societies was to a certain degree part of a global development among industrial societies; it was however more distinct among Western European societies, and hence reinforced European civilisation as an entity.

Finally, distinct social peculiarities of European societies as a whole did exist. They did not include every individual European society, but did include at least the majority of Europeans. These social peculiarities of Europe which can be especially demonstrated in the history of the family, in the history of the active population, in the history of class milieus, in the history of the welfare state and in the history of consumption, and probably also in other fields of social history, single out Europe from the rest of modern industrial societies, although not in the same way as from each individual non-European industrial society. Normally, Europeans are not aware of these commonalities; hence, so far they have not been the base of a European social identity. Nevertheless, these peculiarities exist.

How should these results be interpreted? On the one hand, it is clear that these European social changes and European social peculiarities do not imply and probably also will not imply anything similar to a national society. Europe as a whole still is far less homogenous than a nation. It remains important that no common language exists in Europe. A common European culture has not yet emerged either in the arts or in popular culture. A European political culture, in institutions of a European-wide public, European-wide parties and social movements do not yet exist. At the same time, all the social developments and structures described above are not yet the characteristics of a European social identity with a similar status to the national identities in Europe.

On the other hand, the social changes and social structures of Europe which have been discussed make European societies fundamentally different from any other group of countries. It seems that European countries are more closely connected, less dissimilar and more clearly identifiable as a peculiar civilisation than

South American societies, Arab societies, East Asian societies, African societies or even CIS societies. Since the Second World War, there has been a distinct reinforcement and revival of a common European civilisation which is no longer a matter of a remote ancient or medieval past, but also a matter of the present. It would, however, be naïve to believe that this will automatically lead to a stable system of European peace or to full political integration of Europe. It offers us a chance, no more. Peace and political integration remain a matter for political decisions.

Notes

1. I am very grateful for comments and suggestions by Tony Nicholls.
2. See for a discussion on a major theme of this way of the social history of European integration E. Vogel-Polsky and J. Vogel, *L'Europe sociale 1993: illusion, alibi ou réalité?*, Brussels, 1991; P. Flora, 'Unity and Diversity – A Comparison', in P. Flora (ed.), *Growth to Limits: The Western European Welfare State since World War II*, vol. 5 (in preparation); B. Schulte, 'Die Entwicklung der europäischen Sozialpolitik', in H.A. Winkler and H. Kaelble (eds), *Nationalismus – Nationalitäten – Supranationalität*, Stuttgart, 1993; S. Leibfried, 'Sozialstaat Europa? Integrationsperspektiven europäischer Armutsregimes', in Nachrichtendienst des Deutschen Vereins für öffentliche und private Fürsorge vol. 70, 1990; F.X. Kaufmann, 'Nationale Taditionen der Sozialpolitik und europäische Integration', in L. Alberti (ed.), *Probleme und Perspektiven europäischer Einigung*, Köln, 1986; B. Henningsen, 'Europäisierung Europas durch eine europäische Sozialpolitik?', in P. Haungs (ed.), *Europäisierung Europas?* Baden Baden, 1989.
3. The paper is based on my book *A Social History of Western Europe, 1880–1980*, Dublin-Savage (USA), 1990. The paper, however, goes beyond that book in including the first and fourth aspect, and also in complementing in many ways the second and third aspect which is covered in the book up until the 1970s.
4. K.W. Deutsch et al., *Political Community and the North Atlantic Area: International Organisations in the Light of Historical Experience*, Princeton, 1957; Deutsch, 'Integration and Arms Control in the European Political Development: A Summary Report', in *Political Science Review*, vol. 69, 1966; Deutsch, 'Shifts in the Balance of Communication Flows: A Problem of Measurement in International Relations', in *Public Opinion Quarterly* vol. 1, 1956.
5. The following statistical data are collected from national statistical yearbooks and from publications of the European Community.

6. *Young Europeans in 1990,* Commission of the European Communities, Brussels, 1991, p. 58 (opinion poll among Europeans in the European Community between the age of 15 and 24).

7. See as examples E. Morin, *Penser l'Europe,* Paris, 1987; W. Lepenies, *Aufstieg und Fall der Intellektuellen in Europa,* Frankfurt am Main, 1992, pp. 61ff.

8. Inner Europe includes Britain, France, the Benelux countries, Germany, Switzerland, Northern Italy, Austria and Bohemia. I take this term from Sidney Pollard, *Peaceful Conquest: The Industrialization of Europe 1760–1970,* Oxford, 1981, pp. 45ff.

9. For the decline of industrial labour in Central Europe see *Short-term economic Statistics: Central and Eastern Europe,* OECD, Paris, 1992, tables 5.3 and 5.4; for the post-war development of the labour force see *Economically Active Population,* 5 vols., ed. by the International Labour Office, Geneva, 1986, vol. 5, pp. 87ff.

10. Calculated from *Historical Statistics 1960–1980,* OECD, Paris, 1982, pp. 14ff.; *Historical Statistics 1960–1990,* OECD, Paris, 1992, pp. 18ff; for the decline of international differences in the use of cars, telephones and TVs, see B.R. Mitchell, *International Historical Statistics: Europe, 1750–1989,* London, 1992, pp. 714ff., 744ff., 754ff.

11. See sources given before. For the international comparison of the trends in private consumption expenditure Western Europe as a whole was compared to the non-European members of the OECD, i.e. the United States, Canada, Australia, Japan and Turkey.

12. A. Sywottek, 'The Americanization of Daily Life? Early Trends in Leisure and Consumption', in M. Ermarth (ed.), *America and the Shaping of German Society 1945–1955,* Providence, 1993; P. Duignan and L.H. Gann, *The Rebirth of the West: The Americanization of the Democratic World, 1945–1958,* London, 1991; R. Willett, *The Americanization of Germany, 1945–1949,* London, 1989; J.E. Miller, *The United States and the Reconstruction of Italy, 1945–1948,* Cambridge, 1986; R. Kroes, (ed.), *Image and Impact: American Influences in the Netherlands since 1945,* Amsterdam, 1981; on some aspects of Americanisation, especially in West Germany, see V.R. Berghahn, *The Americanization of West German Industry, 1945–1973,* Oxford/Providence, R.I., 1986; H.-J. Rupieper, 'Bringing Democracy to the Frauleins: Frauen als Zielgruppe der amerikanischen Demokratisierungspolitik in Deutschland 1945–1952', in *Geschichte und Gesellschaft,* vol. 17, 1991; K. Wageweitner, *Cocacolaization and the Cold War,* Chapel Hill, 1994; B. Plé, *Wissenschaft und säkulare Mission. 'Amerikanische Sozialwissenschaft' im politischen Sendungsbewußtsein der USA und im geistigen Aufbau der Bundesrepublik Deutschland.* Stuttgart, 1990; R. Kuisel, 'L'américanisation de la France (1945–1970)', in *Cahiers du dentre de la recherche historique* no. 5, 1990, pp. 53–5.

13. See H. Kaelble, *A Social History*, pp. 12ff; for more details see my arti-
    cle 'The European Integration Since 1950 and Social History', in P.
    Lützeler (ed.), *Europe After Maastricht: American and European
    Perspectives*; for a French version, see 'L'Europe vécue et pensée au
    XXe siècle: une histoire sociale', in R. Girault (ed.), *Identité et con-
    science européennes au XXe siècle*, Paris, 1994; H. Kaelble (eds), *The
    European Way: Essays on Social Peculiarities of Europe During the nineteenth
    and twentieth Centuries* (in preparation with Berghahn Publishers).

14. J. Hajnal, 'European Marriage Patterns in Perspective', in D.V. Class
    and D.E.C. Eversley (eds), *Population in History*, London, 1965; P.
    Laslett, *Family Life and Illicit Love in Earlier Generations*, Cambridge,
    1977, chapter 1; Laslett, Household and Family as Work Group and
    Kin Group, in R. Wall et al. (eds), *Family Forms in Historic Europe*,
    Cambridge, 1983; Laslett, 'The European Family and Early
    Industrialisation', in J. Baechler et al. (eds), *Europe and the Rise of
    Capitalism*, Oxford, 1988; Michael Mitterauer, *Sozialgeschichte der
    Jugend*, Frankfurt am Main, 1986, pp. 28–43; A. Burguière et al.,
    Histoire de la famille, vol. 2, Paris, 1986.

15. See H. Kaelble, 'Was Prometheus Most Unbound in Europe? The
    Labour Force in Europe During the Late nineteenth and twentieth
    Centuries', in *Journal of European Economic History*, vol. 18, 1989, pp.
    65–104; R. Granier, *L'emploi en Europe et aux Etats Unis, analyse compar-
    ative de longue durée*, Paris, 1990; Christoph Conrad, 'Die Entstehung
    des modernen Ruhestands. Deutschland im internationalen
    Vergleich 1850–1960', in *Geschichte und Gesellschaft*, vol. 14, 1988;
    Economically Active Population, 1950–2025, ed. by International Labour
    Office, 5 vols., vol. 4, 3rd edn, Geneva, 1986, p. 160.

16. J. Kocka, 'Middle Class and Bourgeois Society in the nineteenth
    Century', in Kocka and A. Mitchell (eds), *Bourgeois Society in nineteenth
    Century Europe*, Oxford/Providence, 1993 (see also the articles by
    Marco Meriggi, Albert Tanner, Bo Stråth, Gyürgy Ránki, Waclav
    Dlugoborski and Elzbieta Kaczynska); Hartmut Kaelble, 'Die oberen
    Schichten in Frankreich und der Bundesrepublik seit 1945', in
    Frankreich Jahrbuch 1991, p. 64ff.; E.H. Hobsbawm, *The Age of Empire,
    1975–1914*, London, 1987; K. Tenfelde, 'Vom Ende und Erbe der
    Arbeiterkultur', in S. Miller and M. Ristau (eds), *Gesellschaftlicher
    Wandel, soziale Demokratie. 125 Jahre SPD. Historische Erfahrungen,
    Gegenwartsfragen, Zukunftskonzepte*, Berlin, 1988; W. Kaschuba, *Die
    Kultur der Unterschichten im 19. und 20. Jahrhundert*, München, 1990; J.
    Moser, *Arbeiterleben in Deutschland 1900–1970*, Francfort, 1984; H.
    Mendras, *La seconde révolution française 1965–1984*, Paris, 1988; R.
    McKibbin, *The Ideologies of Class: Social Relations in Britain 1880–1950*,
    Oxford, 1990; J.D. Young, *Socialism and the English Working Class: A
    History of English Labour 1883–1930*, New York, 1990; G. Crossick and
    H.-G. Haupt, 'Introduction', in Crossick and Haupt (eds), *Shopkeepers*

and *Master Artisans in Nineteenth Century Europe*, London, 1984; J. Blum, *The End of the Old Order in Rural Europe*, Princeton, 1978; A.J. Mayer, *Adelsmacht und Bürgertum. Die Krise der europäischen Gesellschaft 1848–1914*, Munich, 1984; H.-U. Wehler (ed.), *Europäischer Adel 1750–1950*, Göttingen, 1990; R. Huebscher, 'Déstruction de la paysannerie?', in Y. Lequin, *Histoire des Français XIXe et XXe siècles*, vol. 2, *La sociétié*, Paris, 1983; see also H. Kaelble (ed.), *The European Way* (in preparation).

17. For more details see Kaelble, *Western Europe*, pp. 74ff.; P. Flora (ed.), *Growth to Limits*, 5 vols., Berlin New York, 1986ff.; OECD, *Social expenditure 1968–1990*, Paris, 1985.

18. This debate on social peculiarities in Europe during the nineteenth and twentieth centuries is the theme of one of my current research projects. For a few preliminary conclusions see the introduction to the session 'Europäische Identität und gesellschaftliche Besonderheiten Europas im 20. Jahrhundert', in *38.Versammlung deutscher Historiker in Bochum 1990*, Stuttgart, 1991, pp. 210–12; 'La représentation de la société européenne à la fin du XIXe et dans la première moitié du XXe siècle', in R. Girault (ed.), *Les Europe des européens*, Paris, 1993.

19. See as examples Morin, *Penser*; Lepenies, *Aufstieg*, pp. 61ff.

Bibliography

Published collections of documents

Akten zur Auswärtigen Politik der Bundesrepublik Deutschland 1963, Hans-Peter Schwarz et al. (eds), (im Auftrag des Auswärtigen Amtes vom Institut für Zeitgeschichte), 3 vols., München, 1993 (the diplomatic documents of the Federal Republic of Germany beginning with the year 1963. The publication of the documents in chronological order is planned; a year's documents are to be published each year)

Bossuat, Gérard (ed.), *D'Alger à Rome (1943–1957), choix de documents*, Louvain-la-Neuve, 1989 (coll. Histoire de la construction européenne)

Documents Diplomatiques Français, Paris, 1987 ff. (the French diplomatic documents; 11 vols published so far, covering the period from 21 July 1954 to 30 June 1959)

Documents on British Policy Overseas, Series I: 1945–1950, London 1984 ff.; *Series II: 1950–1955*, London, 1986 ff. (10 vols published so far, covering the years 1945–1946 and 1950–1952)

Documents on the History of European Integration 1939–1950, Walter Lipgens and Wilfried Loth (eds), 4 vols., Berlin, 1985–1990

Dokumentation der Europäischen Integration, zusammengestellt v. Heinrich von Siegler, 2 vols. (vol. 1, *Mit besonderer Berücksichtigung des Verhältnisses EWG-EFTA. Von der Zürcher Rede Winston Churchills 1946 bis zur Bewerbung Großbritanniens um Mitgliedschaft bei der EWG 1961*; vol. 2, *1961–1963 unter besonderer Berücksichtigung der Bestrebungen für eine 'Atlantische Partnerschaft'*), Bonn, 1961 and 1964

Europa. Dokumente zur Frage der europäischen Einigung, Forschungsinstitut der Deutschen Gesellschaft für Auswärtige Politik (ed.), 3 vols., München, 1962

Europäische politische Einigung. Dokumentation von Vorschlägen und Stellungnahmen, zusammmengestellt von Heinrich von Siegler, 2 vols. (vol. 1, 1949–1968; vol. 2, 1968–1973), Bonn, 1968 and 1973

Foreign Relations of the United States, Department of State (ed.), 1945 ff., Washington, 1967 ff.

Gasteyger, Curt, *Europa zwischen Einigung und Spaltung 1945–1990. Eine Darstellung und Dokumentation über das Europa der Nachkriegszeit*, 2nd edn, Bonn, 1991 (Bundeszentrale für politische Bildung, Schriftenreihe, vol. 285)

Lipgens, Walter (ed.), *Europa-Föderationspläne der Widerstandsbewegungen 1940–1945*, München, 1968

Lipgens, Walter (ed.), *45 Jahre Ringen um die europäische Verfassung. Dokumente 1939–1984. Von den Schriften der Widerstandsbewegung bis zum Vertragsentwurf des Europäischen Parlaments*, Bonn, 1986

Schwarz, Jürgen (ed.), *Der Aufbau Europas. Pläne und Dokumente 1945–1980*, Bonn, 1980

Vaughan, Richard, *Post-War European Integration in Europe*, New York, 1976 (Documents of Modern History)

Weigall, David and Peter M.R. Stirk (eds), *The Origin and Development of the European Community*, London, 1992

Guides to sources and archives

Dumoulin, Michel, *La construction européenne en Belgique (1945–1957)*. (Aperçu des sources), Louvain-la-Neuve, 1988

European University Institute, *Guide to the Historical Archives of the European Communities*, 4th edn, Florence, 1993

Henke, Josef, 'Reconstruction in Europe: The Reintegration of Western Germany – Report on the Relevant Historical Material in the Bundesarchiv', *Zeitschrift für die gesamte Staatswissenschaft*, vol. 137, no. 3, 1981, pp. 469–90

Lipgens, Walter (ed.), *Sources for the History of European Integration (1945–1955): A Guide to Archives in the Countries of the Community*, Leyden, 1980

Memoirs and diaries

Adenauer, Konrad, *Erinnerungen*, 4 vols (vol. 1, 1945–1953; vol. 2, 1953–1955; vol. 3, 1955–1959; vol. 4, 1959–1963), Stuttgart, 1965–1968 (English trans., *Memoirs*, London, 1966)

Auriol, Vincent, *Journal du septennat 1947–1952*, 7 vols., Paris, 1970–1978

James, Robert Rhodes (ed.), *Winston S. Churchill: His Complete Speeches 1897–1963*, 8 vols. (vol. 7, 1943–1949; vol. 8, 1950–1963), New York, 1974

Macmillan, Harold, *Tides of Fortune 1945–1955*, London, 1969; *Riding the Storm 1956–1959*, London, 1971; *Pointing the Way, 1959–1961*, London, 1972; *At the End of the Day 1961–1963*, London, 1973

Marjolin, Robert, *Le travail d'une vie. Mémoires 1911–1986*, Paris, 1986 (English trans., *Memoirs, 1911–1986*, London, 1989)

Monnet, Jean, *Mémoires*, Paris, 1976 (German trans., *Erinnerungen eines Europäers*, 2nd edn, München, 1980; English trans., *Memoirs*, London, 1978)

Smets, Paul-F. (ed.), *La pensée européenne et atlantique de Paul-Henri Spaak (1942–1972)*, 2 vols., Bruxelles, 1980

Spaak, Paul-Henri, *Combats inachevés*, 2 vols, (1, *De l'indépendance à l'alliance*; 2, *De l'espoir aux déceptions*), Bruxelles, 1969 (German trans., *Erinnerungen eines Europäers*, Hamburg, 1969)

Spinelli, Altiero, *Come ho tentato di diventare saggio*, Bologna, 1988

Spinelli, Altiero, *Diario europeo*, 3 vols, (1, 1948–1969; 2, 1970–1976; 3, 1976–1986) Bologna, 1989–1992

Bibliographical studies on the early history of European integration and the methodology of studying integration

Griffiths, Richard T., 'À la recherche des débuts de l'intégration européenne', *Revue de Synthèse*, vol. 111, no. 3, 1990, pp. 235–50

Kaplan, Lawrence S., 'The Cold War and European Revisionism', *Diplomatic History*, vol. 11, no. 2, pp. 143–56

Laurent, Pierre-Henri, 'Historical Perspectives on Early

European Integration', *Revue d'Intégration Européenne*, vol. 12, nos 2–3, 1989, pp. 89–100

Pryce, Roy, 'Zum aktuellen Forschungsstand über die europäische Integration in Westeuropa', *Integration*, vol. 5, no. 4, 1982, pp. 164–77

Recherches universitaires sur l'intégration européenne. University Research on European Integration. Enquête réalisée par le Centre d'Études Européennes. Université Catholique de Louvain à la demande de la Commission des Communautés Européennes, No. 12: Bruxelles, 1982; No. 13: Bruxelles, 1985; No. 14: Bruxelles, 1987; No. 15: Bruxelles, 1992

Schwarz, Hans-Peter, 'Die europäische Integration als Aufgabe der Zeitgeschichtsforschung. Forschungsstand und Perspektiven', *Vierteljahrshefte für Zeitgeschichte*, vol. 31 no. 4, 1983, pp. 555–72

Viertel, Grit, 'Die EG als Forschungsobjekt der Zeitgeschichte', *Integration*, vol. 15, no. 1, 1992, pp. 52–6

Integration: theories of integration

Behrens, Henning and Paul Noack, *Theorien der internationalen Politik*, München, 1984, ch. 9

Bellers, Jürgen and Erwin Häckel, 'Theorien internationaler Integration und internationaler Organisationen', in Volker Rittberger (ed.), *Theorien der internationalen Beziehungen. Bestandsaufnahme und Forschungsperspektiven*, Opladen, 1990, pp. 286–310

Deutsch, Karl W. et al., *Political Community and the North Atlantic Area. International Organization in the Light of Historical Experience*, Princeton, N.J., 1957 (classic theoretical text on the relationship between communications, transactions and the integration of political communities)

Dougherty, James E. and Robert L. Pfaltzgraff, Jr., *Contending Theories of International Relations*, 3rd edn, New York, 1990, ch. 10

Groom, A.J.R. and Alexis Heraclides, 'Integration and Disintegration', in Margot Light and A.J.R. Groom (eds), *International Relations. A Handbook of Current Theory*, London, 1985, pp. 174–93

Haas, Ernst B., *The Uniting of Europe. Political, Social, and Economic Forces 1950–1957*, London, 1958 (Reissued: Stanford, Cal., 1968) (the classic exposition of neo-functionalism)

Herbst, Ludolf, 'Die zeitgenössische Integrationstheorie und die Anfänge der europäischen Einigung 1947–1950', *Vierteljahrshefte für Zeitgeschichte*, vol 34, no. 2, 1986, pp. 161–205.

Hodges, Michael (ed.), *European Integration. Selected Readings*, Harmondsworth, 1972 (a useful collection of theoretical texts from the 1950s and 1960s)

Mitrany, David A., *A Working Peace System. An Argument for the Functional Development of International Government*, London, 1944 (the classic statement of functionalism)

Schneider, Heinrich, *Leitbilder der Europapolitik. 1: Der Weg zur Integration*, Bonn, 1977

Tovias, Alfred, 'A Survey of the Theory of Economic Integration', *Revue d'Intégration Européenne*, vol. 15, no. 1, 1991, pp. 5–23

Wallace, William (ed.), *The Dynamics of European Integration*, London, 1990

Zimmerling, Ruth, *Externe Einflüsse auf die Integration von Staaten. Zur politikwissenschaftlichen Theorie regionaler Zusammenschlüsse*, Freiburg, 1991, chs 2–3

Political histories of Europe since 1945 and of Western European integration

Archer, Clive, *Organizing Western Europe*, London, 1990

Arter, David, *The Politics of European Integration in the Twentieth Century*, Aldershot, 1993 (an account of the political history of European integration and disintegration since the First World War)

Benz, Wolfgang und Hermann Graml (eds), *Das Zwanzigste Jahrhundert II.: Europa nach dem Zweiten Weltkrieg 1945–1982*, Frankfurt am Main, 1983 (Fischer Weltgeschichte, vol. 35)

Black, Cyril E. et al., *Rebirth. A History of Europe since World War II*, Boulder, 1992 (an informative und useful account of post-war European history, with the emphasis on the political side)

Ellwood, David W., *Rebuilding Europe. Western Europe, America and Postwar Reconstruction*, London, 1992 (Coll. The Postwar World) (European integration in the wider context of the reconstruction of Western European economies and societies, stressing the role of the USA)

Gerbet, Pierre, *La Construction de l'Europe*, Paris, 1983

Von der Groeben, Hans, *Aufbaujahre der Europäischen*

Gemeinschaft. Das Ringen um den Gemeinsamen Markt und die Politische Union (1959–1966), Baden-Baden, 1982

Hillgruber, Andreas, *Europa in der Weltpolitik der Nachkriegszeit 1945–1963*, 4th edn, durchgesehen und wesentlich ergänzt von Jost Dülffer, München, 1993 (Coll. Oldenbourg Grundriβ der Geschichte, vol. 18) (Introduction to the political and international history of Europe from the end of World War II until 1963; a survey of the main events and of research controversies, with a detailed bibliography)

Jansen, Max and Johan K. De Vree, *The Ordeal of Unity. The Politics of European Integration 1945–1985*, Bilthoven, 1985

Laqueur, Walter, *Europe in our Time*, New York, 1992; German language edn: *Europa auf dem Weg zur Weltmacht 1945–1992*, München, 1992

Loth, Wilfried, *Der Weg nach Europa. Geschichte der europäischen Integration 1939–1957*, Göttingen, 1990 (concise summary of the history of Western European integration up to the Treaties of Rome, taking account of archive material)

Mayne, Richard, *The Recovery of Europe. From Devastation to Unity*, London, 1970

Pinder, John, *European Community. The Building of a Union*, Oxford, 1991

Schieder, Theodor (ed.), *Handbuch der europäischen Geschichte*, vol. 7, *Europa im Zeitalter der Weltmächte* (parts 1 and 2), Stuttgart, 1979

Urwin, Derek, *Western Europe since 1945. A Political History*, 4th edn, London, 1992 (a review of economic and political developments, of the movement towards greater unity and co-operation in Western Europe, and of the international environment)

Urwin, Derek W., *The Community of Europe. A History of European Integration since 1945*, London, 1991 (Coll. The Postwar World) (An account of the history of the European Community from World War II to the Single European Act and the single market)

Wegs, J. Robert, *Europe since 1945. A Concise History*, 2nd edn (1984 repr.), Basingstoke, 1986

Young, John W., *Cold War Europe 1945–89. A Political History*, London, 1991 (An overview of the political history of Europe and of major European states from the end of World War II until the collapse of the Communist regimes)

Zorgbibe, Charles, *Histoire de la Construction Européenne*, Paris, 1993 (An introductory text to the history of European integration from the Second World war to the present)

Collections of essays on the history of Western
European integration. Accounts based on archive
material are rare, but important results of research are
published in collections of essays which are often the
outcome of conferences

Becker, Josef and Franz Knipping (eds), *Power in Europe?
Great Britain, France, Italy and Germany in a Postwar World,
1945–1950*, Berlin, 1986

Di Nolfo, Ennio (ed.), *Power in Europe? II. Great Britain, France,
Germany, Italy and the Origins of the EEC, 1952–1957*, Berlin, 1992

Girault, René (ed.), *Les Europe des Européens*, Paris, 1993 (based
on a conference at Paris in 1992 as part of the research project
launched in 1989 that is investigating the emergence and the
development of a European consciousness in the twentieth century)

Girault, René (ed.), *Identité et conscience européennes au XXe siècle*,
Paris, 1994

Pryce, Roy (ed.), *The Dynamics of European Union*, London, 1987
(a series of essays on major developments of the history of the
European Community from World War II to the 1980s)

Poidevin, Raymond (ed.), *Histoire des Débuts de la Construction
Européenne (Mars 1948–Mai 1950)/Origins of the European Integration
(March 1948–May 1950)*, Bruxelles, 1986 (Publications of the
European Community Liaison Committee of Historians, vol. 1)

Schwabe, Klaus (Hrsg.), *Die Anfänge des Schuman-Plans
1950/51/The Beginnings of the Schuman-Plan*, Baden-Baden, 1988
(Publications of the European Community Liaison Committee of
Historians, vol. 2)

Schwabe, Klaus, Hartmut Kaelble and Rainer Hudemann (eds),
Geschichte der europäischen Integration, München, 1994 (forthcoming)

Serra, Enrico (Hrsg.), *Il rilancio dell'Europa e i trattati di Roma.
La relance européenne et les traités de Rome*, Milano, 1989
(Publications of the European Community Liaison Committee of
Historians, vol. 3)

Stirk, Peter M.R. and David Willis (eds), *Shaping Postwar Europe.
European Unity and Disunity 1945–1957*, London, 1991(based on a
conference at Hull University on 'European Unity in Context'.
The two previous volumes in this series of conferences are:

Stirk, Peter M.R. [ed.], *European Unity in Context. The Interwar
Period*, London, 1989 and

Smith, M.L. and Peter M.R. Stirk eds, *Making the New Europe. European Unity and the Second World War*, London, 1990)
Trausch, Gilbert (ed.), *Die europäische Integration vom Schuman-Plan bis zu den Verträgen von Rom. Pläne und Initiativen, Enttäuschungen und Mißerfolge /The European Integration from the Schuman Plan to the Treaties of Rome. Projects and Initiatives, Disappointments and Failures*, Baden-Baden, 1993 (Publications of the European Community Liaison Committee of Historians, vol. 4)

Federalism, The European Movement, European pressure groups and political parties

Arbeitskreis Europäische Integration (ed.), *Politische Grundströmungen im europäischen Integrationsprozeß*, Baden-Baden, 1982

Ashford, Nigel, *The Conservative Party and European Integration 1945–1975*, Ph.D. Thesis, University of Warwick, 1983

Berstein, Serge, Jean-Marie Mayeur et Pierre Milza (eds), *Le MRP et la construction européenne*, Bruxelles, 1993 (Questions au XXe siècle)

Bosco, Andrea (ed.), *The Federal Idea*, 2 vols. (1, *The History of Federalism from Enlightenment to 1945*; 2, *The History of Federalism since 1945*), London, 1991 and 1992

Boogman, Johan C. and G.N. van der Plaat (eds), *Federalism. History and Current Significance of a Form of Government*, The Hague, 1980

Burgess, Michael and Alan-G. Gagnon (eds), *Comparative Federalism and Federation. Competing Traditions and Future Directions*, New York, 1993

Chenaux, Philippe, *Une Europe Vaticane? Entre le Plan Marshall et les traités de Rome*, Bruxelles, 1990

Deuerlein, Ernst, *Föderalismus. Die historischen und philosophischen Grundlagen des föderativen Prinzips*, München, 1972

Dumoulin, Michel and Anne-Myriam Dutrieue, *La Ligue Européenne de Coopération Économique (1946–1981). Un groupe d'étude et de pression dans la construction européenne*, Bern et al., 1993 (Euroclio: Études et Documents)

Forman, Nigel, *The European Movement in Great Britain 1945–1954*, Ph.D. Thesis, University of Sussex, 1973

Greilsammer, Alain, *Les mouvements fédéralistes en France de 1945 à 1974*, Paris, 1975

Griffiths, Richard (ed.), *Socialist Parties and the Question of Europe in the 1950's*, Leiden, 1993

Hahn, Karl J., *Die christliche Demokratie in Europa*, Rom, 1979

Hick, Alan, *The European Movement and the Campaign for a European Assembly 1947–1950*, Ph.D. Thesis, European University Institute, Florence, 1981

Hrbek, Rudolf, *Die SPD, Deutschland und Europa. Die Haltung der Sozialdemokratie zum Verhältnis von Deutschand-Politik und West-Integration (1945–1957)*, Bonn, 1972

Jansen, Jürgen, *Britische Konservative und Europa. Debattenaussagen im Unterhaus zur westeuropäischen Integration 1945–1972*, Baden-Baden, 1978

Jeutter, Peter, *EWG – Kein Weg nach Europa. Die Haltung der Freien Demokratischen Partei zu den Römischen Verträgen 1957*, Bonn, 1985

Koselleck, Reinhart, 'Bund, Bündnis, Föderalismus, Bundesstaat', in Otto Bruner, Werner Conze and Reinhart Koselleck (eds), *Geschichtliche Grundbegriffe. Historisches Lexikon zur politisch-sozialen Sprache in Deutschland*, vol. I, Stuttgart, 1972, pp. 582–671

Lipgens, Walter, *Die Anfänge der europäischen Einigungspolitik 1945–1950*, Teil I, 1945–1947, Stuttgart 1977; enlarged English edition, *A History of European Integration*, vol. 1, *1945–1947, The Formation of the European Unity Movement*, Oxford, 1982

Loth, Wilfried, *Sozialismus und Internationalismus. Die französischen Sozialisten und die Nachkriegsordnung Europas 1940–1950*, Stuttgart, 1977

Loth, Wilfried (ed.), *Die Anfänge der europäischen Integration 1945–1950*, Bonn, 1990

Mayne, Richard and John Pinder with John C. de V. Roberts, *Federal Union. The Pioneers*, Basingstoke, 1990

O'Neill, Francis, *The French Radical Party and European Integration*, New York, 1981

Newman, Michael, *Socialism and European Unity. The Dilemma of the Left in Britain and France*, London, 1983

Posselt, Martin, *Richard Coudenhove-Kalergi und die Europäische Parlamentarier-Union. Die parlamentarische Bewegung für eine "Europäische Konstituante" (1946–1952)*, Ph.D. Thesis, University of Graz, 1987

Zurcher, Arnold J., *The Struggle to Unite Europe 1940–1958. An Historical Account of the Development of the Contemporary European Movement from its Origin in the Pan-European Union to the Drafting of the Treaties for Euratom and the European Common Market*, New York, 1958

Surveys of the economic and social history of Europe

Aldcroft, Derek H., *The European Economy, 1914–1990*, 3rd edn, London, 1993

Ambrosius, Gerold and William H. Hubbard, *Sozial- und Wirtschaftsgeschichte Europas im 20. Jahrhundert*, München, 1986

Bibliography of European Economic and Social History. Compiled by Derek H. Aldcroft and Richard Rodger, 2nd edn, Manchester, 1993

Boltho, Andrea (ed.), *The European Economy: Growth and Crisis*, Oxford, 1982

Cipolla, Carlo M. (ed.), *The Fontana Economic History of Europe*. Vol. 5, *The Twentieth Century* (Part 1 and 2); vol. 6, *Contemporary Economies* (Part 1 and 2), Glasgow, 1976; German language edn, Knut Borchardt (ed.), *Europäische Wirtschaftsgeschichte*. Vol. 5, *Die europäischen Volkswirtschaften im 20. Jahrhundert*, Stuttgart, 1980

Flora , Peter (ed.), *Growth to Limits. The Western European Welfare States since World War II* (5 vols. planned; vols. 1, 2, and 4 published so far), Berlin, 1986–1987

Kaelble, Hartmut, *Auf dem Wege zu einer europäischen Gesellschaft. Eine Sozialgeschichte Westeuropas 1880–1980*, München,1987; English language edn, *A Social History of Western Europe, 1880–1980*, Dublin, 1989

Kellenbenz, Hermann (ed.), *Handbuch der europäischen Wirtschafts- und Sozialgeschichte*. Vol. 6, Wolfram Fischer (ed.), *Europäische Wirtschafts- und Sozialgeschichte vom Ersten Weltkrieg bis zur Gegenwart*, Stuttgart, 1987

Postan, Michael M., *An Economic History of Western Europe, 1945–1964*, London, 1967

Tipton, Frank B. and Robert Aldrich, *An Economic and Social History of Europe from 1939 to the Present*, Basingstoke, 1987

Industry, economic interest groups, trade associations and European integration

Bührer, Werner, *Ruhrstahl und Europa. Die Wirtschaftsvereinigung Eisen- und Stahlindustrie und die Anfänge der europäischen Integration*, München, 1986

Chanier, Christophe, *La firme Philips face à la construction de l'Europe. Une multinationale sur la voie de l'intégration économique dans les années 50–60*, Thèse de doctorat, Université de Paris I, 1990

Devos, Elisabeth, *Le Patronat belge face au Plan Schuman (9 mai 1950–5 février 1952)*, Louvain-la-Neuve, 1989 (coll. Histoire de la construction européenne)

Dumoulin, Michel, René Girault and Gilbert Trausch avec la collaboration de Thierry Grosbois (eds), *L'Europe du patronat. De la guerre froide aux années soixante*, Berne et al., 1993 (Euroclio: Études et Documents)

Gillingham, John, *Coal, Steel, and the Rebirth of Europe, 1945–1955. The Germans and French from Ruhr Conflict to Economic Community*, Cambridge, 1991

Van Molle, Leen, 'Le milieu agricole belge face à la «concurrence européenne»: 1944–1958', in Michel Dumoulin (ed.), *La Belgique et les débuts de la construction européenne. De la guerre aux traités de Rome*, Louvain-la-Neuve, 1987, pp. 119–43

Noël, Gilbert, *Du pool vert à la politique agricole commune. Les tentatives de Communauté agricole européenne entre 1945 et 1955*, Paris, 1988

Schwabe, Klaus (ed.), *Die Anfänge des Schuman-Plans 1950/51*, Baden-Baden, 1988, ch. VI (the contributions by Philippe Mioche, Ruggero Ranieri, Emile Krier, François Roth, Enrico Decleva, John Gillingham and Alan S. Milward)

Individual European countries' policies on European Integration (see also under personalities and other headings)

France

Bjøl, Erling, *La France deant l'Europe. La politique européenne de la IVe République*, Copenhague, 1966

Bossuat, Gérard, *La France, l'aide américaine et la construction européenne 1944–1954*, 2 vols., Paris, 1992

Dreyfus, François, Jacques Morizet and Max Peyrard (eds), *France and EC Membership Evaluated*, London, 1993

Guillen, Pierre, 'Frankreich und der Europäische Wiederaufschwung. Vom Scheitern der EVG zur Ratifizierung der Verträge von Rom', *Vierteljahrshefte für Zeitgeschichte*, vol. 28, no. 1, 1980, pp. 1–19

Guillen, Pierre, 'L'Europe remède à l'impuissance française? Le gouvernement Guy Mollet et la négociation des traités de Rome (1955–1957)', *Revue d'Histoire Diplomatique*, vol. 102, 1988, pp. 319–35

Loth, Wilfried, Die europäische Integration nach dem Zweiten Weltkrieg in französischer Perspektive, in Helmut Beding (ed.), *Wirtschaftliche und politische Integration in Europa im 19. und 20. Jahrhundert*, Göttingen, 1984, pp. 225–46

West Germany

Hanrieder, Wolfram F., *Germany, America , Europe. Forty Years of German Foreign Policy*, New Haven, 1989

Herbst, Ludolf (ed.), *Westdeutschland 1945–1955. Unterwerfung, Kontrolle, Integration*, München, 1986

Herbst, Ludolf, *Option für den Westen. Vom Marshallplan bis zum deutsch-französischen Vertrag*, München, 1989

Herbst, Ludolf, Werner Bührer and Hanno Sowade (eds), *Vom Marshallplan zur EWG. Die Eingliederung der Bundesrepublik Deutschland in die westliche Welt*, München, 1990

Hildebrand, Klaus, *Integration und Souveränität. Die Außenpolitik der Bundesrepublik Deutschland 1949–1982*, Bonn, 1991

Müller-Roschasch, Herbert, *Die deutsche Europapolitik. Wege und Umwege zur politischen Union Europas*, Baden-Baden, 1974

Schweitzer, Carl-Christoph and Detlev Karsten (eds), *The Federal Republic of Germany and EC Membership Evaluated*, London, 1990

France and Germany are at the heart of Western European integration. The following works describe their relationship

Poidevin, Raymond and Jacques Bariéty, *Les relations franco-allemandes 1815–1975*, Paris, 1977

Schwarz, Hans-Peter (ed.), *Adenauer und Frankreich. Die deutsch-französischen Beziehungen 1958–1969*, Bonn, 1985

Willis, Frank Roy, *France, Germany, and the New Europe*

1945–1967, Stanford, Cal., 1968

Ziebura, Gilbert, *Die deutsch-französischen Beziehungen seit 1945. Mythen und Realitäten*, Pfullingen, 1970

Italy

Di Nolfo, Ennio, 'Das Problem der europäischen Einigung als ein Aspekt der italienischen Außenpolitik 1945–1954', *Vierteljahrshefte für Zeitgeschichte*, vol. 28, no. 2, 1980, pp. 145–167

Di Nolfo, Ennio, *Le paure e le speranze degli Italiani (1943–1953)*, Milano, 1986 (German edn, *Von Mussolini zu De Gasperi. Italien zwischen Angst und Hoffnung 1943–1953*, Paderborn, 1993)

Di Nolfo, Ennio, Romain Rainero and Brunello Vigezzi (eds), *L'Italia et la politica di potenza in Europa 1945–1950*, Milano, 1988 (gathers the Italian papers of the research project on 'The Perception of Power in Western Europe between 1938 and 1958')

Di Nolfo, Ennio, Romain Rainero and Brunello Vigezzi (eds), *L'Italia et la politica di potenza negli anni '50*, Milano, 1992 (see previous title)

Duroselle, Jean-Baptiste and Enrico Serra (eds), *Italia e Francia (1946–1954)*, Milano, 1988

Pistone, Sergio, *L'Italia e l'unità europea. Dalle premesse storiche all'elezione del Parlamento europeo*, Torino, 1982

Willis, Frank Roy, *Italy Chooses Europe*, New York, 1971

Belgium

Dumoulin, Michel (ed.), *La Belgique et les débuts de la construction européenne: de la guerre aux traités de Rome*, Louvain-la-Neuve, 1987 (coll. Histoire de notre temps)

Helmreich, Jonathan E., *Belgium and Europe. A Study in Small Power Diplomacy*, The Hague, 1976 (Issues in Contemporary Politics, 3)

The Netherlands

Griffiths, Richard T. (ed.), *The Netherlands and the Integration of Europe 1945–1957*, Amsterdam, 1990

Griffiths, Richard T. and Alan S. Milward, 'The Beyen Plan and the European Political Community', in Werner Maihofer (ed.), *Noi si Mura. Selected Working Papers of the European University Institute*, Florence, 1986, pp. 596–621

Manning, Adrian F., 'Die Niederlande und Europa von 1945 bis zum Beginn der fünfziger Jahre', *Vierteljahrshefte für Zeitgeschichte*, vol. 29, no. 1, 1981, pp. 1–20

Great Britain

Brivati, Brian and Harriet Jones (eds), *From Reconstruction to Integration: Britain since 1945*, London, 1993

Bulmer, Simon et al. (eds), *The United Kingdom and EC Membership Evaluated*, London, 1992

Camps, Miriam, *Britain and the European Community 1955–1963*, Princeton, 1964

George, Stephen, *Britain and European Integration since 1945*, Oxford, 1991

Greenwood, Sean, *Britain and European Cooperation since 1945*, Oxford, 1992 (Historical Association Studies)

Schmidt, Gustav (ed.), *Großbritannien und Europa – Großbritannien in Europa. Sicherheitsbelange und Wirtschaftsfragen in der britischen Europapolitik nach dem Zweiten Weltkrieg*, Bochum, 1989 (Publications of the German Association for the Study of British History and Politics, vol. 10)

Watt, Donald C., 'Großbritannien und Europa 1951–1959. Die Jahre Konservativer Regierung', *Vierteljahrshefte für Zeitgeschichte*, vol. 28, no. 4, 1980, pp. 389–409

Wurm, Clemens (ed.), *Wege nach Europa. Wirtschaft und Außenpolitik Großbritanniens im 20. Jahrhundert*, Bochum, 1992 (Publications of the German Association for the Study of British History and Politics, vol. 19)

Young, John W., *Britain, France and the Unity of Europe 1945–1951*, Leicester, 1984

Young, John W., *Britain and European Unity, 1945–1992*, Basingstoke, 1993 (British History in Perspective)

Other European Countries

Hederman, Miriam, *The Road to Europe. Irish Attitudes 1948–61*, Dublin, 1983

Miljan, Toivo, *The Reluctant Europeans. The Attitudes of the Nordic Countries Towards European Integration*, London, 1977

Mousson-Lestang, Jean-Pierre, *La Scandinavie et l'Europe de 1945 à nos jours*, Paris, 1990

Wyder, Rudolf, *Die Schweiz und der Europarat 1944–1971. Annäherung und zehn Jahre Mitarbeit in der Parlamentarischen Versammlung*, Bern, 1984

Weiß, Florian, 'Die schwierige Balance. Österreich und die Anfänge der westeuropäischen Integration 1947–1957', *Vierteljahrshefte für Zeitgeschichte*, vol. 42, no. 1, 1994, pp. 71–94

Personalities in European Integration

Bédarida, François and Jean-Pierre Rioux (eds), *Pierre Mendès France et le mendésisme. L'expérience gouvernementale (1954–1955) et sa postérité*, Paris, 1985

Berstein, Serge (ed.), *Paul Ramadier, la République et le socialisme*, Bruxelles, 1990 (especially the contribution by Pierre Guillen, 'Paul Ramadier et l'Europe', pp. 389– 404

Bossuat, Gérard, 'Léon Blum et l'unité européenne, 1945–1950, ou l'internationalisme du possible', *Cahiers Léon Blum*, nos. 28–29, Déc. 1990-Fév. 1991, pp. 63–82

Brinkley, Douglas and Clifford Hackett (eds), *Jean Monnet. The Path to European Unity*, London, 1991 (useful contributions on a crucial figure for European integration and French policy on integration)

Girault, René (ed.), *Pierre Mendès France et le rôle de la France dans le monde. Colloque organisé par L'Institut Pierre Mendès France à l'Assemblée Nationale les 10 et 11 janvier 1991*, Grenoble, 1991

Gouzy, Jean-Pierre, *Les pionniers de l'Europe communautaire*, Lausanne, 1968

Harrison, Robert Vaughan, *Winston Churchill and European Integration*, Ph.D. Thesis, University of Aberdeen, 1984

Horne, Alistair, *Macmillan*, 2 vols (vol. 1, 1894–1956; vol. 2, 1957–1986), London, 1988 and 1989

Institut Charles de Gaulle, *De Gaulle et son siècle*, vol. V, *L'Europe*, Paris, 1992

Jansen, Thomas and Dieter Mahncke (eds), *Persönlichkeiten der europäischen Integration. Vierzehn biographische Essays*, Bonn, 1981 (biograhical essays on leading personalities involved in European

integration, e.g. Robert Schuman, Alcide de Gasperi, Jan Willem
Beyen, Paul-Henri Spaak, Konrad Adenauer, Jean Monnet,
Winston Churchill, Harold Macmillan, Duncan Sandys, Charles de
Gaulle)

Jouve, Edmond, *Le Général de Gaulle et la Construction de l'Europe
1940–1966*, 2 vols., Paris, 1967

Koerfer, Daniel, *Kampf ums Kanzleramt. Erhard und Adenauer*,
2nd edn, Stuttgart, 1988

Lappenküper, Ulrich, '»Ich bin wirklich ein guter Europäer«.
Ludwig Erhards Europapolitik 1949–1966', *Francia*, vol. 18, no. 3,
1991, pp. 85–121

Loth, Wilfried , 'De Gaulle und Europa. Eine Revision',
Historische Zeitschrift, vol. 253, 1991, pp. 629–60

Lucas, Hans-Dieter, *Europa vom Atlantik bis zum Ural?
Europapolitik und Europadenken im Fankreich der Ära de Gaulle
(1958–1969)*, Bonn, 1992

Mittendorfer, Rudolf, *Robert Schuman – Architekt des neuen
Europa*, Hildesheim, 1983

Poidevin, Raymond, *Robert Schuman. Homme d'État 1886–1963*,
Paris, 1986

Rieben, Henri, *Des Guerres Européennes à l'Union de l'Europe*,
Lausanne, 1987

Schwarz, Hans-Peter, 'Adenauer und Europa', *Vierteljahrshefte
für Zeitgeschichte*, vol. 27, no. 4, 1979, pp. 471–523

Schwarz, Hans-Peter, *Adenauer*, 2 vols. (1, Der Aufstieg:
1876–1952; 2, *Der Staatsmann*, 1952–1967), Stuttgart, 1986 and
1991

Soutou, Georges-Henri, 'Georges Bidault et la construction
européenne 1944–1954', *Revue d'Histoire Diplomatique*, vol. 105,
1991, pp. 267–306

**National histories and European integration;
nationalism, nation-state and supranationality**

Baker, John and Martin Kolinsky, 'The State and
Integration', in Navari, Cornelia (ed.), *The Condition of States. A
Study in International Political Theory*, Milton Keynes, 1991, pp.
105–24

Fulbrook, Mary (ed.), *National Histories and European History*,
London, 1983

Hoffmann, Stanley , 'Obstinate or Obsolete? The Fate of the Nation-State and the Case of Western Europe', *Daedalus*, vol. 95, no 3, 1966, pp. 862–915

Hoffmann, Stanley, 'Reflections on the Nation-State in Western Europe Today', in Loukas Tsoukalis (ed.), *The European Community. Past, Present and Future*, Oxford, 1983, pp. 21–37

Milward, Alan S., 'Etats-Nations et Communauté: Le paradoxe de l'Europe?', *Revue de Synthèse*, vol. 111, no. 3, 1990, pp. 252–70

Milward, Alan S., Frances M.B. Lynch, Federico Romero, Ruggero Ranieri and Vibeke Sørensen, *The Frontier of National Sovereignty. History and Theory 1945–1992*, London, 1993

Mommsen, Wolfgang J. (ed.), *Der lange Weg nach Europa. Historische Betrachtungen aus gegenwärtiger Sicht*, Berlin, 1992

Schieder, Theodor, *Nationalismus und Nationalstaat. Studien zum nationalen Problem im modernen Europa*, eds Otto Dann and Hans-Ulrich Wehler, Göttingen, 1991

Salewski, Michael (ed.), *Nationale Identität und europäische Einigung*, Göttingen, 1991

Winkler, Heinrich August and Hartmut Kaelble (eds), *Nationalismus-Nationalitäten-Supranationalität*, Stuttgart, 1993

Institutions, organisations and initiatives

The Schuman Plan and the European Coal and Steel Community

Conrad, Yves, *Jean Monnet et les débuts de la fonction publique euopéenne. La Haute Autorité de la CECA (1952–1953)*, Louvain-la-Neuve, 1989

Diebold, William, *The Schuman Plan. A Study in Economic Cooperation, 1950–1959*, New York, 1959

Gerbet, Pierre, *La genèse du plan Schuman. Des origines à la déclaration du 9 mai 1950*, Lausanne, 1962

Gillingham, John, *Coal, Steel, and the Rebirth of Europe, 1945–1955. The Germans and French from Ruhr Conflict to Economic Community*, Cambridge, 1991 (historical roots of the Schuman Plan and the ECSC; interwar international cartels in steel and coal as the first expression of 'functional integration')

Gillingham, John, 'Zur Vorgeschichte des Montan-Union. Westeuropas Kohle und Stahl in Depression und Krieg', *Vierteljahrshefte für Zeitgeschichte*, vol. 34, no. 3, 1986, pp. 381–405

Gillingham, John, 'Die französische Ruhrpolitik und die Ursprünge des Schuman-Plans', *Vierteljahrshefte für Zeitgeschichte*, vol. 35, no. 1, 1987, pp. 1–24

Goschler, Constantin, Christoph Buchheim and Werner Bührer, 'Der Schumanplan als Instrument französischer Stahlpolitik. Zur historischen Wirkung eines falschen Kalküls', *Vierteljahrshefte für Zeitgeschichte*, vol. 37, no. 2, 1989, pp. 171–206

Palayret, Jean-Marie, 'Jean Monnet, la Haute Autorité de la CECA face au problème de la reconcentration de la sidérurgie de la Ruhr (1950–1958)', *Revue d'Histoire Diplomatique*, vol. 105, 1991, pp. 307–48

Petzina, Dietmar, 'The Origins of the European Coal and Steel Community: Economic Forces and Political Interests', *Zeitschrift für die gesamte Staatswissenschaft*, vol. 137, no. 3, 1981, pp. 450–68

Rieben, Henri, *Des ententes de maîtres de forges au Plan Schuman*, Ambilly, 1954

Schwabe, Klaus (ed.), *Die Anfänge des Schuman-Plans 1950/51*, Baden-Baden, 1989

Spierenburg, Dirk and Raymond Poidevin, *The History of the High Authority of the European Coal and Steel Community. Supranationality in Operation*, London, 1994 (French edn, *Histoire de la Haute Autorité de la Communauté Européenne du Charbon et de l'Acier. Une expérience supranationale*, Bruxelles, 1993)

Foundation of the European Economic Community/European Atomic Community

Gerbet, Pierre, *La naissance du marché commun*, Bruxelles, 1987

Küsters, Hanns Jürgen, *Die Gründung der Europäischen Wirtschaftsgemeinschaft*, Baden-Baden, 1982; French trans, *Fondements de la Communauté Économique Européenne*, Luxembourg, 1990 (a detailed account of the events leading to the founding of the EEC)

Milward, Alan S., with the Assistance of George Brennan and Federico Romero, *The European Rescue of the Nation-State*, London, 1992 (an investigation of the Europeanisation of national policy in three fields: employment and welfare; foreign trade and economic growth; and agriculture; with an essay on Britain's policy towards Europe)

Serra, Enrico (ed.), *Il rilancio dell'Europa e i trattati di Roma*, Milano, 1989

Weilemann, Peter, *Die Anfänge der Europäischen Atomgemeinschaft. Zur Gründung von Euratom 1955–1957*, Baden-Baden, 1982

The creation of EFTA

Camps, Miriam, *Britain and the European Community 1955–1963*, Princeton, 1964

Griffiths, Richard T., *The Creation of EFTA* (booklet of the European University Institute, Florence, n.d.), also in *EFTA Bulletin*, vol. 32, no, 1, 1991, pp. 2–5; no. 2, 1991, pp. 17–22; nos 3–4, 1991, pp. 15–20; vol. 33, no. 1, 1992, pp. 34–40

Kaiser, Karl, *EWG und Freihandelszone. England und der Kontinent in der europäischen Integration*, Leiden, 1963

Steininger, Rolf, '1961: "Europe at Sixes and Sevens". Die EFTA und Großbritanniens Entscheidung für die EWG', *Vierteljahrschrift für Sozial- und Wirtschaftsgeschichte*, vol. 80, no. 1, 1993, pp. 4–29

Economic integration: Organization of European Economic Co-operation, European Payments Union, early customs union negotiations

Berding, Helmut (ed.), *Wirtschaftliche und politische Integration in Europa im 19. und 20. Jahrhundert* (Geschichte und Gesellschaft, Sonderheft 10), Göttingen, 1984 (A useful collection of essays on economic and political integration in the 19th and 20th centuries, some combining political and economic analysis)

Buchheim, Christoph, *Die Wiedereingliederung Westdeutschlands in die Weltwirtschaft 1945–1958*, München, 1990 (The re-integration of West Germany into the European and international economy)

Diebold, William, *Trade and Payments in Western Europe. A Study in Economic Cooperation 1947–1951*, New York, 1952

Eichengreen, Barry, *Reconstructing Europe's Trade and Payments. The European Payments Union*, Manchester, 1993

Griffiths, Richard T. and Frances M.B. Lynch, 'L'échec de la «Petite Europe»: les négociations Fritalux/Finebel, 1949–1950', *Revue Historique*, vol. 274, no. 1, 1985, pp. 159–93

Griffiths, Richard T. and Frances M.B. Lynch, 'L'échec de la "Petite Europe": Le Conseil Tripartite, 1944–1948', in *Guerres Mondiales et Conflits Contemporains*, vol. 38, no. 152, 1988, pp. 39–62

Guillen, Pierre, 'Les vicissitudes des rapports franco-italiens de la rencontre de Cannes (décembre 1948) à celle de Santa Margherita (février 1951)', in Jean-Baptiste Duroselle and Enrico Serra (eds), *Italia e Francia (1946–1954)*, Milano, 1988, pp. 13–30

Kaplan, Jacob J. and Günther Schleiminger, *The European Payments Union. Financial Diplomacy in the 1950s*, Oxford, 1989

Milward, Alan S., *The Reconstruction of Western Europe 1945–51*, London, 1984

Pollard, Sidney, *European Economic Integration 1815–1970*, London, 1974

Pollard, Sidney, *The Integration of the European Economy since 1815*, London, 1981

Serra, Enrico, 'L'unione doganale italo-francese e la Conferenza di Santa Margherita (1947–1951)', in Duroselle and Serra (eds), *Italia e Francia*, pp. 73–114

Military integration: the Brussels Pact, NATO, Pleven Plan, EDC, WEU

Baylis, John, *The Diplomacy of Pragmatism. Britain and the Formation of NATO, 1942–49*, Basingstoke, 1993 (discusses the role of Britain and especially that of Ernest Bevin in the creation of NATO)

Clesse, Armand, *Le projet de C.E.D. du Plan Pleven au «crime» du 30 août. Histoire d'un malentendu européen*, Baden-Baden, 1989

Cook, Don, *Forging the Alliance. NATO, 1945–1950*, London, 1989

Dockrill, Saki, *Britain's Policy for West German Rearmament 1950–1955*, Cambridge, 1991

Fursdon, Edward, *The European Defense Community. A History*, New York, 1980

Van der Harst, Jan, *European Union and Atlantic Partnership: Political, Military and Economic Aspects of Dutch Defence, 1948–1954, and the Impact of the European Defence Community*, Ph.D.Thesis, European University Institute, Florence, 1988

Heller, Francis H. and John R. Gillingham (eds), *NATO: The Founding of the Atlantic Alliance and the Integration of Europe*, Basingstoke, 1992 (a useful collection of essays on an important subject: the relationship between European integration and NATO)

Heuser, Beatrice and Robert O'Neill (eds), *Securing Peace in Europe, 1945–62. Thoughts for the Post-Cold War Era*, Basingstoke, 1992

Ireland, Timothy P., *Creating the Entangling Alliance. The Origins of the North Atlantic Treaty Organization*, Westport, 1981

Jansen, Hans-Heinrich, *Großbritannien, das Scheitern der EVG und der NATO-Beitritt der Bundesrepublik Deutschland*, Bochum, 1992 (Publications of the German Association for the Study of British History and Politics, vol. 22)

Kaplan, Lawrence S., *The United States and NATO. The Formative Years*, Lexington, 1984

Mager, Olaf, *Die Stationierung der britischen Rheinarmee – Großbritanniens EVG-Alternative*, Baden-Baden, 1990

Maier, Klaus A. and Nobert Wiggershaus unter Mitwirkung von Günther Hebert (eds, im Auftrag des Militärgeschichtlichen Forschungsamtes) *Das Nordatlantische Bündnis 1949–1956*, München, 1993

Militärgeschichtliches Forschungsamt (ed.), *Anfänge westdeutscher Sicherheitspolitik 1945–1956*. So far 3 vols. have been published; planned four vols (vol. 1., *Von der Kapitulation bis zum Pleven-Plan*; vol. 2., *Die EVG-Phase*; vol. 3., *Die NATO-Option*), München, 1982–1993

Noack, Paul, *Das Scheitern der Europäischen Verteidigungsgemeinschaft. Entscheidungsprozesse vor und nach dem 30. August 1954*, Düsseldorf, 1977

Riste, Olav (Hrsg.), *Western Security: The Formative Years. European and Atlantic Defence 1947–1953*, Oslo, 1985

Thoβ, Bruno and Hans-Erich Volkmann (eds, im Auftrag des Militärgeschichtlichen Forschungsamtes), *Zwischen Kaltem Krieg und Entspannung. Sicherheits- und Deutschlandpolitik der Bundesrepublik im Mächtesystem der Jahre 1953–1956*, Boppard am Rhein, 1988 (coll. Militärgeschichte seit 1945, vol. 9)

Varsori, Antonio, *Il patto di Bruxelles, 1948. Tra integrazione europea e alleanza atlantica*, Roma, 1988

Volkmann, Hans-Erich and Walter Schwengler (eds, im Auftrag des Militärgeschichtlichen Forschungsamtes), *Die Europäische Verteidigungsgemeinschaft. Stand und Probleme der Forschung*, Boppard am Rhein, 1985 (coll. Militärgeschichte seit 1945, vol. 7)

Wiggershaus, Norbert and Roland G. Foerster (eds. im Auftrag des Militärgeschichtlichen Forschungsamtes), *Die westliche Sicherheitsgemeinschaft 1948–1950. Gemeinsame Probleme und gegensätzliche Nationalinteressen in der Gründungsphase der Nordatlantischen Allianz*, Boppard am Rhein, 1988 (coll. Militärgeschichte seit 1945, vol. 8)

The USA, the Marshall Plan and European integration

Beugel, Ernst H. van der, *From Marshall Aid to Atlantic Partnership. European Integration as a Concern of American Foreign Policy*, Amsterdam, 1966

Bossuat, Gérard, *L'Europe occidentale à l'heure américaine 1945–1952. Le plan Marshall et l'unité européenne (1945–1952)*, Bruxelles, 1992

Comité pour l'Histoire Économique et Financière de la France, Ministère de l'Économie, des Finances et du Budget (ed.), *Le plan Marshall et le relèvement économiqe de l'Europe. Colloque tenu à Bercy les 21, 22 et 23 mars 1991 sous la direction de René Girault et Maurice Lévy-Leboyer*, Paris, 1993

Haberl, Othmar Nikola and Lutz Niethammer (eds), *Der Marshall Plan und die europäische Linke*, Frankfurt am Main, 1986

Helmreich, Jonathan E., 'The United States and the Formation of EURATOM', *Diplomatic History*, vol. 15, no. 3, 1991, pp. 387–410

Hogan, Michael J., *The Marshall Plan. America, Britain, and the Reconstruction of Western Europe, 1947–1952*, Cambridge, 1987

Link, Werner, 'Die Rolle der USA im westeuropäischen Integrationsprozeß', *Aus Politik und Zeitgeschichte*. Beilage zur Wochenzeitung Das Parlament, B14/72, 1972, pp. 3–13 (a systematically formulated paper)

Maier, Charles S., 'The Two Postwar Eras and the Conditions

for Stability in Twentieth Century Western Europe', in Maier, *In Search of Stability: Explorations in Historical Political Economy*, Cambridge, 1987, pp. 153–83

Maier, Charles S. (ed., with the assistance of Günter Bischof), *The Marshall Plan and Germany. West German Development within the Framework of the European Recovery Program*, New York, 1991; German language edn Maier, Charles S. and Günter Bischof (eds), *Deutschland und der Marshall-Plan*, Baden-Baden, 1992

Mélandri, Pierre, *Les Etats-Unis face à l'unification de l'Europe, 1945–1954*, Paris, 1980

Milward, Alan S, 'Was the Marshall Plan Necessary?', *Diplomatic History*, vol. 13, no. 2, 1989, pp. 231–53

Rappaport, Armin, 'The United States and European Integration: The First Phase', *Diplomatic History*, vol. 5, no. 2, 1981, pp. 121–49

Schröder, Hans-Jürgen (ed.), *Marshallplan und westdeutscher Wiederaufstieg. Positionen – Kontroversen*, Stuttgart, 1990

Wall, Irwin M., *The United States and the Making of Postwar France, 1945–1954*, Cambridge, 1991

Warner, Geoffrey, 'Eisenhower, Dulles and the Unity of Western Europe, 1955–1957', *International Affairs*, vol 69, no. 2, 1993, pp. 319–29

Winand, Pascaline, *Eisenhower, Kennedy, and the United States of Europe*, London, 1993